REMEMBERING CROOKSTON

REMEMBERING
Crookston

A Minnesota Memoir

CHUCK DOWDLE

LUMINARE PRESS
WWW.LUMINAREPRESS.COM

Remembering Crookston
A Minnesota Memoir
Copyright © 2022 by Chuck Dowdle

All rights reserved. This book or any portion thereof may not be reproduced or used in any manner whatsoever without the express written permission of the publisher, except for the use of brief quotations in a book review.

Printed in the United States of America

Luminare Press
442 Charnelton St.
Eugene, OR 97401
www.luminarepress.com

LCCN: 2022913864
ISBN: 979-8-88679-061-0

This book is lovingly dedicated to Marilyn Kirkwood Dowdle and Carmelle Johnson Matthes Dowdle, who were best friends and my classmates at Crookston's Cathedral High School. It was my good fortune to meet and marry these two bright, beautiful, lovable, capable and caring women who gave me encouragement and were patient with me while I was writing about these childhood and teenage experiences.

CONTENTS

Home 1
Santa's Matinee 4
True Confession 7
Betty 9
Mouse Attack 12
Crookston Daily Times 14
Bullies 17
Swimming 22
Kindergarten Caper 25
Bill Carter 29
Dance of a Lifetime 34
Little Friends Who Died 35
A Blast from the Past 39
The Kitten 41
The Loss of Innocence 43
The Circus 45
Meaty Treats 48
Special People 50
Polk County Fair 54
Buckaroo 56
Nicknames 61
Ready, Aim, Fire! 65
Work 68
Hustling 70
Slow Win 72

The Farm Crop Show	76
Childhood Sweetheart	79
Chicken	82
The Walkathon	86
Hoboes	90
Duval's Meat Market	92
Bess and the Beaver	94
Rats!	98
Jump Master	100
Crookston Pirates	103
Crookston Barbers	106
To Bee or Not To Bee	110
Caddy	113
The Elusive Gobbler	118
Wilson's Ice and Fuel	120
Home Run King	123
Gus	126
Sweet Tooth	128
The Gopher	132
The Whopping Northern Pike	135
The Weed Eater	139
Skiing Misadventure	142
Boy Farmer	145
Drive on Ice	154
Dance Man	157
Gandy Dancing	159
Dad	164

Minneapolis, Summer of '45	166
The Undefeated Season	171
You're in the Navy Now	178
Coincidence	182
Minakwa Golf and Country Club	185
The Healers	188
The Catch	192
Bill Dowdle	196
Marilyn Kirkwood	200
Pharmacists	205
Teachers	210
The Bethesda Hospital	214
Suppertime	217
Driven	221
Daredevils	229
Martha Lehman	234
Survivors	237
Teaching	244
The Armory	254
It's the Berries	258
The Rowboat	262
The Playhouse	266
Ice Skating	270
Childbirth	276
Flight	281
Veterans	285
Ski Bum	288

HOME

My name is Charles Edward Dowdle, "Charlie" to all my Crookston friends. I was born at home at 403 Pleasant Avenue, Crookston, Minnesota at 12:35 a.m. on February 1, 1928. My mom was a twenty-five year old housewife and my dad a thirty-nine year old Crookston barber when I was born. My mom, Grace Gretchen Van Raden, was born in Buffalo Center, Iowa, and Dad, Frank Dowdle, was born in Lanesville, Indiana.

I just mentioned my parents' names because later in life I learned that there had been name changes. Dad's name was George Francis Dowdle until he changed it to Frank Dowdle, and Mom's first name was Gretchen until she started going by her middle name, Grace. I don't know why Dad changed his name to Frank. Perhaps it was because my Grandpa Dowdle's name was also George, and my dad didn't want the same name or to be called Junior. Who knows! I sure don't.

My paternal grandparents came from Cork County, Ireland. My mom's father, Anton Van Raden, was from the Netherlands, which I found out later in life, and my mom's mother, Gretje Imhof, was from Wilhelmshaven, Germany, thus I'm Irish, Dutch and German. I always wondered why my dad went around the house singing, "Oh, the Irish and the Dutch don't amount to very much . . . !" That was our ancestry about which he was singing, and Dad did have a sense of humor!

Add to that the fact that my mom was a Lutheran before she married my dad and converted to Catholicism, and you have quite a mix, a German Lutheran and an Irish Catholic producing a "Charlie, Charlie, raised on barley, breakfast food and rice, toast and eggs and turkey legs, and everything that's nice. That's what little boys are made of!" How well and fondly I do remember that little ditty being sung in my direction by my mom and dad as I scooted across our slick, shiny linoleum-covered floors on my "kiddie car" which was made from wood. It was a small three-wheeler on which I sat and scooted myself along with my feet on the floor. I steered it with a horizontal wooden handle. I couldn't have been more than two or three at the time.

Another of my favorite toys at that time was wooden building blocks. They had the letters of the alphabet printed on them, upper and lower case, one letter per block, along with colorful animals and objects. I would growl when I put the "L" block in place and meow for the "K" block because they had pictures of a lion and a kitten, respectively, imprinted on them. The "Z" block had a zebra, and I didn't know what sound it made.

I loved to see how high I could build the blocks before they came tumbling down to the floor. It took a lot of patience to get all twenty-six blocks stacked on top of one another. Up to ten it was easy. When I reached twenty, the alphabet skyscraper began to weave a little. The last six were the challenge! Then, finally, I would make it! All twenty-six blocks would be stacked, some a little unevenly, and the stack would be wavering back and forth like it was about to topple, like it was a building being shaken by an earthquake!

It was at that time that I chose to scream and whip my hand through the middle of the stack, sending the blocks flying and crashing to the floor! Inevitably, my mom would say, "My goodness, Charles, do you have to make so much noise?" Of course, I didn't, but I guess I did it because I was playing with one of my favorite toys, and I was happy, and I was home.

Our little two-story house, which my dad said we rented so long we paid for it about three times over, sat on a corner lot with a large front yard where all the neighborhood kids gathered to play hide-and-go-seek, red light, green light, lost track, and post office. Street lights were only on the corners of the blocks, so our play area was always well lit up at night. When we grew tired from running and shouting and playing games, we'd sit under the street light and tell scary stories! Usually, the older boys and girls would be the story tellers, and they'd try to scare the wits out of the younger kids! It sure was a lot of fun. Names like Pederson, Steenerson, and Nelson remind me of some of my best little friends. When we weren't playing in my front yard, we could often be found picking choke cherries or goose berries from nearby trees and bushes, or we might be down by the river.

The Red Lake River ran throughout the town of Crookston and divided it into neighborhoods called additions. Our neighborhood was called Sampson's Addition, more than likely named after one of the Sampsons. I remember "Huggie" Sampson who owned the little grocery store in our neighborhood. I also fondly remember the river where we could dangle our feet in the warm water in the summer, or drop in a fishing line with an earthworm on the hook and hope to catch a perch or rock bass. Sometimes we'd dig our fingers into the moist clay and shape it into animals and let them dry in the sun, and sometimes we'd swim and pretend to be Tarzan as we swung out over the water's edge on thick, long vines which hung from nearby trees.

Living in the Heart of the Red River Valley, alongside the Red Lake River, in the small town of Crookston, in a neighborhood alive with activity was my home! I loved it, and I'll never forget it!

SANTA'S MATINEE

———◆·◆———

Santa Claus never did attend a matinee at the Lyric Theater on Main Street. Nor did he attend one at the Royal Theater next to Daniel's Drugstore on Broadway, and I don't remember him ever coming to the newest theater, the Gopher. For some reason, Santa always had a preference for Crookston's classic show house, the Grand.

Perhaps Santa liked it there because the Grand was located near two other classic structures, the Cathedral of the Immaculate Conception and the Carnegie Public Library.

Perhaps he liked the Second Street location because it was a quiet street, a street on which a lot of kids could congregate without worrying too much about traffic.

Perhaps Santa Claus chose the Grand Theater because it was big enough to accommodate all the children who came to see him at his pre-Christmas matinee.

All the town's children were invited to this matinee. The Crookston Daily Times announced the invitation: "Santa Claus will arrive this Saturday afternoon at the Grand Theater to wish all Crookston children a Merry Christmas! Free movies will be shown, and bags of candy will be given to all who attend."

Were they kidding! Who wouldn't attend! This was the 1930's, the time of the Great Depression, the time when anything free was unheard of.

About the only Crookston child who would miss that matinee would be the one who had pneumonia and about a 105 degree temperature. All the others would be there.

The movie began at one o'clock, and clutches of little kids (some with and some without their parents) began arriving around 12:30 p.m. Almost always the weather was cold, and layers of hard, white snow lay packed on the ground. Sometimes the sun would be glistening against the snow, and sometimes the snow would be blowing, flurrying or falling gently on the day of Santa's matinee. Nothing kept the kids away.

By 1:00 p.m. the Grand was packed with several hundred excited children whose voices created a cacophony of sound. Soon the balcony and downstairs lights were dimmed until darkness enveloped the exquisitely decorated theater. Then a hush of quiet anticipation filled the air as the large velvet curtains covering the screen slowly parted.

The first movies were always animations like Bugs Bunny, Porky Pig, Donald Duck, or Mickey Mouse. When the first image was projected onto the screen, a din of cheering voices always followed. After the animations, the kids were kept laughing with comedies like The Marx Brothers, Abbott and Costello and The Three Stooges. Time slipped by rapidly. As the last movie came to an end, the lights were turned up, and the heavy, velvet curtains drew closed in the front of the white screen.

Immediately, Mr. Hiller, the owner of the Grand, walked onto the stage and made a short announcement: "Children, it makes me extremely happy to see so many of you here this afternoon enjoying yourselves. I'd like to wish you all a very Merry Christmas and thank you for coming!"

As Mr. Hiller walked from the stage, a faint jingling of bells could be heard coming from the theater lobby. Suddenly, the jingling bells grew louder, accompanied with a roaring "HO! HO! HO! MERRY CHRISTMAS!"

Pandemonium broke loose as the kids filled the crowded aisles and fought their way towards the back of the theater.

When the children reached the theater lobby, Santa Claus and all his helpers were busy greeting them, wishing them all a

Merry Christmas and handing each child a large bag filled with hard, wavy, colored candy, different kinds of nuts, an apple and an orange.

The 1930's may have been filled with hard times for families, but you really had to hand it to Crookston's adults; they knew how to lift up the spirits of their children.

As the kids left the warm theater to face the cold outdoor air, they buttoned up, put on their caps and mittens and clutched their bags of goodies.

Walking home, some of them with their parents, some of them with their little friends, all happily chattering with one another, it was easy to see that "Santa's Matinee" was a real hit.

TRUE CONFESSION

I always liked going to church at the Cathedral of the Immaculate Conception. It was a quiet place where I talked to God. It was a beautiful place where the stained glass windows were lit up by the sun when it shone on them. It was a warm place where the radiators breathed heat during the freezing northern Minnesota winters. It was a place where priests wore beautiful vestments and where the strong smell of incense filled the church during the services. It was a place where the organ played pleasant music and where parishioners sang joyfully. It was a place where I saw familiar faces of people I knew and liked and who liked worshipping God like me. The Cathedral was where mass was said by a priest who distributed the Body of Christ in Holy Communion, a small, round, white wafer. The Cathedral was where one's sins were forgiven by a priest in a small, wooden structure called a confessional.

I remember well the first time I ever went to church at the Cathedral. I was about four years old, and I went with my mother. She rushed me out of the house and kept saying, "Hurry up, Charles, or we won't make it on time." My mother was a fast walker, and by the time we reached the church, I was sweating. It was spring, getting nice outside, and the morning sun was already out.

When my mother opened the heavy wooden church doors, I was awed by the statues, the stained glass windows, the rows upon rows of pews, the music, and the gold glittering on the altar. I was fascinated by all the people sitting in the pews as my mother took my hand and led me down one of the side aisles past them to the front of the church near one of the confessionals which had a long, dark-green curtain hanging in front of it like a cloth door. When we sat down, I kept observing the confessional. I had never seen anything like it before. I looked like a little, round, brown wooden house with heavy green curtains for a door. A woman had just separated the curtains and come out of the house and walked up the aisle past us when my mother said, "Charles, you just sit here alone for a minute, and I'll be right back." Then she stood and walked toward the little house, parted the green curtains, and entered it.

That's when I began feeling scared and everything around me began seeming strange. Tears began forming in my eyes as I saw my mother disappear behind the green curtains which flopped closed behind her.

Silently, I sat, the hot tears beginning to stream down my cheeks. My mother, I thought, had left me! I was alone! She said she'd be right back. Would she? Or was she gone forever!

I imagined her entering that little brown house and falling into a deep, dark, endless pit from which she would never return. I became extremely frightened, not knowing where she'd gone or if she'd really come back or what I should do if she didn't. Instead of familiar faces, all of the people sitting around me suddenly became strangers. "How," I thought, "could they let this happen to my mother if they were my friends?"

Instantly, the green curtains parted and my mother appeared. What a relief! She saw my tears and immediately comforted me. At that time I had no idea what "confession" was all about, nor would I have understood if my mother had tried to explain. I just remember her cooing something like, "Poor little boy! You'll be alright! Mommy just went to "confession."

BETTY

———◆·◆———

Everything was hush, hush around our 403 Pleasant Avenue house. Something big was about to happen, but I didn't know what. Parents never tell little kids anything. All I knew was that they wanted me to go over to the Nelsons and play, and I liked that, so I didn't ask any questions.

Mrs. Nelson always treated my brother and me to cookies whenever we played with her daughters, Evelyn and Marilyn, and I didn't see why today should be any different, so I went gladly. It seemed funny, though, because my parents never usually sent me to the Nelsons to play. Rather, they usually had to get me from the Nelsons to come home and eat supper. But, I was only four years old at the time and didn't think much of it.

It was April 6, 1932. It had rained all day, so I was happy to be inside the Nelsons' comfortable, warm, dry house, just playing with Evelyn and Marilyn until it was time to be called home for supper.

For some reason, my older brother Willie didn't come with me, and he usually did because he liked "Evie" who was about his same age. Again, I didn't think much about it because I was the center of attention, and I loved Mrs. Nelson's cookies. I loved Mrs. Nelson, too, because she was always so kind, gentle, and understanding. She'd talk to me like I was an adult. "Well, Charlie," she'd say as she sat calmly working her way through the Crookston Daily Times crossword puzzle, "what exciting things have you been doing today?" I'd shyly begin telling her what I'd been doing, and we'd end up having a great conversation.

As it started getting a little dark outside, I began feeling a little hungry, and so far no cookies had been forthcoming, but I didn't say anything because I was having too much fun playing with Evelyn and Marilyn. Besides, Mrs. Nelson was fixing supper which was beginning to smell mighty good, and I thought that if I kept my mouth shut, I might just be invited to eat at the Nelsons' house that night.

Then about six o'clock my dad and brother Willie came knocking on the Nelsons' door and said it was time to come home. They were all smiles. As we were leaving the Nelsons' house, my dad said, "Guess what, Charlie. You've got a new baby sister! You'd better hurry home so you can see her!"

As fast as my four-year-old legs would carry me, I took off running towards home, my feet splashing in the puddles of water that had gathered on the cracked sidewalks. "A baby sister!" I thought excitedly. "I wonder what she looks like!" Suddenly, as I continued running wildly through the watery puddles, I stumbled and went sprawling flat on my stomach and face into a big muddy one. My dad and brother were slowly bringing up the rear, and I could hear their muffled laughs, but I simply jumped to my feet and dashed towards home, drenched from head to toe.

As I approached our house, I could see all the lights burning brightly. The house was lit up like a Christmas tree! Opening the kitchen door, waves of warm air pressed against my face, and the smell of sweetly-scented powder filled my nostrils. My aunts Jeanette Trepanier and Annie Erickson (two of my mom's sisters) were busily cleaning up, and Dr. H.E. Nelson (no relation to the Nelsons with whom I had been staying) was preparing to leave. The other adults seemed pretty excited and didn't even notice me until my Aunt Jeanette did and said, "Oh, here's Charlie. Charlie," she whispered softly, "your mom just had a little baby girl!"

She ushered me into my mom's bedroom where my mom lay holding a small bundle wrapped in a blanket. I inched closer to her bed, and Mom said softly, "C'mon, Charlie, and see your new sister." I edged closer to get a better peek. All I could see was a little fuzzy baby head, a tiny pink face, closed eyes, and my new baby sister sleeping peacefully in my mom's arms.

"What's her name, Mom?" I asked.

"We're going to call her Elizabeth Ann," my mom answered. "Give me your hand and you can touch her, Charlie," she said. I reached out my hand, and my mother took it in hers and placed it gently on the baby's delicate fingers. They were soft and warm. I just stood there in awe, stared, and felt the baby's warm little fingers twitch in my hand.

Then my Aunt Jeanette entered the room again and came over and stood by me. She took my hand in hers and whispered, "C'mon, Charlie. Let's let your mom rest awhile now."

As we walked from the room, she said, "You must be hungry. Would you like to go into the kitchen and get something to eat?"

MOUSE ATTACK

In 1933 when I was five years old, my mom decided to let me begin carrying a water bucket filled with kitchen scraps over to our Pleasant Avenue neighbors' (Mr. and Mrs. Theodore Garviks') chickens. We fed them potato peelings, carrot peelings, and other throwaway food that the chickens just loved to eat. Whenever they saw me coming, dangling their feast from the end of my arm, a hundred or more of them raced clumsily towards me from all sides, dodging one another gracelessly in their effort to get close to the pail of food.

I'll never forget the first time I fed them. I was horrified! They rushed me and made all kinds of clucking and cackling noises as they brushed nervously and hungrily against my legs. I thought for sure they were going to eat me alive, or at the very least fly up and peck my eyes out! Neither happened. I simply dropped the pail and began walking, petrified, through the sea of white, feathered bodies.

That's when it happened, when my initial fright was compounded. I felt a sharp scratch on my leg and became terror stricken! Something alive was crawling around inside my pants! Crying, oblivious now to the hungry chickens which still surrounded me, I plowed through them and began running home.

On the way, the animal inside my pants began moving around and was heading for my crotch when I burst through our kitchen door and screamed, "Mom! Help me! Something's in my pants!"

"What is it, Charles? Where is it?" my mom asked excitedly as she flew to my rescue with a frightened look on her face. I pointed to my pants, and my mom's hawkish hand pounced on the small, moving lump near my crotch.

"Just a minute now," she whispered calmly as she clutched the lump in one hand and squeezed it slowly until it stopped wiggling and became motionless. Then, cautiously, Mom reached her other hand inside my pants and gently withdrew a small, limp, grey mouse.

That was one day I didn't stop at the Garvik's house to pick up the free eggs we got for feeding their chickens.

CROOKSTON DAILY TIMES

Selling the Crookston Daily Times on the streets during the Great Depression of the 1930's was an education in people and money for a young kid. Money was extremely scarce! I wanted to make some of it, so with encouragement from my dad, selling papers on the streets of Crookston became my first business venture.

First, we kids would go into the newspaper office and Myrtle MacKenzie, the wife of the owner and publisher, would ask us how many papers we wanted to sign up for that day. We'd tell her and then pay her. We bought the papers two for a nickel and sold them on the streets for a nickel apiece. A hundred per cent profit! What a deal!

When I first started selling, I bought only two papers. Mrs. MacKenzie would ask, "How many papers would you like today, Dowdle?"

When I answered, "Two," she would smile, write down my name with a two behind it and say, "All right, that'll be five cents." It paid to get to the office early and sign up because the papers were distributed in the same order that one signed up.

After paying for our papers, we newsboys had to wait for them in a small, dark room in the basement of the building near where the presses were located. That was scary because the older kids, the carriers, waited down there, too, and they would sometimes harass the little kids, kicking them in the seat of the pants when they got their papers and ran out to sell them.

Before the papers came out, it was exciting! We watched the pressmen move rapidly as they installed the heavy metal sheets of print. The smell of fresh ink and paper filled the air. "O.K.," the foreman would yell. "Let her go!" Slowly the mountain of machinery would begin moving. It rumbled and roared as the huge roll of paper began moving. We newsboys could see it all through a small wooden window. The pressmen's hands, arms, and faces were smeared with ink. The huge roll of white paper turned slowly at first, but then as the press picked up speed, it did, too. Soon the Crookston Daily Times would come out all neatly creased and smelling of fresh ink, ready to sell!

"O.K.!" one of the pressmen would shout as we boys bumped and jostled against one another. "Get in line if you want your papers!" He'd yell, and then he'd call our names from the top of the list and hand us the number for which we'd signed up in the office.

When we got our papers, we ran up the old concrete basement steps like we were going to a fire towards those places downtown which we knew were the "hot spots," places like Meng and Garvick's, Heck's, and Acker's where the men hung out and played cards.

One of my favorite places was the Great Northern Depot. The ticket agent bought a paper every day. If I got to him first, I'd have only one paper left to sell and could quit early.

When I got a little older, I bought more papers because I could run faster and sell more, but eight was usually my limit. If I didn't sell all my papers and there was no one left to buy them, I was stuck with them. At times like these, older men who hadn't yet bought a paper would bargain with me and offer me three pennies for a paper instead of a nickel, or they would say, "I'll give you a "chip" for a paper. A chip was a metal coin men used instead of real money when they played cards in the above mentioned "hot spots." Each chip was worth a nickel, but it had to be spent at those bar/cafes.

Oh well, sometimes taking a chip or three cents for a paper was better than nothing, and you could always buy a candy bar, a bag of salted peanuts, or a bottle of pop with a chip because they all sold for a nickel apiece during the 1930,s.

I think I learned a lot by selling the Crookston Times on the streets during the Depression. I learned how to approach people with "Paper, mister?" and if mister said, "Nah!" in a mean or angry way, I learned quickly not to bother him and to go on to the next customer. I learned the thrill of making a sale each day and of making people happy who were able to pay the nickel and eager to read about what was happening. Money was scarce, and most people didn't have a radio, so the newspaper was their main means of becoming informed. Selling the Crookston Daily Times sort of became my first school because I learned to make change and to read about what was going on in my world, even though I was just a little kid.

BULLIES

I read an Associated Press article in the Sunday, December 7, 2003 issue of the San Luis Obispo, California Tribune that read as follows: "The federal government is spearheading an effort to halt harassment in the halls of our schools." The writer, Ben Feller, said, "The goal is to create a culture change in which bullying is not seen as cool, parents watch for warning signs, kids stand up for each other and teachers are trained to intervene." With these thoughts in mind, I'd like to share with you some of my personal experiences with Crookston bullies and tell you how I was affected by them.

It was a bright, sunny Saturday in March, 1933 which would soon turn very dark for me before the end of the day. After a hurried breakfast I could hardly wait to slip and slide the three blocks in the slushy snow to the outdoor ice rink next to Huggie Sampson's (later Ade Ness's) little neighborhood grocery store on Woodland Avenue. Our family had recently moved from our small 403 Pleasant Avenue house to a bigger house at 416 Woodland Avenue, and now everything was closer, downtown, Huggies and the ice rink.

When I got there, many of my young friends, who like myself were around five years old, were running and sliding around on the ice because they, like I, didn't yet own a pair of skates. That was okay because what we enjoyed most of all was just playing with one another. "C'mon over here, Charlie," some of my friends yelled, and I ran and skidded towards them at the far end of the rink, That's when it happened! When I reached them and began sliding around on the ice and playing happily with my friends, a huge, gruff-voiced man (one of my former Pleasant Avenue neighbors who was there with his son) grabbed me for no apparent reason and pulled down my pants. All of my little friends began laughing and thought it was funny as I stood there in my long winter underwear. The man, too, laughed uproariously!

It wasn't funny to me! I began to tremble and grow warm all over my body. I couldn't speak. I couldn't move I was so embarrassed. I think I was in shock! The kids continued laughing as I stood there, muted, and the neighbor himself continued bellowing loud, ridiculing laughter at me. Finally, as hot tears began trickling down my flushed cheeks, I bent down to pull up my pants and leave. Slowly, I began walking away, sobbing, the laughter still ringing in my ears. When I reached the little store, I began running, crying all the way home.

When I got there, I burst into the house, and my mom got all excited because she thought I had hurt myself. "Charles," she asked seriously in a whisper, "what's the matter, son? Why are you crying?" I told Mom what happened, and all she could say was, "It'll be okay, Son. Don't you worry. It'll be okay."

The point is, dear reader, it wasn't okay! I was a five year old kid when this happened. I had just had my fifth birthday in February and was going to start kindergarten in April. Today, I'm seventy-five years old, and I still feel emotionally scarred from that experience. In my heart I've tried to forgive my former neighbor for what he'd done to me, and I have, but it wasn't easy.

Why did this man, a big man, over six feet tall, a heavy man, over two hundred pounds, take advantage of a small five year old boy? Why was he a bully?

The second bully I'd like to talk about is the one I'd always meet on my way to and from school. This boy and I attended the same Catholic elementary school, and because he lived in the Flats Addition and I lived in Sampson's Addition, our paths crossed often. For some reason, Georgie didn't like me, and I was afraid of him simply because he looked mean and sounded tough.

However, one day when I saw Georgie walking towards me on Second Street, instead of walking across the street to avoid his taunts, threats, and pushes, I decided to confront him! This was no easy decision on my part because Georgie was short, stocky, weighed about 140 pounds and was in the seventh grade, whereas, I was about as tall as he, skinny, 90 pounds and in the sixth grade.

This difference didn't matter. I had had enough of Georgie's almost daily humiliation and decided that I wasn't going to walk across the street to avoid him anymore. For once, I was going to keep my self respect and pass right on by him.

As he got closer, my whole body got warm, my legs began to get a little weak, and I was growing very, very nervous! I could feel sweat begin to collect in the palms of my hands as they clenched into tight fists. I was ready for a fight!

Georgie was now only a short distance from me, and his first taunt jolted me to the reality of this confrontation. "You little bastard, Dowdle! Get off the sidewalk or I'll beat the hell outta ya!" Georgie shouted angrily. I just kept walking right on towards him, hoping against hope that he was just bluffing and wouldn't touch me.

It didn't work! Georgie veered towards me as I tried to avoid him, and when we passed one another, he pushed me in the chest, and I hit him as hard as I could right on the nose. It began bleeding badly, and after a few more hits at one another and continued bleeding of Georgie's nose, before the fight had really begun, it was over. Georgie wiped his bloody nose and simply walked away, not saying a word.

I stood there sort of stunned, still waiting for the worst to happen, but it didn't. That's all there was to it. From that time forward, Georgie never bothered me again, and we actually became pretty good friends.

This sort of reminds me of something that happened when I was teaching junior high school English in Santa Rosa, California in the 1960's. It was the first day of school, and one of my seventh graders, a boy, was struggling with the combination to his locker which just happened to be next to my room. Suddenly, a tall ninth grader approached the bank of lockers near us, brushed the seventh grader aside with his arm, and yelled pompously, "Get out of my way, kid!"

Surprisingly, the seventh grader simply looked up into the ninth grader's face and very calmly and seriously said, "I wouldn't do that again if I was you!" As soon as the ninth grader began making another motion with his arm, the seventh grade boy gave him an uppercut that lifted him right off the floor and onto his back. I was a little stunned, just like the ninth grader lying on the floor, but at the same time I was impressed by this seventh grade boy's prowess.

When we got into the classroom, I had a little talk with him and asked him where he ever learned to handle his fists that way. "My dad," he said. The kid's name was Olson, and his dad's name was Bobo Olson, former middleweight champion of the world! Enough said!

It's strange. I guess bullies are really cowards at heart. They select others they think are weak, shy, or vulnerable to push around, embarrass, and conquer, but if given some of their own medicine, they sometimes back off, like Georgie and this ninth grader.

The last time I was ever bullied by anyone in Crookston happened in 1942 when I entered the ninth grade at Cathedral High School. At the end of the first day of school, all of the ninth graders who were going out for football assembled in the gym. There we were faced by a long, straight line of upperclassmen who had taken their belts from their pants and were snapping them back and forth in their hands. "All right, all of you freshmen," shouted one of the seniors, "before we begin practice today, you're going to be initiated. So, get on your hands and knees! Now, who's going to be the first brave soul to begin crawling between the legs of the upperclassmen?"

At first, not one person moved, and you could have heard a pin drop in that gym. Then, finally, one freshman began crawling between the legs of the first upperclassman in the line, and when he did, the upperclassman clenched the boy between his calves like a vise and began whomping the boy's butt with his belt with loud, heavy slaps. As he was released to the second upperclassman in the line for similar treatment, the rest of us began following him, cowering and crawling between the upperclassmen's legs until we all had reached the end of the torture chamber.

Again, this was bullying of a sort, but it wasn't the kind that lingered in your mind, the kind that was repeated on an almost daily basis during my whole freshman year of football at Cathedral High School. And it began the first day as soon as we began undressing in a crowded nine by twelve foot locker room. A senior took one peek at my physique and began making all kinds of derogatory remarks about it, and he kept it up all year long. This kind of verbal assault is almost worse than physical abuse sometimes because it never goes away, and it can be very distracting when one is trying to think clearly and concentrate on school work.

From my personal Crookston experiences and from having been a junior high school teacher of English for thirty-six years, I know how young people can be affected by bullying. It went on when I was a kid, and unfortunately it's still happening today, ranging from slapping, pushing, hitting, kicking, and other physical abuse to verbal abuse to the new frontier, cyber bullying, in which kids use e-mail and websites to humiliate others.

SWIMMING

In the 1930's Crookston had two swimming pools, a "big pool" and a "little pool." The "little pool" was a round, concrete wading pool in Central Park which was about fifty feet in diameter and a foot deep. It's where all the moms took their toddlers when they wanted them to have their first swimming experience. It's where all the little kids who couldn't swim yet gathered to refresh themselves during Minnesota's hot, humid, summer days.

Did I say "refresh?" The water was wet, but it was also tepid and dirty, warm and murky, hot and smelly before it was replaced each week because there was so little of it and so many hot bodies in it. Also, little kids didn't bother to get out of the water when they had to pee. They simply let it go on the spot! Consequently, near the end of each week, the "little pool" water was filthy and smelled brackish, and the pool bottom became slick and covered with green slime.

You can see why I wanted to swim in the "big pool" (which was located between the library and the tennis courts) when I was only five years old. The "big pool" was a large concrete rectangle which was about seventy-five feet wide and a hundred and fifty feet long. It was about two feet deep at the shallow end and nine feet deep at the deep end. It had a spring board and a high diving platform and was usually cold and smelled of chlorine.

It's where all the big kids ran and swam and played water tag and dived. It's where I wanted to be as soon as I felt I had graduated from that "cesspool" in Central Park. I was tired of crawling around on my hands and knees in urinary water and pretending to swim like a frog. So, one hot summer day when I was walking downtown with my dad on his way to work at his Second Street barbershop, I asked, "Dad, will you take me swimming at the "big pool" sometime?"

My dad just kept walking and said, "No, Charlie, I don't think you're ready for that yet." But I was insistent.

"C'mon, Dad," I begged. "Just go to the "big pool" with me once, and then I can swim there by myself after that!"

I guess my dad didn't want to listen to me anymore because he said, "O.K., Charlie. I'll go with you tomorrow morning." Just like that he said it. I couldn't believe my ears. I was going swimming in the "big pool!"

The night dragged for me. I slept, but the morning didn't come any too soon. It was Saturday, a day my dad would do a lot of business at the barbershop, so I knew he wouldn't be spending much time with me. So, when he asked, "Charlie, are you ready to go swimming?" I was ready.

"Yes!" I said excitedly as I ran and got my suit and followed him out the front door. We walked because we didn't have a car.

My dad didn't want to take any chances my first time in the "big pool," so he brought along an automobile inner tube to wrap around my waist. When we got to the pool, Dad doubled the inner tube around me and I felt real safe.

"There you go, Charlie. Let's see you swim," my dad said. I didn't jump right in. Rather, I stepped cautiously down the three steps at the shallow end until I was able to stand on the bottom. The water was cold, and it lapped under my chin as I moved away from the steps and bounced up and down a little in deeper water.

"Look, Dad!" I yelled. "I'm swimming!"

He was sitting in the shade, talking with the lifeguard, but he turned towards me for a second and shouted, "Sure you are, Charlie. Have fun." I just kept bouncing around in the inner tube until my feet couldn't touch the bottom any more. "This sure beats the "little pool," I thought. The water was clean, but it was so dark green that I couldn't see the bottom when i opened my eyes under it.

When I looked back at my dad a second time, he was still talking to the lifeguard and not paying any attention to me, so I thought it would be a good time to venture out a little farther towards the deep end. Kids were splashing and yelling all around me, and it became contagious, so I began splashing with my arms and bouncing up and down to see if I could make my feet touch the bottom.

That's when it happened! Suddenly, the inner tube, instead of popping me right up to the surface, slipped from my waist to my ankles. My head plunged down under the dark green water, my feet went to the surface with the inner tube, and my head was held under. Immediately, I began gulping lots of water, and everything turned black. I don't remember struggling at all, it happened so fast. I was unconscious! I was drowning!

What I do remember is regaining consciousness while lying flat on my stomach on the warm concrete. The lifeguard was saying, "In comes the good air, out goes the bad air," as his strong hands pressed rhythmically against my lower rib cage, giving me artificial respiration. I began feeling sick to my stomach as water and vomit heaved from my mouth each time the lifeguard applied pressure to my back.

When I became fully awake, I saw my dad standing anxiously over me and a cluster of kids standing around staring down at me. I was both scared and embarrassed because I had just about drowned. That wasn't the way it was supposed to happen.

As I lifted my head and was helped to my feet, I began to sob, and my dad said, "You're going to be all right, Charlie!" He took my hand in his, and we began walking home.

KINDERGARTEN CAPER

That first day of kindergarten in April, 1934, my mom walked to school with me, and I remember her saying, "Now, Charles, you be a good boy and do what Sister Elizabeth tells you."

The days that followed passed rapidly, coloring pictures, singing songs, learning to read, and playing games outside in the field during recess with all my new little friends. Then one warm day in May my whole kindergarten world turned topsy turvy when four other little boys and I went astray.

When Sister Elizabeth rang the bell, as usual, calling us in from recess, we boys were having so much fun that we just kept playing while the other kids ran past us on their way back to school.

Before we knew it, we were all alone. That's when one of my little friends, sweating and puffing, blurted out a suggestion which would come back to haunt us all. "Let's go downtown!" he yelled. Now, you have to understand, downtown was right there, close to the St. Joseph Home which was the name of our school. You only had to walk up a hill, past the church, and a block away from school, and you were in the heart of downtown Crookston, a small Minnesota farm community where all the people knew one another.

There was no hesitancy among us. No one questioned the action. We all just started hiking up the hill. When we reached the church, we all noticed that the side door was open. "Let's walk through the church!" suggested our leader. He walked right past the big, brown, heavy, wooden door which was propped open, and the rest of us followed him, one after another, like sheep.

The church was dark, quiet, and empty. It was like being alone with God because Sister Elizabeth said that's where God lived. As we walked up the side aisle next to the heavily-varnished, light-brown, oaken pews, our leader stopped abruptly and gazed down one of them. "Look!" he whispered. "A purse!"

We were all staring at the large, brown, leather purse when our leader said excitedly, "Let's open it and see what's in it!" No one moved until leader unsnapped the brass clasp of the purse. I began growing warm all over, feeling that that was something we shouldn't be doing. But I was curious just like the rest of the boys.

What we found in the purse was money, lots of it! We helped ourselves, walked up the aisle and out the front door of the church, and headed downtown on Second Street towards Peter George's grocery store.

Once inside, it didn't take us long to dispose of the stolen money. We were like a swarm of honeybees. We bought Pepsi Cola, Hires Root Beer, Whistle Orange, and Dr. Pepper to drink. We bought Snickers, Milky Ways, Butterfingers, and my favorite Nut Goodies to eat, and to add insult to injury, we finished off our eating glut with ice cream sandwiches, cupcakes and licorice. Everything we bought was sweet. Our tummies were brim full when we finally left the store and began walking the two blocks back to school . . . . late! Mr. George called after us as we left his store, "You boys be good!"

The welcoming committee was out when we got back to school. Everybody had been looking for us. We didn't have to tell Sister Elizabeth where we had been. Our smeared and stained faces, hands and shirts said it all. Abruptly, the principal marched us to her office and asked sternly, "Where have you boys been!"

When we all began talking at once, she silenced us with her raised hand, and looking directly at me she said, "Charles, you tell me what happened." I blurted out everything we had done. Told her all of it. When she heard me say, "We found a lot of money in a purse in church," her face turned beet red.

She rose from the chair behind her big desk, glared at us silently, and then said nervously, "You boys are going to have to talk to Father Wurm! Come with me!" Like beaten soldiers, we tramped out the door behind the principal on our way to see the pastor of our church. Father Wurm wasn't home at the rectory, so we all had to fall in behind the principal again and continue our hike over to the sacristy of the church where Father Wurm was working.

When he saw us enter, a cheerful smile broke over his face because he loved children. "Come in, Sister! Come in, boys!" he called to us jovially. After the principal told him what we'd done, she turned to leave the sacristy, and the priest's countenance changed dramatically. His smile turned to a frown, his brow furrowed, and his face reddened. "You boys have sinned by taking something that wasn't yours," he said, "and you'll have to be punished." He picked up a large chair and carried it through the sacristy doorway to the sanctuary and placed it near the altar. One at a time, he called out a name, and that boy walked through the doorway to meet his fate. The first boy to be called was our "Fearless Leader." We couldn't see him, so we just stood silently, listening.

We heard some sputtering words spoken and then a whack! whack! whack! whack! that sounded very much like a heavy hand was making contact with the seat of a young boy's pants. Frightened and sobbing, our "Fearless Leader" walked quickly past us on his way back to school.

I was not among the next three boys called. I was last. Standing alone, feeling hot all over my body, nervously waiting to hear my name, I finally heard Father Wurm call out in a brusque voice, "Charles!" When he saw me hesitate in the doorway, he said impatiently, "Come here, Charles!"

Petrified, I didn't move. I just looked at him sitting on the sturdy, wooden chair, his hands palm down on his legs. He looked like he was out of breath from exerting himself. Beads of perspiration covered his forehead and upper lip, and his face was flushed. I had never seen Father Wurm look like this before.

"Charles!" he shouted. "Come here!" I walked slowly and stood before him, trembling, as he placed me stomach down over his outstretched legs and whack! whack! whack! whack! came the palm of his hand down on the butt of my nervous little body. By the time the third whack burned my butt, I lost control and felt a warm stream of urine flow into my pants , down my legs, and onto Father Wurm's cassock. Angered, he gave me two more solid whacks and sent me sobbing and smelly back to school.

Needless to say, HONESTY became one of my main values in life after that misadventure.

BILL CARTER

Bill Carter was my cousin. His mom's maiden name was Alvina Sabin, Gus Sabin's sister. Alvina must have married a man whose name was Carter, but we kids never knew anything about him. Neither did Bill. He told me just a couple of years ago, in the year 2000, that he never saw his dad and that his mom would never tell him anything about him. I thought that was pretty sad, to never know anything about your dad!

All we kids knew was that Alvina had been married to my dad's brother, Jim Dowdle, for as long as we could remember, and Bill and I knew one another as cousins from the time we were both very little. Let me tell you about a few of the experiences we had together.

The first happened one hot summer when we were little kids. We didn't know what to do with ourselves, so we went to our dads' Second Street barbershop and just hung out. Before long, it got hot and muggy, and Bill and I began nagging our dads to cut our hair short. "Dad," Bill said very seriously, "I want my hair cut real short this summer so it's cool!"

"Yeah," I complained to my dad, "I want mine cut short, too! I wanta get rid of this mop!"

My Uncle Jim and my dad cast sly glances at one another, and my Uncle Jim asked, "How short do you boys want it?"

"Real short!" Bill answered. "Cut it all off!"

"Are you sure, Charlie?" my dad asked.

"Yeah," I answered smartly, cut mine all off, too!"

That was all it took for the Dowdle brothers, Jim and Frank, to swing into action. "Okay, boys," they chorused, "jump into the chairs and we'll see what we can do!" In no time flat their clippers were humming, and as they smiled at one another, our blond hair began falling in mounds to the floor as they ran the clippers forward and backward over our scalps.

It all took about three minutes. Our dads held mirrors in front of our faces and asked, "Well, boys, how do you like it?" I think we were both a little stunned by the way we looked because neither of us said a word. We were bald!

For the rest of the summer, whenever anyone met us, together or alone, it was always, "Hi, baldy!" Soon, the hot summer sun began reddening our heads, and we both had to wear straw hats. For the rest of the summer we were inseparable and miserable!

When we got a little older, we both got BB guns and used to shoot at targets in the basement of his North Main Street house. Bill was very competitive and a much better shot than I, and for some reason he always had to demonstrate this fact to me, and one day he did!

We had both tired of target practice in the basement and went outside and began looking around for something else at which to shoot. We climbed a small hill behind Bill's house and began walking along the railroad tracks towards town with our guns over our shoulders when Bill stopped abruptly and said, "Just a minute, Charlie. Watch this!" Immediately, he lay down on his stomach, aimed his gun at a garage door which had about twenty windows in it, and began plinking them out one at a time! Bang! Out went the first window! Bang! Bang! Bang! Bang!

The glass tinkled as Bill fired, and he kept firing until just about every one of those twenty windows was broken! I grew warm all over, like I usually do when I'm in danger, and just about did it in my pants I was so scared! I knew that what was happening was very wrong and that we could go to jail! When Bill said, "C'mon, Charlie, take a shot!" I declined, and he finished the job! All I could think of was getting out of there fast before the police came and caught us. Bill had proved to me that he was a good shot. I wanted no part of the crime!

Come to think of it, Bill always did have a need to prove that he was better than I, and he had an opportunity to do just that on an almost weekly basis when we'd go to his house after school to play Monopoly, a game which our family didn't own. I'd never win, but it didn't matter because we always fixed "Dagwood" sandwiches, which I didn't get to do at home.

When Bill started dragging out luncheon meat, cheese, catsup, mustard, mayonnaise, pickles, lettuce, jelly, etc. from the refrigerator, my Monopoly losses were fast forgotten. I loved to eat! What we'd usually try to do was see how much food we could pile between two, soft, Land O' Lakes buttered slices of thick, white Holsum bread and then chomp into it! Amazingly, neither of us ever got sick!

However, one day after school when we were walking to Bill's house, he probably anticipating beating me again at Monopoly and I anticipating another "Dagwood" sandwich eating feast, an incident took place which upset my gut. One of our St. Joseph's Home sixth grade classmates started walking with us because he lived right across the street from my cousin. As we walked along, this classmate began teasing my cousin for no reason at all, taunting him with names like "fat" because Bill was a little chubby, and pushing him and hitting him on his arm!

My cousin just took all of this abuse silently and said nothing as we walked along. I said nothing, too, but I was about to burst with what I was feeling! I was feeling hot and angry and like a steaming teakettle about to blow its top because I hated a bully, and that's exactly what our classmate was doing to my cousin, bullying him!

After this bullying had gone on for about a minute, I could stand it no longer, and without saying a word, I simply stepped in front of the bully, slugged him in the face and told him to stop picking on Bill! Tears welled in the bully's eyes as he walked away from us without saying a word. Funny, I don't remember talking about that incident on the way home to my cousin's house that afternoon or ever again with the bully. Guess no one likes to remember getting a licking!

Somehow, this childhood experience faded from my cousin's memory, and he still had a real need to beat me, even in high school! Bill had been sparring with different friends at the Cathedral High School for some time, unbeknownst to me. At that time in our lives, we were both sixteen, and I was sort of a loner who didn't mix much with Cathedral High School boys. Rather, I walked home and associated mainly with boys from the public high school, Central, because they seemed to have more in common with me, and many of them lived in my neighborhood, Sampson's Addition. I hung out with guys like Howie Pederson, Clinton "Kitty" Kleinschmidt, Lee Gjesdahl, Jerry "Red" Knutson, Virgil Issacson, and Bill Monroe, all really solid people, good thinkers, kind, and always polite to others. I think they practiced what I was always being taught at home and in school, to love one another!

As I was saying, my cousin had been sparring with his friends, and one fall Saturday afternoon while we were walking along near the high school gymnasium, he asked this question, "Charlie, how'd you like to go into the gym and practice boxing a little with the 16 ounce gloves?" This really caught me by surprise! We used to box around in the barbershop once in awhile with our winter mittens on when we were kids, and I always got the best of Bill, but we'd never really fought with one another when we got older, and I didn't relish the idea of doing it now! But, I knew Bill would think that I was afraid of him if I said no, so I answered just as casually as he had asked, "Okay."

As we entered the gym, my heart was already pounding! I was pretty sure my cousin wanted to do a lot more than simply "practice boxing a little." He wanted to pound me if he could and demonstrate to himself that he could beat me at more than just

Monopoly or target practice, of that I was certain! As we entered the gym, Bill said, "C'mon into the locker room, Charlie. That's where the gloves are kept."

Now my adrenalin really began working overtime! Here we were, the two of us, my cousin and I, on a quiet Saturday afternoon, waiting to square off against one another in a twelve foot by eight foot dressing room lined with dark green metal lockers standing upright on a hard, gray concrete floor. It was a stark setting for a "showdown!" Bill walked right over to a locker and plucked two pair of 16 oz. gloves from it. "Go ahead, Charlie," Bill said anxiously as I hesitated, "put them on!"

Bill was now standing in one corner of the room, gloves on and poised for action. He held his gloves upright in front of his face and chest and yelled, "Ready!"

"Who says this is going to be 'a little boxing practice,'" I thought to myself as I answered, "yah," and stood there with my arms at my sides, the 16 oz. gloves hanging like lead weights from my hands.

Suddenly, like a mad bull charging a toreador, bent on destroying him, Bill came running across the small room, straight at me, his right arm cocked back for a knockout blow. Reacting rapidly, I took one short step toward him with my left foot and straight-armed the glove on my right fist flush into his face as hard as I could!

Bill stopped dead in his tracks. He stayed upright, but he was dazed. As he wobbled, I stepped forward and helped him to a nearby wooden bench so he wouldn't fall and hit his head on the concrete floor. Shortly, his head cleared, and he began peeling off the gloves. He had obviously had enough "practice!" One punch had done it. "Good going, Charlie," he said. "Let's quit and go downtown."

I took my gloves off, handed them to him, and said, "Okay."

DANCE OF A LIFETIME

Do you remember what your world was like when you started kindergarten? I wonder if it was anything like mine at the St. Joseph Home in Crookston in the spring of 1934. My kindergarten world was filled with coloring pictures, playing games, singing songs, and dancing. Dancing? Yes, dancing. Let me tell you a little about my first kindergarten dance.

It called for pairing up, boy-girl. I was very shy, but I had been eyeing one little girl in particular, Marilyn Kirkwood, and fortunately for me, she's the one with whom I was coupled. We faced one another at the start of the dance, and I began feeling extremely warm. Then our teacher began singing, "A heel and a toe and a one-two-three, one-two-three, a heel and a toe and a one-two-three, curtsy-bow."

Clumsily, at first, I put my heel forward and my toe back (matching Marilyn's movements) before clasping her hand over our heads and twirling in a circular movement. When she curtsied and I bowed, I knew that that was the end of the dance until Sister Elizabeth, the Benedictine nun who was our teacher, sang out in her gentle, soft-spoken voice, "All right, children, let's try it one more time."

I may have been awkward at first, but after a few go rounds, I got the hang of the dance and rather liked it, especially with Marilyn Kirkwood, the petite, pretty, nimble little girl who would make any dance partner look good.

Marilyn and I fell in love and were married to one another for forty-nine years during which time we continued our "Dance of Life," and she continued making me look good. My wife, the love of my life, died of ovarian cancer on August 20, 2000.

LITTLE FRIENDS WHO DIED

When I was very young, I lost two little friends, Billy Mercil and Donald Joseph. First, let me tell you about Billy, Dr. Mercil's little boy. He was kind, gentle, and shy. We first met in kindergarten and became fast friends. We never did anything together away from school because we lived in different parts of town, Billy in the Woods Addition and I in Sampson's Addition. Kids usually stayed and played in their own neighborhoods when they were our ages, so school became a great mixer for us Catholic kids who attended grade school at Cathedral's St. Joseph's Home.

It was in first grade that tragedy struck my little friend Billy Mercil. He got extremely sick. I think it was a combination of mastoiditis and pneumonia. The year was 1934, and antibiotics didn't arrive on the scene until the 1940's, so when people got very sick, they usually had to just wait it out. That's what Billy was doing, waiting it out until his fever broke.

But it didn't. He just got sicker and sicker. Our first grade teacher faced us with a very grave expression on her face and painfully announced, "Boys and girls, Billy Mercil is in the hospital, and he's not getting any better, so I'd like to ask you all to say a special prayer for him so he gets well. Now, if you'll all please rise, let's fold our hands and close our eyes and say a special Our Father and Hail Mary for Billy." I prayed with every fiber in body. I wanted my gentle, little friend back in school so we could once again talk with one another and play together during recess.

It wasn't to be. Billy got sicker, and then one day Sister told us that Billy had died! "Billy won't be with us anymore," was the way she put it. "His soul has gone to heaven to be with God."

I grew very warm all over when I heard that. The whole class was silent. An empty feeling developed in the pit of my stomach. I was flattened. My soul sank. "How could this be?" a sobbing voice inside me asked in silence as warm tears began running from my eyes. But it was true. Billy had died!

Our teacher told us that we would be going to Billy's funeral in church, and that six of us had been chosen as his pall bearers. I was one of the six because I was one of Billy's special friends.

The day of the funeral, six little boys dressed in black suits and wearing white nylon armbands tied in bows, walked into the church, carrying a small, white coffin with Billy in it. It was light. It was sort of overwhelming for me. I was so sad!

Tears streamed down my face when I had to leave Billy at the hearse after the service. I realized I'd never see him again. I just wanted to be left alone and not talk to anybody. I felt very empty and lonely!

The second little friend who emptied my heart when he died was Donald Joseph, Georgie and Johnny Joseph's younger brother. Donny lived down in the Flats Addition which was so called because it was a low-lying piece of land near the Red Lake River and the Old Dam which was used to generate electricity for Crookston. The Flats was near the bridge which I had to cross daily to get to my Woodland Avenue house in Sampson's Addition. Donny and I lived only about three blocks from one another, and we saw each other a lot as we walked to and from school each day. Donny went to the Catholic school, too, and he was in my grade.

A lot of the fun times we had together were rather competitive. Who could sell the most Crookston Daily Times? Who could catch a loose chicken from Pederson-Biddick? Who could catch the most and the biggest fish? We both sold the Crookston Daily

Times on the streets, racing from the newspaper building to the downtown bars like Meng's, Heck's and Aker's to see who could sell out first. Sometimes we'd chase chickens that had somehow escaped their doom at the local poultry slaughterhouse and would run around outside near the railroad tracks and under the boxcars. Donny and I would work together trying to corner a bird, but then whichever one of us made the successful grab of its legs got to bring it home, squawking and flapping its wings in protest. Fish reacted the same way whenever we caught them: perch, rock bass, suckers, carp, walleyed pike, or pickerel.

It was on one of those warm, sunny fishing days when Donald's and my fun together came to an abrupt halt. It must have been around 1937 or '38, so we'd be in about the fourth or fifth grade. School was out for the summer, and young boys like Donald were just itching for something new to do, something adventurous. The river was close and convenient, so fishing was usually one of the first things that would come to our minds. At least, that's what I planned on doing that afternoon after dinner.

One of Donny's and my favorite fishing spots was on the banks below the Old Dam. The water was always rushing down there, and it seemed like the game fish liked the fast-moving water, so that's where we usually fished.

On this particular day, I had just finished my dinner around noon and was preparing to go fishing down by the Old Dam when I heard the fire siren blaring. As I listened, it kept getting closer and closer, louder and more shrill. "Mom!" I yelled as I shot out of the house, "I'm going to see where the fire is!"

"Charles, now you be careful," she called after me. But I was gone. I hopped on my bike and headed for the bridge because I could hear the fire truck and see it roaring along the river towards the Old Dam. When I got there, there was no fire. Instead, the firemen were all collected near the bottom of the dam at the place where Donny and I usually fished. The firemen were talking nervously and trying to decide what to do.

Apparently, some little boy had discovered one of those boat-like objects in which men mix concrete, and he had pushed himself out into the river beneath the dam in it, trying to use it as a boat. It had sunk like a rock, and the little boy had gone down with it and was now caught under the water against the intake grates where the water was sucked in to make power.

One of the firemen, Floyd Spence, was going to try to rescue the boy by tying a rope around his waist and then diving under the water while the other firemen held onto the end of the rope. It was treacherous rescue work for Mr. Spence because of the tremendous force with which the water pulled against the iron grates beneath the surface of the water.

The first attempt was unsuccessful. Mr. Spence had to hold his breath while he explored under the water with his hands for a body. "I can't see or feel anything under there!" he gasped as his head burst through the surface the first time.

I heard another fireman say, "Try to catch your breath, and we'll give it another try!" The dark, murky, green water was swirling against the intake grates when Fireman Spence dove beneath the water a second time. He took several huge breaths, held them, and went down.

By this time, many adults and kids had gathered on the riverbank, watching the rescue efforts and hoping the firemen would soon be successful. Time was running out. After what seemed like an eternity, I heard one of the firemen yell, "He's got him!"

When the other firemen pulled Mr. Spence to the surface, he was clinging to a lifeless, limp, young boy's body. Word passed rapidly among the onlookers that the young boy was Donald Joseph. My heart sank! Attempts to revive Donald were unsuccessful. He had been down there too long. I began sobbing silently. My friend had drowned. He was dead!

A BLAST FROM THE PAST

Early every Fourth of July morning during the 1930's, Crookston kids filled their neighborhoods with the pop! pop! pop! sounds that red rolls of explosive "caps" made in their toy pistols. Some kids pretended they were cowboys like Tom Mix, Hopalong Cassidy, and Gene Autry. Others became gangsters like Al Capone, Baby Face Nelson, and John Dillinger and pretended they were doing battle with federal agents from the F.B.I.

A little later in the morning when the teenagers awakened, they celebrated Independence Day with the bang! bang! bang! sounds of smaller firecrackers and the boom! boom! boom! sounds of Flash Crackers and Cherry Bombs which rattled the nerves of young and old alike.

Around noon was when the heavy artillery moved downtown and was mixed with the blasts of Torpedoes (fireworks consisting of explosives wrapped up with gravel in a piece of tissue paper that detonated when thrown against a hard surface) which were thrown at one another. Baseball players from the Crookston Pirates baseball team got in a little practice for their next game by throwing Torpedoes at one another between Eide's Candy Store and the New York Store which had a solid brick wall, and kids would lob Torpedoes high into the air so that they'd land near groups of people and scare the wits out of them when they made contact with the concrete streets and sidewalks and exploded.

In the afternoon the fireworks noise abated, the smoke smell dissipated, and a parade began, highlighted by the crack Crookston Women's Drum and Bugle Corps which marched up and down Main and Broadway under the competent direction of Mr. Thorsen.

The rest of the afternoon was filled with contests for the kids. If you liked to eat, there were pie and watermelon eating contests. If you liked to get your exercise and were older, stronger and faster than the other boys and girls, you may have found yourself entering the three-legged race, the wheelbarrow race, the gunny sack race, or one of the just plain fast foot races.

Being only nine years old, weak, and slow one particular Fourth of July, I had to satisfy myself with watching the other boys until I heard the announcer yell, " Our next race will be a SLOW BICYCLE RACE, so go get your bikes and line 'em up over here!"

My heart leaped to my throat when I heard this announcement because I had learned to ride my new bike in the spring, and I had developed the skill of going real slow on it, so slow that I could almost make it stand still for minutes at a timer while riding it.

You can imagine my excitement when I entered this race against the older, stronger, faster boys. But I did, and I won! I beat all of them by coming in "last" at the finish line! I remember pocketing my half dollar prize money and racing down to the ice cream parlor and buying a triple decker chocolate, vanilla, and strawberry cone for a nickel and licking it all the way home on my bike. Being slow sometimes had its advantages.

When night time arrived, adults usually gathered on their lawns where they sat and talked while they watched their older kids shoot colorful skyrockets and Roman candles into the dark night sky, and their younger kids run around waving sparklers, showering the night with bright, white, sparkling light, much like nature's fireflies. That's the way the Fourth of July celebration usually ended in Crookston during the 1930's.

People were peaceful, happy, and had a lot of love in their hearts for their country and the privilege of being Americans.

THE KITTEN

When we moved from our 403 Pleasant Avenue house to our 416 Woodland Avenue house in Crookston during the 1930's, my playmates, the Pedersons, moved into our old house. Our Woodland Avenue house was still in Sampson's Addition and only a couple of blocks from our old house, so I always ran down there to play with my old friends.

One hot summer day when I was about seven years old, all of the Pederson kids plus a few of the neighborhood kids (including myself) were playing in the Pederson's big, back dirt yard. Some were climbing trees, some were playing tag, and some were playing with a kitten which the Pedersons had just gotten. There was a lot of running and yelling and screaming.

During all of this kid noise, Mrs. Pederson was working in her kitchen, baking and fixing supper for all of her kids because it was late in the afternoon. Gradually, the running and yelling stopped, and the kids all gathered around two of the Pederson sisters who were arguing and fighting over who got to play with the new little kitten. They began screaming at one another. One shouted, "Now it's my turn! You've been playing with it long enough!"

The other sister screamed back, "I have not! I've only had it for a few minutes!" All of the neighborhood kids just stood and watched, silently, because they knew that before long a real cat fight was going to take place—it had before—between these two sisters, and there would be clawing and pulling of hair and fists swinging. Yes, even among girls, even among sisters, this was about to happen.

The pitch of the sisters' screaming at one another kept rising higher and higher, and the first blow was about to be struck when Mrs. Pederson emerged from her kitchen. The girls didn't see her coming, but everyone else did. As the sisters grabbed one another by the hair and their shrill voices kept filling the hot, summer air, Mrs. Pederson came rushing towards them. She still had on her apron, and her strong arms were covered with flour.

As she drew closer to her fighting daughters, Mrs. Pederson bent down to pick up a heavy stick. All the kids suddenly backed away. They knew these girls were in for a good thrashing, and they were just happy it wasn't they getting it. Suddenly, the sisters looked up and saw their mother hovering over them. Without a word, Mrs. Pederson swept the kitten from the ground by its furry neck with her left hand and commenced bashing the kitten's head with the big stick she held in her right hand.

Thud, thud, thud was all that could be heard as the heavy stick landed on the kitten's head. Silence filled the air as we kids just stood there, muted, mouths open, eyes wide, and scared, plenty scared! The hair on my arms bristled, and I began backing away. The kitten hung limp and lifeless from Mrs. Pederson's hand. She threw it to the ground at her daughters' feet and shouted, "There, now neither of you can play with it!"

The girls began crying as Mrs. Pederson turned and walked back towards her house. All of the neighborhood kids, still in shock, began walking slowly away towards home. I shuddered at the sight of the dead kitten lying on the ground and began running quickly for home to tell my mother what had happened in the Pedersons' back yard.

THE LOSS OF INNOCENCE

I was only seven years old the first time I ever saw Mr. Reidesel's little black and white pug-nosed Boston terrier come trotting briskly home (alone) from Erickson's Meat Market with a package of meat clutched in its mouth. I couldn't believe it! I remember standing in front of my dad's Second Street barbershop and staring at that little dog as it pranced proudly and nonchalantly in front of me on its way home to Reidesel's Shoe Store which was only two doors down from my dad's shop. How did Mr. Reidesel, I wondered, ever teach that little dog that fabulous trick?

The same way, I guessed, that my dad taught me. "Charlie," he'd say, "run up to Erickson's and get a pound of hamburger and bring it home." I never asked any questions. I just marched to the market as steadily and soldierly as had Mr. Reidesel's Boston terrier and carried the package of meat (but not in my mouth) home as coolly unconcerned and indifferent to the world as had the dog.

I never gave a thought to what had to happen before that meat could be placed on our table in the form of tasty, juicy, browned, mouth-watering hamburgers. Then one day as I was dallying in the alley behind Erickson's Meat Market, watching a farmer and one of Erickson's butchers prod some cattle from a truck, down a wooden chute, and into Erickson's concrete basement, I learned the awful truth.

The cattle were complaining loudly when a small friend who was standing alongside me said, "They shoot them when they're in there, Charlie!" At first I didn't believe him, but when I got home, I asked my dad, and he said, "Yes, Charlie, they hire a man to do that. I think his name is Frankie Berg. Later, I learned from some older boys that Frankie (who was disabled and had to use a wheelchair) sat on a wooden perch above the animals and shot them in the head before they were butchered. I felt really sorry and sad for the animals, but couldn't picture what was happening to them until . . . .

One day my dad sent me over to the newly-opened Crookston Cold Storage lockers on Main Street to get some frozen vegetables from our locker. When I entered, it was freezing cold, in sharp contrast to the hot and humid summer weather outside. As I was walking down the cold, concrete hallway towards our locker, I heard a loud, desperate squealing sound coming from the far end of the building. Forgetting about the vegetables, I raced in that direction and soon saw what was causing the agonizing sound. A man was hunched over a huge, bleeding hog! "Hi, Charlie," he said.

It was Mr. Schumacher, my friend Jerry Schumacher's dad. He had a big knife in his hand, and it was dripping blood. The hog's slit throat was gushing blood, and its body was twitching and jerking. Gradually, the movement became less perceptible and finally stopped. I just stood there and stared, muted and mesmerized, and said nothing to Mr. Schumacher because I was afraid that something might happen to me.

While I was looking down at the hog, I began to feel a little sick and unsteady on my feet as Mr. Schumacher went to work on it. He severed its head, slit open its belly, and immediately began skinning it. I was too fascinated to pull myself away. Huge folds of skin seemed to just slide from the hog's sides and back as Mr. Schumacher slid his sharp knife beneath it. Layers of steaming white fat were exposed. I turned and began walking away slowly, silently, still a little sickened by what I'd just witnessed. Gradually, it dawned on me what had to happen to the animals before they became food for the dinner table. Now I knew, but that didn't make it any easier.

THE CIRCUS

During the summer of 1935 when I was seven years old, my dad took me to a circus that I'll always remember. It was an afternoon performance on Thursday, June 6th, and because we didn't have a car, my dad and I walked all the way out to Highland Park from our Sampson's Addition home, alone, because my ten year old brother Bill was playing baseball in Central Park and my mother was five months pregnant with my sister Catherine and home taking care of my three year old sister Betty. By the time we got to the circus grounds, we were pretty hot and sweaty and ready to get out of the sun.

We got in line to buy our tickets as soon as we got there so we could get in a little early and find good seats, and we did. Ours were perfect, about fifteen rows high and right next to a large canvas flap through which the circus people and animals entered and exited the "Big Top." By the time the show began, bleachers on both sides of the large tent were jammed to capacity with eager, excited, squealing kids and their parents!

First came the colorful clowns to perform their antics. Then the jugglers, tight rope walkers, and trapeze artists. As the heat under the big tent grew more intense and the crowd's interest began to wane somewhat, it was waxed anew when the animals began entering. First, the horses came galloping through the large canvas flap, and their riders began doing tricks with them, standing on their backs and leaping from one side to the other as they raced around the large, dusty, dirt oval. Next came the lions and the tigers and their trainers. Finally, the elephants came lumbering through the canvas flap, and it was a sight to behold those huge, gray beasts dance and perform the delicate feats through which their trainers put them.

As the show began winding down with a barrel juggling act, tragedy struck! One of the huge elephants which had just finished performing came charging back into the tent and against the bleachers where my dad and I were sitting! Before I had time to act, my dad jumped up and pulled me as far away as possible from the rampaging pachyderm. Dad twisted his left ankle while he was pulling me to safety, and he saw Dr. Nelson for it the next day.

Many other people were injured and sought medical treatment, but the real tragedy was that a young girl who was sitting with her friends in the first row of the bleachers below me was killed! The Friday, June 7, 1935 issue of the Crookston Daily Times reported the incident this way: "A nine-year-old, circus-loving child is dead today, an elephant trainer is being held pending a criminal investigation, and scores of people are nursing minor injuries as a result of a tragedy that stalked the tents of the Atterbury Brothers show during its matinee performance here yesterday afternoon.

The tragedy came near the close of the afternoon performance when Virginia, an eighteen year old elephant, crashed through the sides of the tent, upsetting the bleachers and throwing the crowd into pandemonium, as she was being taken back to her cage after her part in the show.

Dead is Margaret Ann Francis, daughter of Mr. and Mrs. William Francis, whose skull was crushed by the elephant's foot as it made its way the length of the tent."

When Mrs. Francis was called to the hospital and learned that her child was dead, she collapsed!

On Saturday morning circus employees were walking all around downtown Crookston, talking to people and trying to calm them. If they learned that a person had been injured, they offered them money.

The Saturday, June 8th Crookston Daily Times reported that a coroner's jury composed of: Ebbe Anderson, J.D. Boileau, O.Mercil, Jr., Sam Meng, Ole Nerland, and J.F. Fournet found William H. Woodstock, trainer of the elephant Virginia, guilty of negligence, and the Monday, June 10th Crookston Daily Times reported that a settlement in the neighborhood of $5,000 was made with the William Francis family for the death of nine-year-old Margaret Ann Francis.

Unfortunately, no amount of money could ever compensate for Margaret Ann's death nor bring her back to life!

MEATY TREATS

Our whole family loved Mom's cooking, especially her fried chicken of which each of us had a favorite part. I always liked the drumstick and thigh, my brother Bill the wings, and my dad, believe it or not, the neck and back. Now isn't that weird! He had other unusual meat eating habits, too, habits he tried foisting off on us kids, but it didn't work.

One day Dad and I were walking to Erickson's Meat Market on South Main Street to get some meat for supper when Dad saw this big wooden barrel of pickled pigs' feet. He looked at me with a smile on his face and said persuasively, "Let's get some of those, Charlie. I think you'll like them." I didn't! That night I settled for a peanut butter sandwich and a glass of cold milk.

Another time, a Sunday when we were all sitting around our dining room table waiting for supper, my mouth began to water when my mom brought out a large platter of golden brown chicken. "Yummm!" I thought. "That certainly looks good!"

Dad said prayers, and immediately after he said, "Amen!" we all began digging in. I stabbed what looked like a delicious, golden-brown thigh, picked it up with my fingers and chomped it. My taste buds rebelled immediately. "This doesn't taste like chicken," I complained.

"Of course it is, Charlie," my dad countered with a broad smile on his face. "What's wrong with it?"

"I don't know," I said cautiously as I slowly swallowed my first bite. "It just doesn't taste like chicken."

Then my dad just laughed and said, "It isn't, Charlie. It's rabbit!" That's all I had to hear to ruin my appetite for that meal. I excused myself, left the house, and went downtown.

The last time Dad tried to get us to like one of his weird meat delicacies was the evening we all sat down to hamburger patties and potatoes. The patties were browned to perfection. I had never seen hamburger patties as "golden" brown as these. These "burgers" weren't served on buns. They were just eaten with potatoes and vegetables as was our custom.

As soon as I began cutting into my "burger' to take a bite, I knew something was wrong because a white, creamy liquid oozed out. "What's this!" I asked, holding the piece of "burger" up in the air on my fork for everyone to see.

My dad just said, "Try it, Charlie. You'll like it."

My mom added, "Ya, Charlie. Give it a try. You're too fussy."

Then my dad told me it was "pig brains!" Right then and there, I dropped my fork on my plate and was up and out. That's all she wrote for that supper. A procession of my two brothers and two sisters followed right behind me.

Those were some of the bizarre meats my dad tried unsuccessfully to get us kids to eat. The rest were very normal: chicken, turkey, goose, beef roasts, pork chops, wieners, hamburger, liver, ribs, steak, mince meat, summer sausage, liverwurst, etc. You name it. We ate it, except for the "meaty treats."

SPECIAL PEOPLE

Steve Octeen and Tom Keeley were slow, innocent men who captured Crookston's collective heart during the 1930's. Here's how they left an indelible impression on mine.

Steve, who was a chubby fellow, always seemed like a man on a mission. I guess this was because whenever I saw him walking around town or passed him on Woodland Avenue, he was delivering a package for Wallace's Drug Store.

Whenever we'd meet, Steve would always say, "Good morning, Mr. Dowdle," or "Good afternoon, Mr. Dowdle," or simply, "Hello there, Mr. Dowdle." It was always "Mr. Dowdle," and you can imagine how this made a little kid feel being addressed as "Mr." It made me feel important, and I liked Steve for making me feel that way.

Steve always seemed to be happiest when he was working, delivering his packages for Wallace's. Come to think of it, I don't think I ever saw him when he wasn't walking somewhere or other with a package in his hand. Obviously, this job made Steve feel useful and needed by society, and it showed in his whole being which radiated with friendliness whenever he'd meet you on the street.

When Steve walked, he sort of wobbled like a penguin, but he wobbled on fast forward at all times. He had a little belly, but this didn't slow him down a bit. When Steve scooted along, it seemed like his whole body moved. His head swung from side to side, and his arms flailed forward and backward, making me think of one of the Great Northern Railroad's steam locomotives puffing down the track.

When Steve would really get going, he'd begin sweating profusely at which time he'd stop, take out his handkerchief and wipe his brow, and then he'd just keep chugging right along. Once in awhile he'd stop and say hello to me when he was doing this, and while he was catching his breath, it gave me a chance to observe Steve more closely. I noticed that he always wore his pants real high, what the kids used to call "floods." He also wore suspenders. On his feet Steve wore heavy, high-top dress shoes which must have made him pretty tired during all that walking, but he didn't seem to mind. If it was a hot summer day, he'd simply (like I mentioned above) take out his handkerchief, wipe away the heavy beads of perspiration from his forehead, and say something like, "Well, Mr. Dowdle, it's a pretty hot one today isn't it!"

When I'd look Steve straight in the face, it was like looking right at another little kid like myself. It was an innocent face, a cherubic face that looked like an angel had landed there, a happy face that never meant anyone any harm and that just wanted to make other people happy, too. Steve always had a little tuft of brown hair falling over his forehead which made him look all the more little boyish to me even though he was a man. I guess what made Steve Octeen seem so special to me and why I still remember him is that he always seemed so filled with happiness and love.

The other "special guy" I remember was happy, too, but Tom Keeley was very different from Steve Octeen. I even hesitate to use the two names in the same sentence they were so different. Tom wasn't even-tempered. At times he had emotional outbursts which scared me. I don't think he ever hurt anybody, but I didn't feel comfortable around him. Sometimes I even got a little afraid of him and didn't trust what he'd do.

Maybe this was because of some of Tom's habits. He liked to hang around Acker's saloon (which was next to my dad's barbershop) and drink a little beer and smoke cigars. Whenever he'd come swaggering out of that saloon (on Second Street), huffing and puffing on a cigar, his face all flushed red, I knew to stay out of Tom's way. At those times he scared me.

He made me think of a snorting bull ready to charge! When he roared, "Good afternoon, Mr. Dowdle!" I just ran away, quickly. It's sort of sad because I'm sure the man didn't mean any harm. It's just that his demeanor (probably fueled by the beer he drank) was loaded with emotion, and it scared me! I had a tendency to laugh when I saw Tom in this state, but I didn't because I knew this would make him very angry, and I'd just be asking for trouble and have to run away from him.

One day, however, I did laugh, the first time I saw Tom perform his "Handkerchief Trick." It was during halftime at a high school football game in Central Park. Tom ran out onto the football field and placed his big old red railroad handkerchief smack dab on the middle of the fifty yard line. All of the people standing on each side of the field began cheering as Tom lumbered (he was a short, heavy-set man) his way fifty yards to the end zone. I kept wondering what he was going to do when all of a sudden he raised his arms over his head for silence, and the crowd grew quiet.

The next thing I knew, Tom was thundering down the field towards his handkerchief, and the crowd was cheering wildly. When he reached his handkerchief, Tom stopped, again raised his arms over his head, and again the crowd grew silent, so silent you could have heard a pin drop in the grass this time.

No one even brushed the air with so much as a whisper as Tom lay on his back on the grass, turned his head sideways towards his handkerchief, opened his mouth and clenched the handkerchief between his teeth. At that instant the crowd roared its appreciation for Tom once again having performed his "Handkerchief Trick."

Pandemonium continued breaking loose as Tom rose to his feet, extracted his handkerchief from his mouth and waved it over his head to acknowledge the crowd which continued cheering, laughing, and clapping their hands wildly!

Tom strode off the field, bowing to both sides, continuing to acknowledge the crowd's appreciation for the act he had just performed. I guess it was all in good fun, and it made Tom feel good about himself, but it always bothered me a little each time I saw Tom perform that stunt after that.

POLK COUNTY FAIR

Almost every summer during the 1930's when my older brother Willie and I were kids, we'd walk with our mother to the Northern Pacific Depot where we boarded the train for about a twenty mile ride to Fertile, Minnesota, the Polk County Fair, and a visit with our grandparents, Anton and Gretje Van Raden. Grandma was always full of enthusiasm, and when we got there and began running around the house and playing, she'd get all excited and play with us! The first thing I always liked to do was pump the organ pedals with my feet and play the organ as loudly as it would go! In retrospect, I'm sure we drove our grandparents crazy when we were there, but they just seemed to love every minute of our visit.

Each morning Grandma would make us delicious buckwheat pancakes for breakfast and let us take turns grinding the beans for freshly made coffee. After breakfast my brother and I would usually run outside and play cowboys and Indians. One morning while we were doing this, my brother had a homemade bow and arrow and he was chasing me. When he let go of the arrow, it was a good shot, and it stuck in my back. I ran into the house, crying, "Grandma! Grandma! Willie shot me!"

Grandma grabbed her broom and flew out of the house after my brother. I heard her yelling, "Villiam! You come here!" I think my brother got a spanking, but before long everything was okay, I got fixed up, and we were out playing again.

Grandma Van Raden was big, robust, and jolly, and Grandpa was tall like her, only he was lean and big boned. He looked stern most of the time but was always very gentle with us and willing to teach us something, like going out to the henhouse and collecting the eggs or showing us how to use the outhouse. In Crookston we had indoor plumbing, so using an outhouse (which smelled) and wiping ourselves with pages from a catalog was a totally new experience, but it was all very new and therefore exciting to us.

Of course, going to the fair with our mom was also exciting. When she took us, she always dressed us in white linen pants and white shirts. Don't ask me why! That's just the way it was! Well, one summer when we went, there we were, all dressed in white, neat as a pin. As soon as we entered the gate, I saw a food stand and asked Mom if I could get something to eat. "Sure, Charles," she said. "What would you like?"

I read what they had like hot dogs, hamburgers, etc., but for some reason I had a yen for an egg sandwich, so I said to the girl at the stand, "I want an egg sandwich!"

She smiled at me in my sparkling white outfit and said, "Okay," and walked away to fix it. Shortly, she came back and handed me the sandwich which was served between two slices of thick white bread, my favorite. Immediately, I chomped into it and yellow egg yolk spurted all over the front of my white shirt and pants! "Why," I thought, "did she make an egg sandwich without scrambling it? Who ever heard of an egg sandwich being served sunny side up between two slices of bread!" I just stood there, dumbfounded, as the yellow egg yolk ran down the front of my shirt and pants. Mom helped me clean up, but that day at the fair sure got off to a bad start for me!

The rest of our day at the fair was uneventful, and before we knew it the visit with our grandparents was completed and we were headed home. Attending the Polk County Fair and visiting with our grandparents each summer was always fun, but getting back to Crookston among familiar friends and places always turned out to be the most satisfying part of our summer adventure.

BUCKAROO

Galloping wildly around our front yard on my imaginary horse, neighing, snorting, bucking and frantically slapping my butt, I became my cowboy idols Tom Mix and Tim McCoy during my preschool days in Crookston. When I grew a little older was when I had my first experience with a real horse.

It must have been around 1936 when I was eight years old that a circus and carnival came to town and set up near Mount Saint Benedict at Highland Park. Young kids like myself got excited and went out there early in the morning to watch the roustabouts set up their tents and care for their animals. What attracted my attention the most were the Shetland ponies which were being saddled, reined, and led around a small roped in circle for exercise. I just knew that when the carnival opened that afternoon that I was going to want to be out there riding one of those ponies.

So, after selling all of my Crookston Daily Times papers on the streets that afternoon, I half ran and half walked all the way through town, past the Northern Pacific Depot, up the Riverside Drive hill, and finally reached the carnival grounds. I had broken out in a hot sweat and was eager to saddle up like a real cowboy by the time I reached the ponies.

Surprisingly, the few nickels and dimes that had been jingling around in my pocket hadn't fallen out, so I took out a dime, bought a ticket, gave it to the carnival man, and cautiously approached one of the short, sturdy, rough coated ponies. I must have looked a little scared because the carnival man came over to me and said, "Here, son. Let me help you up there. Nothing to be afraid about. Just take hold of the reins and the horse will know where to go."

Riding seemed so easy until about the third time my pony was walking around the roped in circle. Then all hell broke loose! The Shetland snorted, broke from the circle, trotted rapidly towards the rope and jumped it with me desperately clinging to its mane. Once outside the roped in circle, the pony must have sensed my panic and fear and its own newfound freedom as it raced away, snorting and bucking, towards the big circus tent. When we reached it, the pony dashed under one of the large, bristly, twine ropes which held the tent secure, and I caught my neck on it and was flipped off backwards! I remember landing on my butt and just sitting there for awhile, stunned, when the carnival worker ran over to me, picked me up, brushed me off and asked excitedly, "Are you all right, son?"

I wasn't able to answer him right away because I had the wind knocked out of me, but when I finally caught my breath, tears began forming in my eyes and I said, "I think so." That episode ended my first ride on a real horse, but it wasn't to be the last.

About four years later when I had turned twelve in 1940 was when I had my second encounter. It was in Sampson's Addition above the Old Dam where my good friend Howie Pederson and I used to go swimming in the nude during some of Crookston's hot, humid, summer days.

We were reckless boys, always challenging one another to daring new feats that would test our "manhood." One day while we were swimming above the Old Dam I said, "Let's see who can swim out the farthest in the river, Howie."

"Okay," he said, "but what happens if we caught in the current?"

"We won't," I answered confidently and began running towards the riverbank with Howie at my side. We both flew off the bank and into the water at the same time and were stroking our way towards the middle of the river when we noticed that we were being carried towards the dam by the current. "Let's swim back before it's too late!" I yelled. Panting and out of breath, we made it safely.

What happened next was just as exciting as the swim, if not more so, for me. Some big old workhorses had moseyed over on the hill behind us and had begun pasturing while we were in the river. "I dare you to ride one of them, Charlie," Howie taunted. I really didn't want to because I was afraid of horses after my one experience with them at the carnival, so I asked, "How am I supposed to get up? They're huge!"

"That's no problem," Howie answered. "Just put your foot in my cupped hands and I'll hoist you up!"

Well, although having mixed emotions about what I was about to do, that sounded okay to me, and we began walking towards one of the horses. It looked gentle, harmless, and didn't even pay any attention to us, just kept chomping on its grass and acting as if we were invisible. "Okay, Charlie," Howie whispered so as not to spook the horse, "put your foot in my hands and I'll boost you up." And he did. The horse's sleek fur felt fine on my bare bottom, and I knew that this was going to be an easy, fun, and safe ride as the large animal wandered leisurely on the hill from one patch of grass to the next.

That's when Howie said, "Let's see how fast he can run, Charlie!" And he let out a whoop and slapped the horse on the butt as hard as he could. Instantly, that old workhorse jerked up its head, snorted its displeasure and began galloping towards the riverbank! I just held on to its mane for dear life! Suddenly, at the very edge of the riverbank, the horse forcefully jutted its forelegs into the ground, stiffened, and sent me flying over its head into the water. Luckily, I wasn't hurt, but vowed never to get on a horse again!

Never say never. It happened again just two years later when I turned fourteen. The United States had entered World War II when the Japanese bombed Pearl Harbor in 1941, and town boys were needed to help the farmers harvest their crops. We'd drive out in groups and shock grain, wheat, barley, oats. Some of us even drove teams of four horses into the fields with empty rigs which were then pitched high with shocks of grain before returning to a threshing machine for harvesting. It was fun and exciting work, especially for a town boy like myself who had never really had any success with horses, a town boy who, in fact, was afraid of them!

Once again, my time had come to conquer my fear of horses as I tugged on the heavy leather reins and tried to lead a team of trotting horses into the field. All it took was a loud shout and a strong slap with the heavy leather straps on their butts to get them moving. I imagined being just like the pioneers I'd seen in the movies, driving their "prairie schooners" across the land at a torrid pace in order to ward off an Indian attack. It was a chance to be free and wild, a real buckaroo, and I loved it until . . . .

It was late afternoon, and the first, hot day of work was done. I was standing outside the farmhouse in the yard, alone, just waiting around for supper to be ready when I noticed an old nag of a horse standing near the barn, also alone. That's when I decided to go for a ride before supper and once and for all conquer my fear of horses. The nag had no equipment on it, no reins, no saddle, no nothing, so the ride was going to be bareback, just like when I got dumped in the river two years ago. When I approached the animal, it just stood there and stared at me as if to say, "Don't bother me, town boy!" so I grabbed its mane aggressively, like I'd seen Indians do in the movies, swung myself aboard, and we were away! The old nag didn't wait for any directions from me! It just began trotting away from the farmhouse, and once we reached a nearby gravel road began galloping away. That's when my fear of horses kicked in again. "What was I to do now?" I thought, as we trotted along and left the farmhouse in the distance.

What I did was cling tightly to that old horse's mane and pull at it in an attempt to turn it towards home. This maneuver didn't set too well with the old nag. Suddenly, it quickly left the gravel road and turned sharply down a ditch! This took me by surprise, and when we reached the bottom of the ditch and began heading up the other side, I lost my balance and tumbled to the ground while the "old nag" just kept running away. I was sort of shaken up by the fall and picked myself up very slowly.

As I started walking back to the farmhouse, I began thinking that I'd lost the farmer's horse and would have to pay for it! I could be working for him all summer and not earn a dime! When I made it back to the farmhouse late and sat down to eat with the rest of the men, I sheepishly told the farmer what had happened, and he just laughed. "What was so funny?" I thought.

"Don't worry about the horse," the farmer said. "He knows his way home." Sure enough! After supper, I walked outside, and standing near the barn, all alone, I saw the horse chomping on some hay. Was I relieved!

NICKNAMES

Nicknames were quite familiar to the boys who grew up in Crookston during the 1930's and 1940's due mainly to one man, "Minnie Morin Mike, who could and did lay a nickname on a person over the slightest incident. "Minnie" was in a good position to observe Crookston's boys because he was the town's summer baseball director. Once nickname mania was begun by "Minnie," it caught fire, and all the boys began looking for "creative opportunities" to nail any person with a unique nickname.

Some I can remember kids being called are: "Butch," "Fat," "Spanky," "Meat," "Stud," "Wa Wa," "Hugga Hugga," "Alfalfa," "Cowpie," "Red," "Snort," "Buddy," "Dinky," "Gus," "Kitty," "Weezie," "Toddy," and "All Guts." Some other names I learned about recently are: "Pookie," "Puddles," "DoDah," "Arf," "Laddie," and "Snowball." Even some of the girls had nicknames, but the only two I can recall are "Chub" and "Bubsy."

Kids just called me "Charlie" which was fine, but one summer day "Minnie" Mike laid a nickname on me, too. It was my first try at playing shortstop, and I made a couple of outstanding plays, catching one line drive and making a double play from a ground ball hit my way.

When I got home that afternoon, all sweaty and tired from having played baseball all morning, I said, "Guess what, Mom, I caught a line drive this morning!"

My mom just said, "Well, good for you, Charles. Sit down now and eat something and rest awhile before you go outside and play again. You look all tired out." My mom was a constant worrier who never paid too much attention to what got my older brother "Willie" or me excited.

Unfortunately for me, my brother was paying attention to what got me excited and to what I was telling Mom because the next day when we went down to Central Park to play baseball again, he told "Minnie" what I had told her.

"Minnie," of course, picked right up on this and yelled, "Oh ho! 'Star at Home!'" You guessed it. From that day on whenever I played baseball in the park, the kids called me "Star at Home." I didn't like it but tried not to let it bother me.

Let me tell you what happened to my brother "Willie" who was also know as "Bill," "Salty," and "Dipsy."

It was Halloween night, and as usual I was tagging along with my older brother. Being with older boys, especially on Halloween night, was always filled with excitement and action. They didn't go to parties. They didn't knock on doors and call out, "Tricks or treats, money or eats!" And they didn't go around soaping windows. The bigger boys always planned bigger mischief which was designed to drive Crookston's cops crazy!

That's the way it was in 1938 when I was ten years old and my brother was thirteen. As soon as we finished supper, we were out the door and downtown. It was already dark, and by time we reached Main Street from our Woodland Avenue house in Sampson's Addition, a large gang of boys had already gathered, and their plans were made. The ringleaders began walking north on Main Street towards the Hill Addition when I heard one of them shout, "This is going to be fun! There are outhouses up there that are just begging to pushed over!"

This sounded exciting! It would be a new experience for me, and a great chance to do something just like the older boys. So, I ran along after them as they rang a few doorbells and created a ruckus. It didn't take very long before a voice familiar to all of us shattered the night air. "All right you boys," shouted Art Roy. "Slow down! I wanna have a little talk with ya!"

When the ringleaders heard Art's command to come to a halt, they yelled, "Run like hell for the railroad tracks, you guys! It's Art!" Instantly, all the boys dashed towards the hill which had to be climbed before reaching the tracks. I was petrified when I reached the bottom of the hill and began running up it. "I'm not going to make it," I thought. "Art's going to catch me!"

My lungs were aching, and I could hear Art gaining on us when out of desperation I clutched at an older boy's hip pocket and was dragged speedily up the hill after him. "Damn it, Charlie, let go of my pocket," he yelled, but I just clung to it and was carried right up the hill behind him.

When we reached the top of the hill, all of the boys began running towards my grandpa and grandma's house which was only a couple of blocks from the railroad tracks. I was all sweaty and began panting heavily and knew I wasn't going to be able to keep up, so I began thinking about what I could do to escape from Art and survive!

It was then that I realized that the boys had made a sharp turn and were heading right between my grandparents house and another house, so i kept plunging behind them as fast as my legs would carry me. As the boys thundered between the two houses and past a car that was parked alongside one of them, I could hear Art shouting, and his voice seemed angry which sent chills up and down my spine. "I'm going to be caught for sure," I thought.

As soon as I reached my grandparents' house, I dove to the ground and rolled under the car which was near it. Holding my breath and not moving a muscle, I could hear Art panting as he ran past me. I was saved! Art didn't see me go under the car! In the distance I saw him waving his flashlight in the direction of the older boys, but I just lay there, silently, afraid!

When I thought it was safe, I crawled slowly from beneath the car and began walking home, alone. I'd had enough Halloweening for one night, but that wasn't to be the end of it for my brother.

He did indeed find an outhouse to push over with the older boys that night, and when he did, he fell into the outhouse hole! In desperation, he called out, "Louie, pull me out!" He was calling to Louie Salem, his friend. Fortunately, Louie came to my brother's aid and he was saved. The fun began when my brother got home that night.

"William!" I heard my mother's surprised voice call out, what have you been doing? Where have you been?" After "Willie," "Bill," "Salty," "Dipsy" told Mom what had happened, she just looked at him with disgust in her voice and said, "You just take those clothes off and hose yourself down real good in the yard before you come into the house and take a bath!"

From that day on my brother acquired another nickname, "Shithouse." His friends would greet him very casually on the street with, "Hey, "Shithouse," wadda ya gonna be doin' tonight?" Or "Dipsy" might be in the Playhouse shooting a game of pool and a friend in a very normal voice would say something like, "Nice shot, "Shithouse." In polite company I remember the boys referring to him euphemistically as "S.H."

That's about it for nicknames. I think some can be devastating to one's personality, causing a lowered self image and much embarrassment. On the other hand, they can generate a real creative flair, too, like the time Garrett De Mott (a much older boy) taunted my brother when he called across the street to him, "Willie, Willie, Weiner, the outhouse cleaner!" My brother with a flash of inspiration shot back, "Garry Garry Gitt stinks like shit!" And then he ran.

It's strange how some nicknames stick with a person for a lifetime. Whenever I come home, people always think I'm my brother and only remember one nickname, "Dipsy."

Thank God!

READY, AIM, FIRE!

Bang! Just one shot from my trusty BB gun was all it took to seal the fate of the squirrel which had been staring at me just a moment ago. My eyes were unbelieving when I saw the squirrel drop. Guilty thoughts burned my mind as they raced through my head and caused my small body to tremble. "I killed it! I killed it with my gun! I didn't mean to!" But it was useless for me to try to escape the logic of my act. I did aim my BB gun at the squirrel, and the squirrel did drop from the branch.

As I walked slowly towards the tree below which lay the motionless, furry animal, I was hoping against all hope that the squirrel was just stunned and would get up and run away as soon as I approached, but the closer I got to the tree, and the longer I stared down at the still animal, the surer I was that it was dead!

I couldn't believe it! My ten year old lips quivered! About the only animals I'd ever killed before were ants, mosquitoes, grasshoppers, bees, earthworms and fish. I'd aimed at a lot of birds, but I'd never hit one. How could I? I was such a lousy shot. But the squirrel sure seemed dead!

I laid my BB gun on the ground and slowly, cautiously bent over to pick up the squirrel. Its body was warm. Its fur was a sleek, golden brown. It was a young squirrel. As I gently rolled its small, lifeless body over in my hands, I saw it, the puncture wound where my BB had struck. My heart sank! I had shot the squirrel right between the eyes, a perfect hit.

But it wasn't perfect at all for a sensitive child like myself. I wasn't proud of my marksmanship. I was sad, sad that I had silenced the life of one of the small creatures that I had come to admire and love so well. Tears began welling up in my eyes and running down my cheeks as I lay the squirrel's warm body back down on the ground. "Sure wouldn't like it if someone did that to me," I thought.

I picked up my gun and began the long walk home through Crookston's Sampson's Addition woods. Birds, full of life, chirped overhead as I walked along.

"If they only knew how I felt," I thought. As I looked away from them, I quickened my pace because it was getting late, and my mom didn't like it when I got home late for supper. I began wondering what would happen when that little squirrel didn't show up that evening. Would its mother begin searching frantically for it?

As I entered the house and quietly closed the front door, my mom called out, "Charles, is that you? Better wash up and get ready to eat. Your dad will be home any minute now."

"That little squirrel's dad is sure going to miss it," I thought. As our family sat down to eat, my dad said grace, and everyone but me began digging in, ravenously. I guess I must have just sat there, daydreaming, because I heard my dad ask, "What's the matter, Charlie, not hungry?"

When I came to my senses, I answered him, saying, "I'm not very hungry, Dad. I don't feel very good."

"Have you been eating something?" my mom asked.

"No, Mom," I answered. "I just don't feel too good."

"Well, why don't you go up to your bedroom and lie down for a while, and maybe it'll go away," she said.

"O.K., Mom," I replied. As I got up from the table, my two brothers, two sisters, and parents hardly noticed me leaving. They all just kept eating, shoveling it in like nothing had happened. "How could they?" I thought. "Didn't they suspect something? Weren't they curious to know what terrible thing had happened to me?"

I shuffled up the stairs to my room, lay down on my bed, curled up, and fell asleep. Before long, I was dreaming, reliving the sad experience of that day.

WORK

When I was a Crookston kid during the Great Depression of the 1930's, work was a large part of my life. It gave me something to do. It made me feel important. It molded my character. It helped me feel independent. It helped me earn money to buy the things I wanted. Both work and money were at a premium during that time, and if one could get either, he was fortunate. In previous articles I've already mentioned different jobs I held as a child, but here are three more I'd like to tell about that interested me.

For some reason, I just loved pastry! So much so, that I'd go to J.C. Penny's on South Main Street and ask Mr. Nick Barthelomew for empty cardboard boxes which I knew Marotte's Bakery, also on South Main Street, needed, and for which Mr. Marotte would give me pastry! It must have been an odd scene, I dragging cardboard boxes down the street from Penny's to Marotte's, but he and I had a mutual business transaction going, and it was one which satisfied both of us.

I loved pastry so much that I'd hang around the back of the bakery late in the summer evenings sometimes and watch and help the baker, Mr. Lones, (who was my friend Louie Lones's father) make doughnuts and rolls. He'd show me how to twist them before he put them in the oven, and when they came out, he'd pay me off with the warm, yummy pastry of my choice for my work!

In contrast to the artistry, warmth, and delightful smells of the pastry making work was the not so exciting job of setting pins in the bowling alley on South Broadway, across the street from Widman's Candy Store. That was before they had automatic pinsetters. The ball would come crashing against the pins which would go flying in all directions! Sometimes, in spite of trying to protect my legs by holding them high in the air, a pin would slam against my shin, and oh would it hurt! Needless to say, I didn't last long at this job!

However, another job I had, one that was much more satisfying, and lasted all summer, was after sixth grade when I became a helper on a Dr. Pepper soft-drink truck for Mr. Vick who was my friend Jimmy Vick's dad.

Each morning we'd begin the day by loading the truck with cases of Dr. Pepper, Whistle Orange, and Howell's Root Beer. Before we left on our route, I'd watch the bottling men feed empty bottles into the giant machine which washed them and then filled them with "pop!" Like the bakery, one of the perks of this job was being allowed to consume the product, in this case, a cold bottle of whatever I wanted whenever I wanted it.

Besides making a little money on this job, I liked it because I got to ride to all of the towns around Crookston. As I mentioned in previous stories, our family never owned a car, so it was a thrill for me to be able to ride anywhere. It was also geographically enlightening, peaceful watching nature pass by, and a socializing influence on me.

Mr. Vick and I would talk as we'd drive from one little town to another, and then we'd stop at the towns' restaurants and bars and fill their orders. While he was taking an order, I'd begin hauling out their empty cases on a two wheeler, and then we'd both bring in the full cases of Dr. Pepper, Whistle Orange, and Howell's Root Beer. We'd always stop for lunch, and Mr. Vick would pay for it. He'd also give me fifty cents at the end of the day for my work. Time just seemed to fly by, and before you knew it, we'd be heading back to Crookston's Carmen Addition where the bottling plant was located, and I'd be saddling up my bike and heading home after another rewarding day.

HUSTLING

When I was eight years old the summer of 1936, the year the World Series baseball game was played between the New York Yankees and the New York Mets, I discovered a unique way to make money, by becoming a "numbers runner."

My dad didn't have a radio in his Second Street barbershop, and he was real interested in the game, so he said, "Charlie, why don't you run up to the Crookston Hotel on Broadway and get the first inning score from their ticker tape and bring it back to me."

I was out the door in a flash, and when I got to the hotel, I waited until the end of the first inning to run the score back to my dad and the other barbershop habitues who were waiting for it. When other Second Street businesses learned that I was going to run the score back to my dad each inning, they wanted me to stop and give it to them, too.

That's when my business acumen came into play because I said, "O.K., I'll do it for a nickel an inning." Before long, I had five businesses who wanted the score each inning, and there were eight innings to go, so I made forty cents from each business for the game times five businesses was $2.00. I didn't charge my dad because he's the one who was responsible for setting me up in business, and besides, he fed and clothed me, so he got a free ride.

By the way, it was the final game of the series, and the Yankees won it 4-2.

My brother Bill (who was eleven) and I observed a little World Series betting going on that summer, and it sort of rubbed off on us, so during the fall we devised a "hustling" plan to earn money. Here's how it worked. We'd take a one foot square piece of cardboard and draw 100 squares on it. At the top of the card we'd print the name of our favorite Big Ten football team which, of course, was the Minnesota Golden Gophers. On the left side of the card we'd print the name of the team the Gophers would be playing each Saturday, like the Purdue Boilermakers or the Nebraska Cornhuskers.

The next step in the process was to sell all of the numbers for a dime apiece. We'd enter a business with the card secreted under our sweater so no one, especially the cops, would see it. When a business person bought a number, he'd write his name in any one of the hundred squares which wasn't already taken and hand us a dime. Some people bought more than one square, like Pauline Raumbehler, who was the cashier at the C.O.D. Pauline was a "regular."

When the card was full, we'd draw numbers from 0 to 9 and write one number at the top of each row of vertical squares. Then we'd repeat the drawing for the left side of the card so each player square had two numbers, one for the Gophers, and one for their opponent. If one or both of the teams' scores were in the double digits, we counted the second digit.

When the game was over and the winner declared, we'd pay him $9.00. Are you wondering what happened to the other dollar? It went to the entrepreneurs. My brother Bill and I kept it for our labors. It was exciting being a "bookie."

SLOW WIN

During the fall and winter of 1937 when my brother Bill was twelve and I was nine, we earned our first bicycles from our manager, John Scully, by delivering the Minneapolis Tribune and the St. Paul Pioneer Press to our Sampson's Addition customers and by selling newspaper subscriptions to people all around Crookston. My brother and I worked together to help him win his bike first because he was older, and when winter came, he helped me win mine, too, but the only place I could ride it then was in our bedroom with the kickstand up because I hadn't yet learned to ride and because there was so much snow and ice on the ground.

"You wait until spring after the snow has melted, Charlie," my mom said, "then you'll be able to ride to your heart's content." Waiting was agony! Each day after school I plowed home through the snow, raced up to my bedroom, hopped on my bike, and pedaled until I was drenched with sweat. When the spring day my mom had mentioned finally arrived, it was a Saturday, a beautiful sunny day, and all the streets were dry.

When I wheeled my new blue and white, balloon-tired, "American Eagle" bicycle out onto Pleasant Avenue, a large group of kids had gathered there with their own bicycles to watch me try to ride mine for the first time.

Holding the bike steady with one of his hands on the handlebars and the other beneath the seat, my dad smiled at me and said cheerfully, "O.K., Charlie, I'm going to run with you and give you a good push to get you started. After that you're on your own!" So, away we went, my dad running alongside me as fast as he could, and then he let go. The bike wobbled as I pedaled, zigzagged, and then fell sideways to the street.

All the kids laughed and began riding away, so I just got up, walked my bike to the curb, pushed off and began pedaling, and it worked! I was riding all alone! I rode all around Sampson's Addition that day, and when I arrived home late in the afternoon for supper, the sweat was pouring from my body. "Oh, Charles," my mom said with worry written all over her face, "you better take it easy with that bicycle of yours. You'll make yourself sick!"

Right after supper, I was up and riding again, all around Sampson's Addition some more. It was too much fun to give it up so early after just learning. It was freeing because I could now get to whatever part of Crookston I wanted, rapidly. The next day after church, Sunday, I rode all around Crookston, every neighborhood, and within a week I had mastered the geography of the town and the mechanics of my bike.

Part of that mastery included being able to ride my bike at a snail's pace, very slowly. For some reason, after being able to race all around town without falling, I became fascinated with being able to keep my balance while the bike barely moved. I'd twist the handlebars back and forth, and it seemed like the bike would just stand still. So, although I couldn't race as fast as the older kids, I knew I could go slower than many of them.

By the time summer arrived and the annual Fourth of July celebration was held in Central Park with plenty of games and prizes for races-including bicycle races-, I knew I could go slower than "most" of the older kids, but that didn't help out much because all of the prizes went to the speediest. Until, that is, I heard this announcement which made my heart leap up come blaring from the loudspeaker late in the afternoon: "The last race of the day will be a "slow" bicycle race. Anyone who wishes to enter this race should ride his bike to the starting line at this time!"

At first I thought my ears had deceived me, but when I learned they hadn't, I jumped up and thought, "Slow bicycle race? That's for me!" I could have a real chance in that kind of race. Immediately, I hopped on my bike and pedaled over to the starting line where nine older boys had gathered. None of them even noticed or said anything to me because I suppose they thought I didn't have a chance. As far as they were concerned, I was invisible.

"All right!" the starter yelled. "Get your bikes behind me! When I shoot my gun, you begin riding. The "last" one to cross the finish line wins "this" race. If you touch the ground with either of your feet, you're out. You must direct your bikes towards the finish line at all times. Get on your bikes! Get set! Bang!"

I was extremely nervous. My palms were sweating. I started out too fast and slowed down immediately to almost a standstill. After what seemed like only a few seconds, five bicycles had already dropped out of the competition. I was able to count them as they dropped because I was "behind" them. Some of them fell clumsily to the ground as they tried to makes their bikes slow down. Others couldn't prevent their feet from touching the ground, and they were immediately dropped from the competition.

Only four older boys and myself remained in the race, and they were all ahead of me. For once, I was "first" by being dead last. I couldn't believe what was happening, and I got more nervous by the second as the tension grew. However, I didn't have any trouble going slow. It seemed natural to me because it was a skill I had worked on and developed. "I'm going to beat these guys," I said nervously to myself as I watched the older boys trying to prevent their bikes from crossing the finish line. My bike was barely moving as I twisted the handlebars back and forth and tried to remain calm.

"Damn it!" shouted one of the remaining older boys as his bike crossed the finish line.

Two other boys followed him over the finish line, and they

were immediately out of the race, too. All of the older boys started cheering for Earl Wicklander, the one older boy who remained in the race with me.

"C'mon, Wicklander," one of the older boys yelled, you can't let that little fart beat you!"

"Yeah," another chimed in, "You gonna let Dowdle beat you!"

When I heard my name and saw Wicklander ahead of me, my heart began pounding. He was a boy who always picked on me and called me names, and I never understood why. Through all the shouting a quiet inner voice kept whispering to me, "You can do it, Charlie. Just keep turning the pedals as slowly as you can and keep twisting the handlebars back and forth." This I kept doing until I was almost standing still, and Wicklander was extremely close to the finish line.

"Stop!" shouted the older boys to him. "Stop moving or he's gonna beat ya!" Then it happened. Earl Wicklander's bike crossed the finish line while mine was still moving towards it. I couldn't believe it! I was winning!

Wicklander glared back at me and slurred some threatening words in my direction. I got pretty scared because I knew that this boy didn't like to get beat.

I KEPT INCHING TOWARDS THE FINISH LINE, AND THE older boys all started yelling at me, taunting me, hoping I'd fall, but I didn't. I was so intent on being LAST that my concentration didn't break an instant. When my bike finally crossed the finish line, the older boys just groaned with disgust and began walking away.

"The winner is Charlie Dowdle!" the judge announced as he handed me a shiny half dollar for my prize. I took it, put it in my pocket, hopped on my bike and began racing towards downtown, all the time thinking of the triple dip vanilla, chocolate, and strawberry ice cream cone I was going to buy with some of my winnings.

THE FARM CROP SHOW

During the 1930's the Red River Valley Farm Crop Show was staged every winter in Crookston in a cluster of large two story buildings located behind and across the street from Central High School. Farmers brought samples of their best crops and livestock to town, hoping to have them judged and prized with blue ribbons. Ten year old "city slickers" like myself didn't have time for watching the judging and prizing because we had other interests at the show.

The Saturday I went there in 1938, my friends and I first had to figure out how to get in for free because we didn't have any money. So, we sneaked in. One boy distracted the ticket taker while the rest of us whisked by him silently, swiftly, and unnoticed. Once in, the fun began!

First, we ran down a concrete walkway into the basement where they kept the huge bulls and cows. While we were walking past one of the big, black bulls, his penis reeled out, and we all just stood and stared, amazed at what we were seeing! As we walked on, we noticed a large group of people standing around one particular straw-covered pen, and the cow in it could be heard bawling and moaning as if in pain. We had a difficult time squeezing through the adult bodies to see what was happening, but when we did, we saw a giant-sized cow giving birth to a calf!

With our eyes fairly bulging from their sockets and our mouths hanging open, we watched as the wet mucous-covered calf came out. It was an awesome sight, somewhat overwhelming for us "city slickers," so we turned and ran to a place somewhat more in keeping with our natures, among the chickens.

They were always fun to watch because they looked at you so sharply and quickly as they jerked their heads from side to side inside their metal cages. And it was exciting to stick our fingers between the metal wires of the cages to see if we could withdraw them quickly enough to not get pecked. What was even more exciting was to try to withdraw a freshly-laid egg from beneath a hen and then silently and secretly slip it into another boy's pocket and crush it!

Yes, we "city slickers" did this, and we paid for it, dearly, but not before running upstairs and causing more mischief among the pigs. They were in pens, about four pigs to a pen, and they would squeal and snort when we approached them. They were smart, and I think they sensed mischief, and they were right!

As nicely dressed townsfolk walked up and down the aisles, admiring the animals, we boys sat on the pen railings, trying to imitate the grunting and snorting sounds of the big pigs. That's when my friend said, "Hey, Charlie, what do you think would happen if we let some of the pigs out of their pens?"

I thought he was crazy, but in the blink of an eye, he lifted the gate of one of the pens and four huge pigs scrambled out and down the aisle towards the nicely-dressed townsfolk. The pigs ran chaotically from side to side right at them, around them, and through them, and we "city slickers" all ran in the opposite direction until we were suddenly collared by the law!

"All right, you boys," the cop said, "you can come with me!" Riding to the police station was definitely a first for me. Everyone on both sides of Broadway looked at the police car as it drove slowly towards the station. I ducked my head into my jacket because I was so embarrassed and scared. I had never been to the police station before, and now it was like I was a criminal!

Once we arrived at the red, brick building which was across the street from The Crookston Daily Times, the policeman opened the door and said, "All right, boys, you can get out now and follow me." Silently, we trudged behind him to Chief McCaffrey's office.

I began getting warm all over and real scared. Everyone knew that Chief McCaffrey was authoritative and to be feared. Standing in front of his desk, I began shaking. The chief was big, red-faced, and gruff. "You boys know you could be put in jail for what you've done?" he growled. When he said that, I just stood there and shook. "I've a good notion to just lock you up!" he said.

Staring at my pants pocket, he asked, "What's that wet stuff on your pants, son?"

"Egg, sir," I answered. Someone put an egg in my pocket and crushed it. A muffled chuckle could be heard coming from the policemen. "Tell you what I'm going to do, boys," Chief McCaffrey said sternly as he stared at us. ""I'm going to send you home this time, but if this ever happens again, you're all going to jail!"

Needless to say, it never happened again to this "city slicker again because Chief McCaffrey taught me a lesson that lasted a lifetime.

CHILDHOOD SWEETHEART

Although she wasn't aware of it, I fell in love with Marilyn Kirkwood the first time I danced with her in kindergarten in 1934. This story is about the second time I made a connection with her four years later.

It was 1938, I was now ten years old, and the action takes place on a warm, summer Crookston evening I'll never forget. My brother, Willie, who was thirteen years old at the time, announced that he was going to ride his bike down to the Woods Addition after supper and meet some older kids at Betty Kirkwood's house. Now, Betty Kirkwood was the older sister of "Marilyn," the little girl I liked, so when my brother began riding away from the house, I flew out the door after him, hopped on my bike and yelled, "I'm comin' with ya!"

My brother wasn't too happy about my tagging along after him wherever he went, but he liked me, and I liked him, and we were brothers, so sometimes he just let me stick to him like glue. But this wasn't one of those times I was tagging along just to be with him. This time I was tagging along in hopes that I might meet and play with Marilyn Kirkwood.

And I did, but it was very awkward for me because I didn't know Marilyn that well, and although we went to the same Catholic school, all of her neighborhood playmates attended the public school.

As soon as we got there, the older kids held a rapid conference among themselves, hopped on their bikes, and rode off towards the woods. And I, I just stood there, not knowing which way to turn. Finally, one of the younger boys said, "C'mon, you can play with us." I felt very strange and began wishing I had not come at all. I felt freakish because the kids seemed to hesitate before I was accepted by them, but I was, and it was worth enduring their hesitancy just so I could be near Marilyn.

We played "tin-can-off" which was a little like hide-and-go-seek, and I remember lying on the grass near Marilyn as we prepared to sneak in free. Her focus was on the moment when she could make a dash for the goal. I was like a Border Collie. My focus was on her. She didn't sense anything for me, I'm certain, but I sure sensed something for her.

What happened next between Marilyn and me was certainly not a childhood experience, and it was ten years later, 1948, but it was so important to both our lives that I may as well tell it now.

After high school, two years in the Navy, and a semester at Loras College in Dubuque, Iowa, I once again found myself near my brother Bill, living with him in Minneapolis. I had turned twenty, and Bill was now twenty-three.

One day after work Bill said, "Charlie, how'd you like to go out on a double date with me?"

"Sure," I said. "It'd be fun. The only trouble is I don't know anyone in Minneapolis." Bill thought hard for a minute because he really wanted me to be with him so I could check out his new girlfriend, Pearl Carlson, a girl with whom he had fallen deeply in love.

Suddenly, Bill's eyes brightened and words very precious to my ears flowed from his mouth. "How about that Kirkwood girl?" he asked. "She works in Minneapolis. As a matter of fact," he said, "I think she lives at a girls' rooming house called Maybeth Paige. It's only a couple of blocks from us."

Needless to say, my heart leaped up! I was over to Maybeth Paige that evening, knocking on the rooming house door, and asking Marilyn if she would go out on a double date with me. Forget the kindergarten shyness. Forget the embarrassment of invading a new neighborhood as a ten year old just so I could be near her. We were now both twenty years old. This was serious business!

Bill and Pearl and Marilyn and I went on that double date, we did. And the rest is history. Bill was in love with Pearl, and I fell head over heels in love with Marilyn, and in 1951 we both married our sweethearts!

CHICKEN

Working with Russ Howard at Duval's Meat Market on South Broadway when I was ten years old in 1938 wasn't to be my last encounter with animal killing, for it wasn't long after I quit my job at Duval's that the next slaughter took place, at home!

It happened this way. As usual, I was walking home past Peterson-Biddick (Crookston's poultry slaughterhouse) one late fall afternoon when I saw a big, white chicken strutting slowly, cautiously under a Great Northern Railroad boxcar near the building. I thought, "Boy! If I could catch that chicken and bring it home, Dad would be real proud of me, maybe even give me some money for it."

So, I walked across the street towards Peterson-Biddick and very casually and nonchalantly sauntered down the railroad tracks towards the boxcar, thinking that if I looked like I wasn't paying any attention to the chicken, the chicken probably wouldn't pay any attention to me and not try to run away. It didn't work out that way at all.

As soon as I bent down and began crawling slowly and stealthily under the boxcar and towards the chicken, it cocked its head, gave out a few low cluck, cluck, clucks and began taking slow, light steps towards the building. Quietly, trying to not make any unnecessary noise that would get the chicken excited, I slid from under the boxcar on my stomach, got to my feet, and crept up behind the big bird while its head was turned. Wham! I slammed my right hand down on one of the chicken's legs and all hell broke loose!

The chicken started erratically flapping its wings in my face while I clung for dear life to its one leg. I was too startled to try grabbing its other leg with my left hand and just held it out as far from my face as I could so I wouldn't get battered with the big bird's flailing wings. Gradually, it stopped trying to fly away, and I grabbed the other leg with my left hand and held the chicken upside down. As I transferred both legs, very carefully so as not to let go, to my right hand, the chicken began squawking bloody murder and flapping its wings again. It must have gotten its second breath. Through all of this hubbub, I think I was just as afraid of the chicken as the chicken was of me, being only ten years old at the time. Finally, the chicken stopped fighting for its freedom, and I began walking home with it. It was heavy!

My face was all hot and sweaty, and people I passed stared at me as I crossed the bridge and turned on Woodland Avenue towards home. When I got there, I walked back to our small, old dirt-floored garage behind our house by the alley and locked the chicken in it. When I entered the house, my mom looked at me and said, "Charlie, what have you been up to? You look all hot!"

"I am, Mom," I said. "I caught a chicken at Peterson-Biddick and put it out in the garage." She said nothing and just walked away. When my dad got home that night, I was real anxious to tell him what I'd done. He was surprised and said, "Good! Good! Charlie! We'll butcher it tomorrow and have it for dinner on Sunday!"

That's when I began thinking, "Butcher it! Just how is that accomplished with a chicken?" I didn't ask my dad how he was going to do it, but I sure found out the next day.

Dad was up bright and early Saturday morning, and after he ate his usual bowl of corn flakes and drank a cup of coffee, he called up to me, "C'mon, Charlie. Get up! It's time for you and me to go out to the garage and take care of that chicken now before I go to work!" I crawled out of bed and put on the dirty old clothes I was wearing the day before. When I reached our back porch, I saw that Dad was carrying a pail of steaming water. He had on his old clothes, too. When he saw me, he pointed to a long-handled ax lying on the floor and said, "Bring that ax, Charlie. We're going to need it."

I began getting scared because I knew we only used that ax to chop wood. But I knew the chicken was going to die, just like the hog I'd seen at the cold storage locker, just like the calf I'd seen out at the stockyards. I just didn't know how it was going to be accomplished. I'd never seen it done before.

When Dad opened the garage door, there was my chicken, all big and white, strutting around on the dirt floor like a king of the roost. He became a very excited king when he saw us enter. Dad pointed to a big stump of wood on which we usually chopped kindling and said, "O.K., Charlie, after I catch him, I'm going to lay him on that stump of wood. Your job will be to hold his legs while I grab his head and chop it off with the ax."

"O.K.!" I said, but I knew I wasn't going to like this!

In no time flat my dad cornered the chicken, swooped down and caught it by both its legs, and laid its body on the chopping block.

"O.K., Charlie!" Dad said calmly as he passed the chicken's legs from his hands to mine. Meanwhile, the chicken was trying to flap its wings and was making an awful racket. "Ready?" Dad said. "Now don't let go!"

He took the chicken's head in his left hand and stretched its neck across the block, at the same time raising the ax up in the air with his right hand. Swish! Chop! Pandemonium! The chicken flew from my hands and went crazy! It didn't have a head, yet it was flying and running all around the garage, spurting blood on whatever it touched. I covered my head and face with my hands and tried to move away from it. I'd never seen anything like this. However, it didn't affect me the way the hog and the calf did when I saw them killed. I don't know why. Finally, the commotion stopped, and the chicken lay motionless, its white feathers all smeared with blood.

Dad didn't waste any time. He picked the chicken up, plunged it in the pail of steaming water, and the smell of wet feathers immediately began filling the air. Rapidly, Dad picked all the feathers from the big bird, held it up and exclaimed, "That's a real nice chicken you caught, Charlie! He'll make good eating tomorrow!"

We walked back to the house with it, and my mom cleaned out its insides. The next day, Sunday, we all sat down to a delicious, golden brown , fried chicken dinner.

Now I really knew what had to be done to a chicken before I could enjoy eating one of its meaty, brown drumsticks. The bird had to be killed! Violently! Of course, how else does one kill?

Methodically, that's how. Dispassionately! I witnessed the whole process when I walked across the street to Peterson-Biddick the following Saturday, not to catch a chicken this time, but to see how they killed them. I saw!

Chickens were brought down to the main floor in heavy metal cages from which they were roughly taken and hung upside down, their legs clamped to a moving conveyor belt. As they moved forward, they helplessly flapped their wings a little in an effort to right themselves while all the blood drained down to their heads. After a bit, they remained still.

A man waited with a sharp knife, and as a chicken approached, he slid his hand over its head, stretched its neck, and mechanically slit it. Immediately, the moving conveyor belt plunged the chicken into a rectangular tank of steaming water.

When the chickens emerged from the tank, they entered a large, square room where women wearing heavy rubber aprons and gloves laughed and chatted with one another and picked the chickens clean of their feathers. The stench of the wet chicken feathers was overpowering! I didn't have to see any more. I had seen enough. Now I knew. I left.

THE WALKATHON

We newspaper carriers who delivered the Grand Forks Herald, Saint Paul Pioneer Press, and Minneapolis Tribune to Crookston's neighborhood houses were always treated royally by our kind and gentle manager, John Scully. He taught us a work ethic, helped us earn money, awarded us prizes like skis, mittens, bicycles, etc., and was always treating us to new experiences which helped us get better acquainted with our world.

My brother Bill, who loved to play catcher for baseball games in Central Park, won a trip to Chicago to watch the Chicago Cubs play a baseball game during the summer of 1940. All he could talk about when he got home was Gabby Hartnett, the catcher for the Cubs. Hartnett must have been a highly skilled catcher because he became a member of the National Baseball Hall of Fame at Cooperstown, New York in 1955.

A trip I remember real well was one I took to the Minnesota State Fair. John Scully was chaperoning a busload of boys. When we arrived in Minneapolis, we stayed at the Andrews Hotel, two boys to a room. The next morning we got up early and were treated to a breakfast banquet with other newspaper carriers from throughout the state. The breakfast was a real feast given in our honor! After we listened to speakers from the Saint Paul Pioneer Press and the Minneapolis Tribune laud our efforts as newspaper carriers, we were each given an envelope which contained cash and tickets for all of the rides at the fair! Wow! Attending the Minnesota State Fair sure made up for a lot of those freezing Crookston mornings when we had to get up early and deliver our newspapers.

The two trips mentioned above were sponsored by the Saint Paul and Minneapolis newspapers, but the one I'll always remember was the one sponsored by the Grand Forks Herald during the summer of 1938. After my brother Bill and I had been working especially hard, selling newspaper subscriptions to the Grand Forks Herald all week, John Scully told us he had a special treat in store for us the following Saturday. He told us to ask our folks if it would be all right for us to ride to Grand Forks with him that day.

We asked our dad and mom, and right away they said, "Certainly." They knew John Scully well, were members of the Cathedral of the Immaculate Conception Catholic Church with him, and liked him as a person. If Grace and Frank Dowdle had known that John was going to take their two sons on a thrill ride, they may not have been so willing to give their consent.

It seemed like forever for the week to pass, but it did, and Saturday morning found three other newspaper carriers and my brother Bill and me eagerly waiting at the Great Northern Depot for our ride to Grand Forks with John. As we all stood around, impatiently, waiting for him to arrive, he finally pulled up in front of us, and in a brand new car! John hopped out, opened the doors for us, and with a boyish grin on his face blurted, "Okay, boys, pile in!"

As we drove north on Main Street towards the highway, John said, "Why don't you roll down the windows. It's going to get pretty hot today." We rolled them all down, and before you knew it we were passing "The Barrel," Crookston's favorite hamburger and root beer stop which was shaped just like a large cylindrical barrel. On the highway we began picking up speed, and the soft, warm breeze pressed against our faces and blew through our hair. It felt good, refreshing, and the car purred, was comfortable, and smelled new.

My brother Bill asked, "When did you get the new car, John?"

"Just this morning," he answered, enthusiastically. John never showed a whole lot of emotion, but you could tell he really liked this new automobile he was driving. "I picked it up from the dealer right before I picked you guys up at the depot. That's what took me so long," he said. As we passed the AC (the Crookston Agricultural School), we all noticed that the car was now moving a lot faster. Now the wind was blowing hard against our faces and our hair was flying straight back! We were already quite a ways out of Crookston and headed towards Fisher, Minnesota when John asked, "Any of you boys ever gone a hundred miles an hour in a car?" Of course, no one had, so John's question was greeted with silence! Our parents didn't own a car, and in 1938 I didn't think a car could even go that fast. I was soon to find out otherwise!

Before we knew it, the red needle on the speedometer was moving from 70 to 75 to 80 miles per hour, and all of us caught the excitement of the moment as we stared at the needle and watched the countryside go by in a blur. Now the wind was really burning against our faces with increased force, but none of us noticed or cared. We were all too intent on seeing that red needle reach a hundred! It was printed in big black numbers, 100. The speedometer crept slowly towards 90 and then just sort of hung there, seemingly reluctant to move ahead.

John yelled, "Hang on! Here we go!" And as he plunged his foot against the accelerator and held it to the floorboard, the engine throbbed in response and the needle finally began inching its way toward 100. I began getting a little scared, thinking about what would happen if the car went out of control and off the road at that speed. As we rounded a long bend in the highway at Fisher, some "X" marks the spot signs began appearing, indicating where people had been killed in automobile accidents. I began shuddering and shivering a little in spite of the warm weather.

John kept holding the car at 100 mph for what seemed a very long time to me, but I realized after it was all over that it was only for a minute or two. As John began letting up on the accelerator, we cruised into Grand Forks, and everyone began asking John where he was taking us. "Just be patient," he said. "It's going to be a big surprise!" No bigger I was hoping than the thrill ride we had just completed! Shortly, we parked in front of a large arena that many people were entering. A big banner hanging outside the building was advertising a "WALKATHON!" John said it had been going on all week, and we were arriving for the final day.

Inside the building a large, wood, oval track was set up around which twelve tired people were slowly shuffling, seemingly dragging their bodies around the track by sheer will power. These people were plodding along and really looked like they had been walking all week! They only stopped to go to the bathroom. They ate and drank water while walking. It looked like torture! Everyone looked exhausted! Arms and heads of the walkers hung limp. Feet slid slowly against the wood floor, not raised from it but a fraction of an inch as they shuffled agonizingly forward. Heads of the walkers remained bowed until cheered on by the audience. Then, slowly, one after another, they would raise in recognition of the cheers, and tired, expressionless faces told the audience that this was one contest they wished they had never entered! It was too grueling to try to outlast one another for the big money prizes to be awarded.

The walk continued throughout the afternoon, and we stayed and watched six or seven contestants who couldn't take it anymore drop out. Some literally dropped to the floor and had to be carried out of the walking circle on a stretcher. It was sad to watch people put themselves through so much misery for money!

When we finally left, the walkathon was still in progress. While riding home, we talked about the torture the walkers were putting themselves through. Funny, we had all forgotten about the speedy ride John had given us on our way to Grand Forks. We were drained!

HOBOES

Hoboes, men who traveled in railroad boxcars from town to town during the Great Depression of the 1930's in search of work for food and money, were a common presence in the Great Northern Depot and along the banks of the Red Lake River opposite it during the summer months in Crookston. I'd often see these men come riding in on moving freight trains, and when they neared the depot would jump off and run down the riverbank to the river's edge where they'd set up camp for the night.

During he day these men would tramp around our Sampson's Addition neighborhood in search of work. Often, one of them would come knocking on our door, and when my mom would answer it, would ask, "Got any work I can do for a sandwich, missus?" Usually, my mom would find something for the man to do like mowing the lawn and then feed him. Instead of giving these men food for performing odd jobs, some people gave them money so they could buy their own food downtown.

At night near the river's edge these hoboes could be seen huddled around a campfire, cooking and sharing whatever food they had been able to earn during the day. We young boys would always try to sneak up close enough so we could hear what the men were saying, but not too close because we were afraid of them and what they might do to us if they caught us spying on them.

Now, when I reflect back on those days, I think it was special for those men who were down and out, many through no fault of their own, to be sitting together in comradeship, sharing their food and stories of the day's activities with one another. It was almost like they had a common occupation, searching for work from town to town so they could eat and survive!

When it got a little chillier in the fall, the hoboes' ranks thinned out, and instead of catching their shuteye by the banks of the Red Lake River, they moved up to the Great Northern Depot for the night. There, early in the morning, they could be seen stretched out on the depot's long, hard, highly varnished, oak benches, and they'd be snoring up a storm until the newspaper carriers arrived around six in the morning.

Then all hell would break loose because we carriers were not a quiet lot! Some of us would be running around playing tag while others would be pitching pennies at a crack in the concrete depot floor, winner take all! I'd often go in and out the door to the tracks where I could watch for the passenger train which would be coming from Minneapolis with our St. Paul Pioneer Press and Minneapolis Tribune newspapers. When they'd arrive, there was more noise as the passengers entered the depot and our papers were counted out to us by our managers John Scully and Tony Swanson.

Gradually, during this flurry of activity, the hoboes would awaken, rub their reddened eyes, and prepare for another day of riding the rails. As fall waned and winter set in, hoboes were no longer a part of the Crookston scene. However, one winter I do remember a hobo who was discovered in a boxcar on a spur, a short branch track which led from the main track to a mercantile company near the depot.

The hobo was beginning to freeze to death, and he was brought over to Meng and Garvick's where his frozen legs were plunged into a tub of ice water. Unfortunately, they had to be amputated, but the man survived! I guess that's what it was all about in those days, survival, and for that matter still is today. It's just a matter of how we do it!

DUVAL'S MEAT MARKET

When I was a ten year old boy in 1938, Russ Howard paid me fifty cents each Saturday to help him deliver packages of meat to Crookston homes and businesses for Duval's Meat Market. I liked the job because Russ was a nice person, and I enjoyed riding around downtown and among the different neighborhoods in the meat market pickup. I liked being busy, too. The butchers at the market must have sensed this because when I wasn't out helping Russ deliver meat, they kept me busy at other small jobs instead of just letting me stand around and do nothing.

One particular Saturday I remember well. I had just finished helping one butcher squirt mixed meat into pig intestines which then became pork sausages when another butcher called out, "Charlie, c'mon with me for a ride out in the country, and you can help me for awhile." I was rapidly ready to go because the smell of the sausages and a barrel of hamburger they had just had me mix was getting to me!

It was a beautiful Minnesota autumn day. The leaves had turned many colors and were falling, the air was brisk, and the sun was shining brightly. It was a great day to be alive! As we drove out of town and into the country, I began wondering where we were headed. I soon had my answer, for within ten minutes we pulled off the road and up to some corrals which held a few cattle near a railroad spur.

The butcher jumped out of the truck, unlatched the rear gate of the pickup, and walked quickly over to one of the pens. "C'mon,

Charlie," he yelled. I noticed the butcher had a rope in his hands. After tying the rope around a calf's neck, he led it near the pickup and coaxed it along, calling softly, "Here, bossy! C'mon, bossy!" It was then that I realized what was about to happen. A chill ran up and down my spine and my hair bristled.

The butcher had reached into the bed of the pickup for a sledge hammer which he was now holding behind his back, hiding it from the eyes of the innocent calf which he continued to beckon with soothing tones, "Here, bossy! Nice bossy!"

Like a flash of lightning it happened. The butcher buried the head of the sledge into the top center of the calf's head, and the calf fell under crumpled legs to the ground. The calf's tongue lolled from its mouth and blood gushed from the hole made by the blow. I stood, dizzy, weak, faint, staring at the brown, furry, calf body lying in a pool of its own blood.

"Don't just stand there, Charlie!" yelled the butcher. "Grab its legs and help me heave it into the pickup!" Without a word, I did as the butcher commanded, slowly, unwillingly, silently and in shock. I grasped the calf's hind legs which were still warm and helped the butcher heave it into the pickup bed. Neither of us spoke a word all the way back to the market.

BESS AND THE BEAVER

In 1938 when I was ten years old, the Red Lake River which meandered through our wooded Sampson's Addition neighborhood in Crookston provided hours of exciting adventures for my best friend Howie Pederson and me and our neighbor's dog, Bess. So, early one brisk Saturday morning when Bess saw us headed for the river, she eagerly joined us and soon led the way.

Bess was an energetic, strong, brown and white English Springer Spaniel who loved to follow Howie and me around, especially when we hiked the trails by the river. She was a hunter, and as soon as she reached the river trail ahead of us, she began running, and we could hear her barking playfully in the distance at the small woods animals.

Before too long, her barking began sounding more serious and commanding, so we started jogging to catch up with her. The crisp autumn air that filled our lungs was exhilarating, and we soon found ourselves running harder to close the gap between Bess and us. As her barking grew louder, we knew that we had just about reached her, but we still couldn't see her.

"Here, Bess! Come here, girl!" I shouted, thinking she'd come running back to us. She didn't.

Abruptly, the trail turned towards an open area where lay a tangle of scattered branches, sticks, and twigs. Among them and some freshly cut trees and mounds of wood chips, we saw Bess, barking fiercely at a large beaver she had cornered.

"Sic 'im, Bess!" we yelled, and she unleashed a ferocious attack which was met head on by the beaver's four, sharp, frontal teeth.

Suddenly, Bess yelped painfully and backed away from the beaver which swished its large. leathery tail on the ground and bolted for the river. Bess's ear had a ragged tear and was dripping blood.

"Get 'im, girl!" I screamed, and she sprang after the beaver with lightning speed. Near the edge of the riverbank, Bess clamped her strong jaws onto the thick, furry neck of the beaver, and it snapped at her in an attempt to make her loosen her grip, but she clung tenaciously to the beaver's neck. The two animals tugged at one another from side to side, the beaver clawing at the ground to gain access to the water, and Bess pulling in the opposite direction in the dirt and woodchips. Finally, the beaver's will prevailed, and the two animals toppled over the edge of the riverbank and into the water, Bess still clinging to the beaver's neck.

"Here, Bess!" Howie called. "C'mon, girl! Get outta that water!" He made a daring attempt to grab for her collar, but it was too late. Bess and the beaver rapidly churned the river water a muddy gray as they struggled with one another and were carried downstream. Within seconds the washing machine action ceased, and their tumbling bodies disappeared under the roiling water.

When a thin line of bubbles appeared on the surface of the water andf angled downstream close to the riverbank, Howie and I walked along the trail, tracking them with our eyes, hoping against hope that Bess wasn't drowned, wasn't dead! Suddenly, the water began boiling over at a spot near us, and dog and beaver came bursting through the surface, locked in a thrashing life and death struggle.

Uselessly, I pleaded, "Come here, Bess! Come here, girl!" But Bess didn't respond. She couldn't! In our eagerness to have her attack the beaver, we now both realized that we had done something very wrong and stupid. We had sicked our neighbor's dog onto a strong, wild animal, and now that it had reached its natural habitat, water, the advantage was on its side. Its webbed feet and large, powerful flattened tail made it an excellent swimmer, and we knew it could hold its breath for a long time under water.

Our shouting was to no avail, and again the dog and beaver sank out of sight. Staring at the water, we ran along the riverbank and waited anxiously for Bess and the beaver to surface again. But they didn't. They stayed under the water a long time, and I wondered if Bess was still alive! I became numbed and began to feel a great heartache as I stumbled after Howie. He was silent, too. It was eerie! We spoke no words, and both became dumb to the life around us. Then Howie began muttering something unintelligible, and I asked God to not let Bess die.

God must have been watching and listening all the time because when the two animals broke water again, Bess still had the beaver's neck clenched in her jaws.

We couldn't believe it! Not only was Bess alive, but she was trying to bring the beaver to us. We jumped up and down and cheered her towards us as she fought against the current which carried her downstream. We moved right along the bank with her as she drew nearer. Finally, she engineered the few remaining feet to a protruding sandbar and dropped her motionless mouthful at our feet. Then she herself, panting hard and exhausted, lay down immediately on the ground. Howie began petting her and praising her lavishly, but she was too weak to respond.

"Good girl, Bess," I whispered. She had done battle at our bidding, and she had won, but now she was dead tired.

Seemingly lifeless, the beaver just lay where Bess had dropped it, but as soon as we turned our backs, it began inching slowly from the sandbar back to the water. We just let it go and watched as it turned upstream and swam away from us. Bess watched, whined, and slowly rose on her wobbly legs.

All fight had been drained from her, but after a few minutes she seemed ready to head for home. Slowly, the three of us began going back along the trail, Bess behind us this time.

As soon as we reached the back door of her owner's house, Bess lay down on an old rag rug and collapsed, looking like she was never going to move again. When we walked past Mrs.

Pierce, who was out front raking leaves, she asked, "Have you boys seen Bess?"

"She's out back sleeping on her rug," I said, hoping Mrs. Pierce wouldn't go back there and see Bess's torn ear.

"She seemed pretty tired," Howie said.

As we walked away, I whispered to Howie, "And to think we almost...."

Yeah!" Howie replied nervously. "Let's get outta here!"

RATS!

In 1938 when I was a ten year old boy working at Duval's Meat Market in Crookston, I learned everything I ever wanted to know about meat, including what happens to the "entrails."

I learned about them late in the afternoon during my first Saturday on the job after all the other work was done. My boss, Russ Howard, said, "We have one last job to do before we call it quits for the day, Charlie. We have to go to the dump."

I was tired, but I certainly wasn't going to say I didn't want to go because I liked riding in the truck, and I liked the money I was earning, so I answered, "O.K." About five minutes out of town we turned off the highway onto a bumpy dirt road. The sun had already set, and it was getting dark and chilly.

Russ said, "Just wait 'til you see what's at the dump. You're really going to be surprised." As we bumped along the potholed dirt road, I could hear the contents of four, large, metal barrels swish back and forth. "What's in the barrels, Russ?" I asked.

"Guts," he answered. "We'll be dumping them soon." It was dark now, and Russ had turned on the pickup's headlights. I didn't need eyes to tell me that we were close. The smell was overpowering! The stench of the intestines we were carrying merged with that of burning garbage, and it was enough to make one vomit.

When we finally arrived, Russ maneuvered the pickup near a huge pile of garbage and said, "Charlie, get out and tell me when I get near the edge." I jumped out and began waving Russ to the edge of the garbage pit when I saw them coming, hundreds of them, RATS! their yellow eyes blazing, their hungry mouths cheeping, their slithering bodies rippling like a brown furry carpet creeping over the mounds of garbage and heading in our direction.

Quickly, I leaped into the bed of the pickup with the barrels of guts and gave Russ directions to the edge. "That's good!" I called. He stopped and hopped into the bed of the truck with me.

It was feeding time, and the rats knew it. They must have scented the guts because they moved in a frenzied, frantic, flowing brown blanket over the ground in our direction. I began getting goose bumps all over my body when Russ yelled, "Let's feed them, Charlie, before they eat us alive!" I took him seriously and began helping him dump those barrels fast. The rats ate ravenously! They seemed to bury themselves in the animal entrails.

I simply stared, scared, and jumped back into the truck when we were finished. We left, and I don't think I began breathing easily until we got back out onto the highway. On the way back Russ just laughed and began singing to himself because his work for the day was done.

When we pulled up to the market and got out of the truck, Russ reached into his pocket and handed me a half dollar. "Here, Charlie," he said. "This is for your work today." I took it, said thanks, and was eager to be on my way home.

JUMP MASTER

At times in the 1930's, winter weather in northern Minnesota could act unusually weird. One Friday I remember in particular because during the day the sun was shining brightly and starting to melt a lot of snow, creating slush all around the streets, sidewalks, and alleys, and then that same day, at night, it grew extremely cold and a blizzard dropped about three feet of snow on the ground, creating huge drifts which banked against many of the downtown buildings.

After a night like this, Saturday morning was a time for us kids to get out and explore what damage, if any, the previous night's storm had done, and to just walk around and have some fun. As usual, I found myself tagging along with some older boys because that's where the action was.

As we were walking down the alley towards Second Street, one of the older boys pointed to a huge pile of snow alongside an old brick building and hollered, "Wow! Will you look at that drift! Let's climb up those stairs and jump off that garage roof into it!" It didn't take long for the other boys to follow their leader. As he plowed his way down the alley and began climbing the wooden steps which led to the roof of the garage, the other boys followed without hesitation. I did, too, but last! I was only ten years old at the time and sort of afraid of high places.

One by one the gang of boys first had to leap a few feet from the wooden stairs into the new-fallen snow on the garage roof. That was okay. I hesitated, but I made it. Then the leader walked cautiously to the edge of the roof, peaked over it to where the largest snowdrift lay, let out a loud shriek and jumped! His body swooshed through the air and plowed waist deep into the glistening white, light, drift of snow below. "C'mon, chickens!" he yelled. "Your turn! Are you coming or are you just gonna stand there and stare!"

As he began walking away, the other boys approached the edge of the roof and one by one flung themselves into the bank of snow below. They screamed as they left the roof, relieving themselves of the fear and tension they felt as they dropped through the air from such a height. I was the last one to jump, but I didn't. I just stood on the edge of the roof and stared down at the ground, watching the boys walk away.

They didn't miss me at all. I guess it was because I was so young and small. No one turned around to call, "C'mon, Charlie! Jump! Are ya chicken!" If they had, I might have jumped right away. As it was, I was left standing there, all alone, trying to get up enough courage to let go, to prove to myself that I wasn't afraid, and to prove to the older boys that I wasn't a coward!

I inched my way to the edge of the roof and moved over a ways from where the older boys had jumped because they had really mashed the snow down, and I wanted a nice, deep, soft place to land so I wouldn't hurt myself. As I was getting ready to jump, my body began growing warm all over, and I tried to steel my nerves against the fear I was feeling. "I could go back and climb down the stairs," I thought, but when I went back to try it, I discovered they were too high for me. I was stuck between a rock and a hard place! So, I once again approached the edge of the roof.

"I just hafta jump," I thought. "If I don't, I'll be a coward!" I wanted so badly to be able to do what all the bigger boys had done, but mainly I wanted to face up to my fear of heights and conquer it!

The gang of older boys I'd been tagging along after all morning were now out of sight. "They're probably enjoying themselves doing more exciting things," I thought, "while I'm standing here on the edge of this garage roof about to do it in my pants before I jump." No one was in the alley now as I surveyed a big, fresh, snowdrift into which I contemplated jumping. I was all alone. Was I ready to jump? The silence was killing me. I had to do it now, or I never would.

"Thump!" My legs and butt crashed through the snow and met a hard layer of ice which had frozen over during the night before the new snow had fallen. I tried getting up but couldn't because I had the wind knocked out of me. Gradually, I eased myself to my feet, but I still couldn't breathe. It was a sickening feeling. I thought, "If I don't get my breath pretty soon, I may die!" Believe me, it was frightening. I was panicky and didn't know what to do. I couldn't call out for help because I couldn't speak, I could barely move, and no one was nearby to help.

Finally, I was able to straighten up a little and begin taking in faint breaths of air. Hunched over and hobbling up the alley towards Second Street and my dad's barbershop, people passing me on the street said, "Hi, Charlie!" and I just sort of groaned my greeting to them.

When I entered my dad's shop, I just walked over to a chair and saying nothing, sat down. Dad took notice of all of the snow on my clothes and the deathly pale look on my face and asked, "What in heavens name have you been up to, Charlie!"

I just answered, "Oh, nothing."

CROOKSTON PIRATES

The Crookston Pirates was a minor league baseball team whose players energized the town both on and off the field during the 1930's. Fondly, I remember them lounging around the swimming pool on a hot and humid day and hearing one player call out to another, "Hey, Joe, I'll give you a dollar if you dive off the platform with all your clothes on!"

All the kids' eyes suddenly switched to Joe, who very casually looked up at the platform and then slowly and dramatically began taking his wallet out of his pants pocket, his watch from his wrist and his feet out of his shoes. "O.K.," he'd say as he walked toward the platform ladder and began climbing it to the top. What followed next was Joe taking a flying leap into the air and making a perfect swan dive before plunging into the water, fully clothed. All the kids yelled and clapped at this antic, hoping that other players would become lemming-like and follow Joe into the pool as they sometimes did.

During home games in the evenings at Highland Park, the same players who had a lot of fun during the day became intense and serious at night against their competition because they were all trying to work their way up to the next level of baseball and play with the Minneapolis Millers. We kids loved to go out and watch the Pirates play at night after we had been playing baseball ourselves all day down at Central Park, but there was a problem, money.

Many of us lacked it and had to resort to one of two ways to get into the games for free. The first way was the honest way, but there wasn't any guarantee that you'd be able to see the game. All the kids would crowd around one another outside among the parked cars and wait for a batter to pop a foul ball over the grandstand. What followed was a wild melee! A mad scramble after the ball ensued, and once it was sighted, a hand-to-hand fight and struggle for it followed because whoever got it ran to the gate, handed it over, and walked in free.

The other way of getting into the night games free, the less honorable way, was by climbing over the fence. I'll never forget the first time I tried this when I was about ten years old.

It was a night game, the bright lights flooded the field, and the crowd was cheering, so the game was obviously very exciting. I wanted so badly to get in there and watch it, but I didn't have any money, so I just had to imagine what was happening until I saw some older boys climb to the top of the fence, look both ways, and then drop magically, unnoticed, onto the ground into the right field for free!

When the second wave of boys began climbing the fence, I heard one of their "lookouts" call, "Get down! Here comes Hook!" Hook was the man who guarded against "sneaks" such as we, and Hook carried a big, wooden cane with which to swat us hard if he caught us.

The "lookout" whispered, "O.K., get ready. He's not looking. Go!" The second wave of older kids quietly scaled the rough, slivery, wooden fence and dropped unnoticed to the ground.

I just stood there all alone, outside the fence, wondering if I should try it. "Just take a run towards the fence," I urged myself as I listened to the continued cheering of the crowd. "Then jump with one foot as high as you can against the boards and reach for the top." The older boys did it, and I thought I could, too. So, I ran and jumped, and as my fingers clung to the top of the fence and I began pulling my body upwards, the crowd grew louder and louder, and when I peeked over the top, nobody appeared to be near, so I decided give it a try.

Just then I heard a boy on the other side of the fence call to me softly, "Get down, Charlie! Here comes Hook!" Raking my hands against the top of the fence, I dropped to the ground with a thud, just missing a tangle of barbed wire lying on the ground below me. Again the soft voice on the other side of the fence whispered, "Charlie, wait a minute, and I'll tell you when he's gone." I waited and waited and waited, but no voice sounded, beckoning me to come, so I decided to try it again, regardless.

Run! Jump! Grab! My fingers felt numb as they clung to the slivery edge of the top of the fence. I began breathing heavily and sweating as I struggled to pull myself to the top again. It seemed like I wasn't going to be able to do it.

Still clinging to the top, I let my body down and just hung there a few seconds, arms stretched out and panting, until I felt rested enough to give it another try. "It's now or never," I thought as I tried a second time to pull myself up. I was so involved in my second attempt, so intent on getting over the fence and into the game, so excited when I heard the kids and adults shouting that I didn't hear old Hook lumbering towards me, cane raised, on the other side.

Then, whack! The full force of the cane slammed down on my fingers, and it felt like an electric shock of pain traveled from them to throughout my body. I screamed and fell to the ground, snagging my shirt on the fence on the way down, and this time landing directly on top of the tangle of barbed wire below me. It punctured my skin in a couple of places, and I began sobbing quietly. As I got up, I flexed my numb fingers and began walking slowly home in the dark night, alone.

CROOKSTON BARBERS

My dad, Frank Dowdle, first began barbering in Lockhart, Minnesota in 1917 when his parents, two brothers, and he moved from Corydon, Indiana. During the same year the family moved to Beltrami, Minnesota, and then in 1919 to Crookston where my dad and his brother Jim had a barbershop located directly across the street from the Wayne Hotel on Second Street for as long as I can remember.

The shop, besides being a place to get a shave and a haircut for six bits during the 1930's, seemed to be the political gathering place for farmers, laborers, businessmen, and professional men alike. They all put in their two bits while discussing the current issues of the day, and their oratory grew especially heated during an election year. It was a real education for a kid like myself just to sit there and listen to them banter back and forth with one another.

I'll always remember when Wendell Wilkie, who most of his life had been a loyal member of the Democratic Party, left it to become a Republican in the middle of the 1930's. My Uncle Jim did likewise, and my dad who remained a loyal Democrat just about boiled over whenever his brother Jim began talking up Wilkie in 1940 when Franklin D. Roosevelt ran for a third term as a member of the Democratic Party.

Besides discussing the political scene, the barbershop habitues just loved playing checkers. My Uncle Jim made a number of homemade, Masonite checkerboards on which the men played and challenged one another. The game became so popular with some of the men that they even held tournaments in the evenings.

In addition to getting shorn and shaved, debating politics, and playing a hot game of checkers, a man could, if he so desired, take a Turkish bath at the Dowdle brothers' barbershop. The bathroom had a one foot thick wooden door, and when it was closed, the room was sealed, allowing air neither to enter nor leave the room. When hot water began being drawn into the big porcelain tub, steam filled the room, and one could barely see his hand held right in front of his face. I remember when a guy my dad called "Jimmy the Chimney Sweep" came to town from Grand Forks each year and cleaned Crookston chimneys. Jimmy would come into the barbershop and be all covered with black soot from head to toe after his day's work, but after he took a Turkish bath, he emerged looking like a different man, all dressed in clean clothes, rosy-cheeked, and smiling.

My dad was secretary/treasurer of the barbers' union, so all of the barbers would meet at his shop once a month to discuss business, play cards, and share a keg of beer. It was often my good fortune the morning after their evening meeting to stop at the shop on my way to school and be allowed to sip a cool glass of delicious Grain Belt Beer. My dad was my buddy!

Once a month he'd pay me to run around town to all of the barbers and collect their union dues, so I got to know most of them pretty well. Joe Brule, the Ness brothers, and the Dowdle brothers all had shops on Second Street. Mr. Theroux had his shop on the southeast corner of Second and Main, across from Meng and Garvick's. Mr. Levine was located on South Main near the Playhouse, and Mr. Jebe was over by the New York Store. The Schafer brothers had their shop on South Broadway in the basement of the Crookston Hotel, and you got to Harry Pfeiffer's place by heading down the hill towards the Winter Sports Arena. I think there were thirteen barbers in all, the names of two of whom I've forgotten, but I can remember where they had their shops. A friend of mine, Eddie Regan, searched his Crookston City Directories and made me aware of other barbers who worked in Crookston at one time or another between 1915 and 1949. Their names are as follows: Polansky, Johnson and Storholm, Alphonse Lalonde, Mercil and Thomas, Thomas Mortenson, S.P. Olson, Peter Snyder, Chouinard, Frank Klerma, Art Krogen, William Martin, Paul Myerchin, Ed Ralston, Emory St. Marie, Ernest Patnode, and William Hovet. What I often wonder about now was how a small town like Crookston was ever able to provide a living for that many barbers.

Sometimes, my dad would be called to one of the local hospitals to prep a patient for surgery. Barbers in those days really knew how to wield a straight-edge razor, and having watched my dad whip off a man's heavy beard and leave nary a scratch on his smooth-shaven face, I knew that he was one of the highly-skilled barbers, and that's why the hospitals called him. It supplemented Dad's income.

Like any other business, barbering had expenses. First, you needed a place out of which to work. Next came the chairs, and then the supplies: razors, strops, soap mugs, towels, scissors, combs, hair tonics, shaving lotions, etc. Mike Noah was the man who sold the barbers their supplies. "Hello, Frank," Mike would always greet my dad as he entered the shop, and then the two of them would sit and chat while Dad placed his order for new supplies.

In addition to purchasing materials, some of them had to be constantly serviced, like the sharpening of the razors, scissors, and hair clippers. It was always fun to watch my dad and uncle whip their razors up and down on their strops to sharpen them with a fine edge. The scissors were sharpened in the back of the shop on a rotating emery wheel. Another business which played a role in Crookston barbering was Dikel's Crookston Steam Laundry at the end of the block on Second Street where Dad always sent his towels to be washed.

When he wasn't busy barbering, Dad sometimes used the shop as a place to counsel World War I veterans, helping them fill out paperwork so they could receive their pensions and/or receive medical care at the Veterans' Hospital in Fargo. Dad was the Veterans' Service Officer in that area, and he really had a soft place in his heart for anyone who had served his country. When World War II broke out and the United States got involved after Pearl Harbor in 1941, my dad and Uncle Jim closed their shop and got other jobs. Dad became a bartender for the V.F.W. Club, and my uncle shoveled coal at an iron ore smelting plant on the Iron Range.

TO BEE OR NOT TO BEE

During the Great Depression of the 1930's, my Grandpa Dowdle always kept beehives in the backyard of his Hill Addition Crookston house. Once in awhile I'd watch him tend them, but I never got too close because I didn't want to get stung. The only thing I liked about the honey bees was the honey they made.

My grandpa also liked the money he made from selling his honey. He would walk around to the different neighborhoods, pulling a wagon loaded with gallon and half gallon cans of this "nectar of the gods," and sell it to his eager clientele. Our family always had a gallon can of honey available to spread on freshly-baked white bread which I just loved to eat with a freshly-baked slice of white bread and butter. Ymmm!

When my grandpa died, near the beginning of World War II in 1941, my Uncle Jim began taking care of the bees, and that's where this story really begins. I was twelve years old at the time and just hanging around my dad's and Uncle Jim's Second Street barbershop late one fall Friday afternoon after school when my Uncle Jim said, "Charlie, I'm going out in the country to take care of my bees tomorrow. How'd you like to go along and help me?"

"I don't think so," I said. "I don't want to get stung!"

"You won't get stung, Charlie," he said. "I'll dress you all up with a screen hat and gloves, and we'll tie your pant legs with cord so the bees can't get near you."

Well, this sounded like a different proposition to me. It even sounded a little exciting if I could be working among the bees and not have them sting me, so I said, "O.K."

"I'll drive by your house and pick you up early tomorrow morning," my uncle said. "Make sure you put on a long sleeve shirt."

My uncle arrived bright and early in the morning, and we were on our way. He had a bunch of clothes in the back seat for both of us to put on before we started working with the bees.

AFTER A SHORT DRIVE OUT INTO THE COUNTRY WHERE he kept the hives, he parked the car in a field and said, "O.K., Charlie, this is it. Help me get this equipment out of the back seat and then you and I can get dressed." I watched my uncle Jim put on a hat which had a screen mesh on its face so he could see out, but so that the bees couldn't get at his face. Next, he tucked a cloth collar from the hat into his shirt. "You just dress yourself like I do, Charlie," my uncle said very casually as he dressed, "and then we'll be ready to go."

It didn't take long. I put on a denim jacket my uncle had brought for me and a bee hat which made us both look like aliens from another planet. "O.K., Charlie, we're just about ready to go," my uncle said. "Just let me tie some of this cord around your sleeves and ankles so the bees can't get up them, and I think we'll be all set."

As we began walking toward the hives, I could hear the bees buzzing and see them flying around, thousands of them. My uncle walked right up to the first hive, removed its cover, and belched clouds of smoke into it with a bellows which he had previously filled with smoke to put the bees to sleep while he removed the waxy honeycomb which contained the honey. Of course, not all of the bees were put to sleep. Many of them were flying all around us, driven wild by the smoke, but so far, so good, no stings!

"O.K., Charlie," my uncle said in a very businesslike voice, "why don't you start taking the covers off for me now while I smoke the bees and take out the honeycomb. That way it'll go a lot faster."

This sounded O.K. to me, so I stepped forward and took off a cover. My uncle followed with a blast of smoke from his bellows and then removed the honeycombs. I was standing there holding the cover, layers of bees still on it, when my uncle said, "Just lay the cover over there in the grass with the rest of them, Charlie." As I moved to do this, I felt a sharp sting against my thigh

"Ouch!" I screamed as I let the cover fly from my hands, bees flying all around me. Then two more hit my legs, and I began to panic! I slapped at my legs and began moving rapidly away from the hives. I began sweating like crazy, and my uncle said, "Just go and stand over by the car for awhile, Charlie, until they go away."

My uncle Jim didn't have to tell me this twice. It just took me a jiffy to run to the car, pull down my pants, and examine the damage. Three red welts were already rising where I had been stung. They hurt! I just waited until my uncle finished and came walking over to the car. "Well, Charlie," he said, "that's enough for this morning. Let's go home and get some lunch." As he dropped me off at my house, he said, "I'll be back after lunch to pick you up."

"I'm not going back, Uncle Jim," I said softly. "I don't want to get stung anymore!"

CADDY

During the summer of 1939 when I was eleven years old, Crookston golfers who were mainly doctors, lawyers, businessmen and their wives, hired caddies while they were playing at the Minawkwa Country Club.

My first experience as a caddy was with my dad's lawyer friend, W.E. "Billy" Rowe. Early one summer afternoon, Dad had just finished giving Mr. Rowe a shave and a haircut, and they were bantering back and forth as usual with their Hoosier dialect when Mr. Rowe turned to me and said, "Cholly, how'd you like to come out to the golf course with me this afternoon and caddy?"

Well, to tell the truth, I didn't know the first thing about caddying. I had never done it and had never even been out to the golf course. But I liked Mr. Rowe, and my dad said it was o.k. to go, so I said, "Sure."

Our family didn't have a car, and I knew the golf course was way out in the country, so this would be a fun ride. Mr. Rowe said, "You go out and get in the front seat of the car, Cholly, and I'll be right out." When we started driving, Mr. Rowe went north on Main Street, turned west on Highway #2, and pretty soon we were passing "The Barrel," Crookston's favorite hamburger and root beer stop which was shaped and looked just like a huge, wooden, varnished barrel. Shortly, we turned left off the highway onto a gravel road and then left again onto a tree-lined dirt road and were soon at the golf course. It was about then that I started getting a little nervous and began wondering just what I was supposed to do.

Mr. Rowe put me at ease as soon as we stopped and got out of the car. He took his big, brown, leather golf bag out of the trunk of his car and showed me how to carry it on my shoulder. Then in a very relaxed fashion he said, "You just wait here by this number one tee while I go into the clubhouse and change my shoes, Cholly. If you want to, you can take some of the golf balls out of my bag and wash them for me." He didn't say I had to. He just made a gentle suggestion. That's what I liked about Mr. Rowe. He was always so gentle, courteous, and soft spoken.

As I mentioned previously, I'd never caddied before, so I didn't even know how to wash golf balls, but I unzipped his golf bag anyway, found some golf balls with the name W.E. Rowe stamped into them, and began washing them one at a time in a plunger that contained soapy water and hard-bristled brushes. The ball fit into a hole in the wooden handle of the plunger, and as I moved it up and down between the brushes, the ball got nice and white. There was a bath towel hanging alongside it on which to wipe the balls. "Hey!" I thought, "This is sort of fun."

Then I noticed a group of older boys, the regular caddies, staring at me, perhaps wondering what I was doing out there, taking their work away from them. I could feel their dislike for my being there, their resentment, and I got scared.

Luckily, Mr. Rowe emerged from the clubhouse just then, and as he teed his ball up and prepared to drive it down the fairway, he said, "You watch where the ball goes, Cholly, and then pick up the clubs, and you and I'll walk to it for our second shot." Mr. Rowe drove the ball right down the middle of the fairway about 175 yards.

The golf bag wasn't too heavy, and it had a thick, spongy, dark-brown leather, comfortable shoulder strap. As we began walking towards the ball, Mr. Rowe told me what to do once his ball reached the first green. "Cholly," he said softly, "once the ball reaches the green, you just go stand by that pin with the flag on it and hold it still until I putt the ball. If it looks like the ball is going to hit the pin, pull it out of the hole and take it to the side of the green until I putt out." It took Mr. Rowe four shots to get his ball into the hole, and he seemed pretty happy with himself.

"Well, Cholly," he said as a smile crossed his face, "we got a par on that hole. You can put the pin back in now and get ready for the second hole." I did as he said and then walked over to the second tee with him. He handed me his putter, and I took out his driver and handed it to him for his first shot. "Is this all there is to it?" I thought. "Simple! I can do it."

Mr. Rowe handed me a score card and said, "O.K., Cholly, right here after where it says 1, write the number 4 because that's how many strokes it took me to get the ball into the hole. That's how many strokes it's supposed to take, and par is pretty good."

After he hit his drive from the second tee, I began having lots of fun just walking along quietly with Mr. Rowe, listening attentively to him as he taught me how to caddy. This was great! I was really enjoying it!

At the end of nine holes, Mr. Rowe invited me into the clubhouse and bought me a bottle of ice cold Hires Root Beer. I was extremely thirsty, and it was the perfect treat. As he was taking off his golf shoes, he said, "Well, Cholly, you did a good job. Here's a half dollar." I couldn't believe it! That much money for just walking around a pretty, green golf course, breathing in fresh air for about an hour? "Thank you very much, Mr. Rowe," I said. "I really enjoyed it!"

As we drove back to town, Mr. Rowe asked me if I'd like to caddy for him again sometime. I said, "Yes, I sure would." I liked caddying so much after my first experience with Mr. Rowe that I began riding my bike out to the golf course every day after that and became a "regular." As such, I soon learned that there was another way to earn money at a golf course besides caddying.

Some caddies arrived early in the morning to search the fields, ditches, and ponds for balls golfers had lost the previous day. Some of the balls had players' names stamped in them and could be sold back to their owners for a dime apiece. Unmarked balls would be sold to the golfers for "whatever the traffic would bear." It became a bargaining process between golfer and caddy. Some caddies made more money selling balls they'd found than they did caddying.

I hope you're not getting the idea that caddying at the Minawkwa Country Club was all work because it wasn't. When it wasn't Ladies Day which was one morning each week, caddies themselves were allowed to play the nine hole course for free until noon. Some of us would go out in foursomes and gamble on who'd take the fewest strokes per hole, just like the members, only we bet considerably less money, like a nickel a hole.

Younger caddies who didn't own a set of clubs but did own a putter, challenged one another by putting their way around an extremely well-designed and difficult nine hole miniature course they had created among the trees below the clubhouse and near the number four hole where all the caddies hung out.

This is beginning to sound like the caddies' lives were devoted solely to making money and developing golfing skills. Not at all! Let's talk about some of the nonsense activities and games which occupied them. "I'll pay for your Pepsi if you drink it all with your feet uphill and your head downhill," one caddy would challenge another. They'd usually challenge the younger kids because the older caddies got such a big laugh out of watching them attempt to drink twelve full ounces while lying on their backs on a steep bank. The drinker's face would get all red, and his eyes would become bloodshot and look like they were going to pop right out of their sockets. A caddy "cheering section" egged the drinker on, encouraging him to finish the bottle so he wouldn't have to pay for his pop. Some drinkers were successful, and some weren't, but in either case it provided high entertainment for all the caddies, many of whom had tears in their eyes from laughing and watching the drinker struggle to get down his Pepsi. It was a real circus!

What was closer to a real circus, however, was "tree tag!" It was played on a big, old tree which had large branches, and it was meant for the more athletic and daring types. The big limbs of the tree were beautifully balanced which made it just perfect for climbing around on like a monkey.

Instead of running after someone on the ground and making them "it" by touching them, in "tree tag" you had to touch them while they were in the tree. You couldn't touch the ground with any part of your body while playing. Balance, speed, strength, and daring were all needed to be successful at "tree tag." Tarzan of the Apes didn't have anything on these guys as they jumped and swung from one smoothly worn limb to another.

That about sums up the life of a Crookston caddy in 1939. Deja vu was experienced by me ten years later during the summer of 1949 when Bill Sullivan and I managed the Minawkwa Country Club.

THE ELUSIVE GOBBLER

This all happened late one autumn afternoon a few days before Thanksgiving in the 1930's. Men at Peterson-Biddick, Crookston Minnesota's poultry slaughterhouse, were unloading truckloads of turkeys when one large tom flapped wildly and escaped the grasp of his executioner's hands. The big tom trotted nimbly away and ran across a busy street and along the railroad tracks towards the Great Northern Railroad depot. Some kids chased it towards a nearby riverbank, hoping to corner and catch it, but the big bird took off flying and landed high in a branch of an old oak tree.

Before long, a large crowd of kids and adults gathered near the riverbank to see what the turkey would do next. Shortly, a local policeman, Art Roy, arrived on the scene. Everyone began wondering what Art would do to try to get the turkey out of the tree.

As he sauntered up to the crowd, he smiled, looked up into the tree and said, "Well, well, what do we have here?" The turkey was balancing precariously on a high limb, and it didn't take Art long to decide how to get it down.

Slowly, he nudged his way to the front of the crowd and cautiously unsnapped his six shooter from its holster. "This might be a good time," he said confidently, "to get in a little target practice."

As the gun hung heavily from Art's hand, he said, "Why don't you all just move back from the bank a little now and give me plenty of room for a good shot."

All of the people began moving back and murmuring to one another as Art leveled his gun at the turkey and fired. Bang! He missed! Instantly, the large, bronze tom rose as high as it could on its bony legs and emitted a nervous gobble, gobble, gobble! The crowd began tittering.

"Nice shot, Art!" one gent bellowed sarcastically. "Better luck next time!" Slowly, Art raised his arm again and took aim at the big turkey. It simply turned its reddish, featherless neck and head towards him and looked dumbly straight down at him. Bang! Bang! Art fired his gun twice and missed both times. Now his gun was smoking, and the turkey began moving nervously back and forth on the high branch.

The crowd hushed as Art raised his arm for the third time. Bang! Bang! Bang! Three more misses in a row. Art's face turned tomato red as the crowd exploded with laughter. Some were laughing so hard that tears were streaming down their faces.

"What's so funny?" Art asked sheepishly as he began reloading his gun for yet another try. It wasn't to be. The noise must have panicked the turkey. It looked down excitedly at the laughing crowd and again made the throaty gobble, gobble, gobble sound that the male turkey usually makes.

Without any hesitation the big bird suddenly spread its large wings and flew down to the dirt trail which bordered the river.

Immediately, a gang of kids ran down the riverbank towards the trail, thinking they were going to catch the turkey, but it took evasive action. As the crowd watched the chase, the big tom was last seen trotting rapidly away from the kids. My sense is that the cagy old bird eluded them all and lived to have the last gobble!

WILSON'S ICE AND FUEL

On any hot summer day during the 1930's, but especially during the blazing days of July, we Sampson Addition kids, barefooted and tanned, would come running from all directions whenever we heard one of our own cry out, "The ice man's coming! The ice man's coming!"

In the summer of 1939, the ice man happened to be the ice men, the Shipstead brothers, two gentle giants who delivered ice for Wilson's Ice and Fuel. "All right, you kids," they would call out to us as we scrambled near the rear of their truck, "stand back now so you don't get hurt!" Immediately, they began axing huge 500 pound cakes of ice into smaller 100, 75, 50, and 25 pound cakes which were then delivered to ice boxes in neighborhood houses.

"Ice chips" flew in all directions, and we kids darted in and out, grabbing them from the rear of the truck and from the hot concrete street when they landed near our feet. Once in hand, we would begin sucking them, slaking our thirst and cooling our dry mouths and throats with the cold ice water which trickled down them.

Sucking on ice wasn't good enough for me. I wanted to deliver it to the houses like the Shipsteads, so I followed their truck each day until they finally relented and gave me a job delivering the 25 pound cakes. They hung a quarter inch thick rubber cape over my back, handed me a pair of ice tongs, and showed me how to sling the 25 pound cake of ice onto my back. It was easy and it was fun, and before long I could do it with one arm. "Ice man!" I'd holler before I entered a house and placed the cake in the ice box.

"Oh, I see we have a new ice man," Mrs. Johnson would say, and I'd just put the ice in her box, smile, and run back to the truck, eager to make the next delivery. The Shipsteads paid me a dime a day, and although I was only eleven years old at the time, they liked my enthusiasm and began letting me ride back to the ice house with them where they gave me other work.

In the ice house (which looked like a big barn) I shoveled thick layers of wet sawdust from the tops of the 500 pound cakes of ice which were to be removed next. Then the Shipstead brothers who were powerful and muscular men would break the cakes loose with long, iron crow bars and large ice tongs used to wrestle the cakes onto a conveyor belt and down to the waiting ice truck. There the blocks of ice would be hosed off and made ready for delivery to another Crookston neighborhood. By the time the Shipstead's came back, I'd have another layer all cleaned off and ready for them to break loose again and haul away. And my pay was increased to twenty-five cents a day!

During the fall when I began sixth grade at Cathedral's St. Joseph's Home, Chris Wilson, the tall, lean, rosy-cheeked, friendly, soft-spoken Scandinavian owner of Wilson's Ice and Fuel, gave me other work to do. He showed me how to start and stop a gasoline engine which powered a large circular saw used to cut long tree limbs into short lengths suitable for burning in stoves and fireplaces. For this work Chris paid me fifty cents each Saturday, and sometimes I even did it after school.

Once Chris showed me how to do the work, he'd leave and let me cut piles of wood all by myself. It was scary when I first did it because I was afraid I might get my hand caught in the saw blade , and I had visions of my hand flying off and of blood spurting all over the place and no one to help me. What would happen? I'd just lie there and bleed to death, I thought.

Luckily, I escaped without mishap and continued to work with the ice that winter when the monster 500 pound cakes were cut from the river near South Main Street and the Woods Addition. This was really fun! The ice was about three feet thick, and the cutting was done in crisscross fashion with a large, mounted circular saw. After a section of 500 pound cakes were cut, they were floated down a channel by boys like myself who wore spikes on their boots so they wouldn't slip and fall into the ice river water. The cakes were pushed along with pointed poles to waiting horse drawn sleighs which hauled them to the ice house.

It was really fun work, even though it was sometimes done when the snow was flying and the temperatures were in the below zero range. It was exciting! One just had to be careful.

That about completed the "ice cycle." The new sawdust from the wood sawing was used to cover the new ice which was stored for distribution during the next hot summer.

Now, when I think back on those days, I can't believe they'd let an eleven year old kid do that kind of work, but they did, and I'm glad they did because the Shipsteads and Chris Wilson became good friends of mine, and they taught me trust and a work ethic I'll always remember.

HOME RUN KING

The summer baseball season was finished, and the two best 12-13 year old teams would meet in the playoffs. The game would be between the Hill Addition and Sampson's Addition. I played for Sampson's Addition because that was my neighborhood. The game would be nine innings played on a Saturday afternoon on the Hill Addition field. The exciting news for all of us boys was that the "Wheaties Man" would be at the game, and any player that hit a home run would win a case of "Wheaties."

Now you have to understand, dear reader, that a case of "Wheaties" was worth a lot of money during the "Great Depression of the 1930's, and every kid on both teams would be trying to win one. Besides, the "Wheaties" boxes always had colorful pictures of famous baseball players on them, so if any of us hit a home run, we could fantasize about being just like the professional baseball players we idolized.

A lot of older kids gathered at the baseball field that afternoon. Some were from the Hill Addition, and some were from where I lived, Sampson's Addition, but many others were from all over town. The word had gotten around fast, and I guess they just wanted to be there to see if any of us little farts would hit a home run and win a case of "Wheaties."

My brother Bill was there. He played baseball with the big boys on the American Legion team. I'm sure Bill would have loved to see me hit a home run and bring home a case of "Wheaties," but he knew I always closed my eyes when I swung at the ball, and I usually struck out. Who knows, maybe I'd get lucky this time.

"Listen, Charlie," Bill instructed me as we were walking from our house up to the Hill Addition, "just keep your eye on the ball from the time it leaves the pitcher's hand until it hits your bat. Then you won't strike out all the time." I knew Bill was right because he was a catcher and fearless. I was always amazed to see him catch balls that a batter would swing at and miss. Sometimes the balls would tick the bat, and Bill would catch them.

"O.K.," I said. "I'll try."

Well, the game began, and it was actually sort of boring until the ninth inning rolled around because by the bottom of the eighth neither team had yet scored, and it looked like nobody was going to take home a case of "Wheaties." Then at the top of the ninth the Hill team was up, and as our pitcher tired, they began hitting. Before they had finished, they had scored, and they were leading us 1-0 when we went into the bottom of the ninth.

When our first man came up to bat, everyone started cheering him because they wanted to see the underdogs, our team, tie up the Hill team. Unfortunately for us, the Hill team's pitcher was a kid named Johnny Noah, a natural athlete who threw a baseball like a man. You could hear the ball splat into the catcher's mitt when Johnny threw it. "Steeeerike one!" bellowed Minnie Mike, the umpire, after the first pitch. "Streeeerike two!" he bellowed again after the second pitch. All the kids started shouting encouragement to the batter, but to no avail. "Steeeerike three!" Minnie wailed, and the first batter was out.

As our second batter started approaching the plate, I picked up a bat and started swinging it to loosen up because I was up third. The same thing that happened to our first batter, happened to the second. Johnny was just too much for us. His arm was too strong. He had too much power, too much speed, and too much accuracy.

As I approached the plate, I began growing warm all over. I heard my brother Bill in the background, calling softly, "C'mon, Charlie! You can do it! Just remember what I told you!"

I whispered excitedly to myself, "O.K., I'm going to keep my eye on the ball if it kills me!" Johnny just looked relaxed out there on the mound because he knew he was pitching to the strike out artist, Charlie Dowdle. Of course, the other kids knew this, too.

Finally, Minnie Mike called out, "Play ball!" from behind the plate, and Johnny looked at his catcher and began going into his windup. I was gripping my bat tightly and looking right at him. When the ball left Johnny's hand and came whistling towards me, I closed my eyes and swung for all I was worth.

"Craack!" was all I heard. Everyone was yelling like crazy. "Run, Charlie, run!" they screamed. I was stunned. I had hit the ball. I had really connected. As I was approaching first base, I saw Buddy Schraeder, the center fielder, running way back to try to catch it, but he couldn't because the ball flew way over his head.

As I approached second base, I was puffing, and pandemonium broke loose. I heard my teammates screaming at me to run faster, but I was running as fast as my body would go, and I was getting tired. I had never had to run this far before. When I reached third base, Buddy Schraeder had already thrown the ball to another player towards home.

That's when the yelling really got loud. I was dead tired and plunging towards home plate, looking at the "Wheaties Man" waiting there to award me with a case of "Wheaties" if I made it home safe.

When I was about four feet from the plate, I heard the ball splat into the catcher's mitt, and my heart sank as the catcher tagged me sliding home. "You're out!" roared Minnie Mike, and I heard my whole team groan in unison.

Everyone started walking away, and on the way home my brother Bill put his arms around my shoulders and whispered, "That's O.K., Charlie. It'll be alright. Maybe next time."

I just looked at him as big tears began welling in my eyes and said, "Ya!"

GUS

◆ • ◆

Gus Heldstab was a blond bombshell boy set to explode at any moment when he was young. His temper would flare into a mad rage whenever somebody did something he didn't like.

I especially remember one warm, summer morning when Gus came down to Central Park to play a game of baseball against our team. Gus was carrying a bag of oranges in one hand and a peeled orange which he was eating in the other. As he approached the clubhouse, "Minnie" Mike, our summer baseball director, saw him and rushed towards him. Now you have to understand that Gus didn't have a lot of love for "Minnie" because of "Minnie's" harassing habit.

What habit? "Minnie" loved to come up to a kid and pull a kid's cheeks and upper and lower lips between his thumbs and forefingers while at the same time bellowing "A-a-tae!" When he did this to Gus that particular morning, Gus exploded! He held onto his oranges, but orange pulp flew from his mouth and juice ran down it as he spewed a blue streak of language in "Minnie's" face which would have wilted a lesser man.

"God damn you, "Minnie!" You son of a bitch! Take your goddamned hands off me!" shouted Gus. "Minnie" just hung on until Gus grew real red in the face, and when he finally let go, all the kids laughed, but Gus was all sweaty and exhausted, and as he walked away, he let "Minnie" have another blast. "You bastard, "Minnie!" he shrieked.

The morning flew by, and when our game was finished, everyone was hot, sweaty, and tired. "Let's go for a swim up at the

Mount!" one of the boys yelled, and before you knew it, a small group of tired young boys found themselves trudging towards the Mount Saint Benedict (where the sisters lived and taught school) and the warm, inviting water of the Red Lake River.

Gus said, "Boy, this is going to feel real good."

"Yah," I answered. "It'll give a chance to cool off."

The Mount was only about four blocks from the park, and before we knew it we were there and one of the boys yelled, "Last one ins a big ninny!" Everyone started stripping rapidly. I saw Gus dash for the riverbank and heard a big splash. The rest of us followed and flew over the bank like lemmings. I was last, and by the time I took the plunge, everyone was already swimming around, free and easy, in the warm river water.

It was nothing at all like the pool with its loads of chlorine to sting the eyes and dry the skin, and no lifeguard was bossing us around, telling us not to run and to stay in the shallow end if we couldn't swim well. What a laugh! All of us could swim like Tarzan except Gus. He still dog paddled and sort of thrashed his arms around to keep his head above the water.

Suddenly, one of the boys noticed that Gus was missing! "Where's Gus?" he screamed.

Everyone started looking around for him when another boy yelled, "There he is!" I was the closest to him, and when I saw his head break water, I swam to his side. His mouth was wide open, gasping for air, and he wasn't able to let out so much as a squeak.

I knew I had to act fast or Gus'd be a goner, so impulsively, I grabbed the first thing I could get hold of, his long, blond, wet hair, and started to swim towards the river bank.

By the time we reached it, Gus was coughing and spitting up water. When he finally caught his breath, every word that came out of his mouth was a cuss word. "God damn you, Charlie! You shithead! Why'd you have to pull my hair?" he sputtered.

I simply turned and swam away, thinking about what had just happened and trying to understand Gus.

SWEET TOOTH

When I was a preschooler living at 403 Pleasant Avenue in Sampson's Addition during the 1930's, my main source of candy was a short five block walk to "Huggie" Sampson's (later Ade Ness's) "little store" on Woodland Avenue, and that's right where I'd go whenever I had one or more pennies jingling around in my pockets, eager to be spent. The candy was enclosed in a large glass cabinet, and as soon as "Huggie" or Ade saw me standing in front of it, he'd come over and say, "What's it going to be today, Mr. Dowdle?" It didn't take me long to decide because I had my favorites. Sometimes I'd buy foot long strings of twisted red or black licorice, sometimes round, black licorice sticks which were flat, had some printing on one end and looked like cigars, and sometimes a package of hard, white candy cigarettes which had pink tips. Any of these could be had for a penny apiece and could be found for the same price at all of the "little stores" which were located in neighborhoods throughout Crookston.

During my primary grades I graduated to the candy counter at the F. W. Woolworth store which contained about twenty kinds of candy, all enclosed in separated cases which were covered with glass. Already, I was selling the Crookston Daily Times on the streets, and instead of having pennies jingling around in my pockets, I had nickels. Oh happy day! I could buy a pound of chocolates, candy corn, jelly beans, or orange slices for a nickel and have it all eaten before I got home at night and sat down for supper. This was really good stuff! They also had Boston Beans, but I think my favorite among all of the candies Woolworth's sold was the salt water candy kisses that had peanut butter inside and were wrapped individually in brown wax paper. They were so good!

In the intermediate grades, I still earned money selling the Crookston Daily Times on the streets, but I also had other sources of income. One was shoveling snow from in front of our 416 Woodland Avenue house to which we had moved. After a blizzard or a heavy snowfall my dad would always pay me a dime or a quarter to do the job. I enjoyed it! It proved to be a welcome release for all of my pent up energy and supplied me with money for renewal with: Denver Sandwiches, Butterfingers, Milky Ways, Snickers, Nut Goodies, Baby Ruths, Salted Nut Rolls, Mounds Bars, and O'Henrys.

Another source of income was washing windows for some of the businesses across the street from my dad's Second Street barbershop. I began doing this one Saturday after washing my dad's barbershop windows for free. I'd take a pail of hot water and a brush and a wiper blade, both on long wooden poles, and first scrub the windows and then use the wiper on them. One day Dad said, "Charlie, why don't you go across the street and ask some of those people if they want their windows washed."

It sounded like a good idea to me, so I filled the pail with clean hot water and went across the street. The windows were all covered with soap because Halloween had been the night before. The first business was a fabric store run by two middle-aged women, and they welcomed me with open arms. "How much do you charge?" they asked.

Well, I hadn't thought about that, so I just blurted out the first significant coin that came into my head. "A quarter," I said.

"That's fine!" they said. "Go right ahead, and when you're finished, come in and get your money." So I did, and I also got a couple more jobs on the same side of the street, and after awhile they all became regular Saturday morning customers and an added source of money for more good candy like: Walnut Crush Bars, Neccos, Walnetos, Hersheys, Heath Bars, Big Hunks, Mars Bars, Bit O' Honeys, Milk Duds, Black Crows, Mountain Bars, and even Bazooka Bubble Gum. How sweet it was!

Then came seventh grade and a day of reckoning, a day of accounting for all sweets eaten in the past, and the first day my dad ever took me to see a dentist! His name was Dr. Tipizar, and he had his upstairs office on Broadway across the street from the Gopher Theater. When Dr. Tipizar had me open my mouth and saw all of the cavities, he let out a little groan and said, "My, my!" Then he looked at my dad and said, "This is going to take quite a little work, Frank!" My dad left me, and the work began!

That drill hurt so bad that I thought I was going to die, and I had to keep going back to Dr. Tipizar for a solid month! On each occasion as I began climbing the steps to his office, I'd begin getting hot, and by the time I got into his chair and gripped the arm rests, I was wet with sweat! Eating that candy all those years was fun, but paying the price was misery!

Pain didn't stop me! I had shifted the memory of it to the back of my brain somewhere and kept eating lots of candy, even the homemade quality sweet stuff like peanut brittle, chocolate fudge, and divinity from the premier candy store in town, Widman's! Mr. and Mrs. Widman were always extremely polite and kind to their customers, as was their daughter Margaret. Little did they realize that what they were selling was leading to my oral demise!

The next time I saw a dentist was in the ninth grade and the two year hiatus had taken its toll on my teeth. This time I saw Dr. Spence who had his office above Wallace's Drug Store on Broadway. After examining my teeth, Dr. Spence said, "Charlie, we're going to have to pull four of your molars, one on the top and one on the bottom of each side of your mouth." This scared me, and I had to talk it over with my dad before I made another appointment.

Dad just said, "Well, Charlie, if it has to be done, it has to be done! There's no use waiting!" He said he'd give me fifty cents for each pulled tooth I brought to him, but that didn't do much to bolster my courage. Finally, I went back to Dr. Spence and made four separate appointments, one each week, to have the molars pulled!

I really got scared for the first "pulling" when I saw Dr. Spence take out this large, heavy, silver pliers-like instrument, but when I saw his muscular forearms approach my open mouth with it, I gained some confidence. "This may hurt," I thought, "but this man will certainly have the strength to pull out my tooth!" And he did!

"You just keep holding your mouth open like that, Charlie, and this will all be over in a few seconds," Dr. Spence announced as he clamped the pliers onto the molar. Then he moved the pliers back and forth and I could hear the grinding of the roots and feel the tooth loosen right before he yanked it out! Then he held it up in the air for me to see and said, "That's the first one, Charlie. Three to go!"

When I showed the bloody tooth to my dad, he just said, "Good going, Charlie. Here's your half dollar." Right then and there I decided that I was going to begin cutting down on the candy and taking better care of my teeth. This was definitely not an easy way to earn a buck!

THE GOPHER

When I was a seven-year-old Crookston boy in 1935, the town boasted of having three movie theaters, the Lyric, the Royal, and the Grand. The Lyric at 109 South Main Street and the Royal at 109 North Broadway were both extremely small, unadorned, and basic. The Grand, on the other hand, was large and luxurious, possessing both an upstairs and a downstairs with rounded loges on each side and a spacious stage with heavy, rich, velvety curtains which swished open and shut at the beginning and end of each movie.

We young boys were always intrigued by what was happening on the screen, but we were sometimes just as interested in what was happening among the teenage boys and girls who seated themselves way in the back of the upstairs of the Grand. At times it seemed that the action among the teenagers eclipsed the action that was taking place on the screen, and it was extremely distracting.

Of course, we couldn't complain because we hadn't paid to get into the theater in the first place. When one show would let out and the adults would be exiting by the downstairs side door, we boys would furtively wait until the exiting crowd thickened and then squirm among it, going in the opposite direction until we gained our free entrance to the theater. There was simply no other way for some of us to see a show. Money was scarce, and we were poor.

A couple of years later when I turned nine, I no longer had to resort to sneaking into a movie because I made my own money selling the Crookston Daily Times on the streets and helping my brother Bill deliver the Minneapolis Tribune, St. Paul Pioneer Press, and Grand Forks Herald to our Sampson Addition customers. At about that same time in the winter of 1937, C.L. Hiller, who was the operator of the Grand Theater, announced plans to build a new 800 seat theater.

Three years later, on February 5, 1940, a Crookston Daily Times headline read: "New $30,000 Theater To Be Built On North Broadway Lot." This vacant lot was located between the Con Scully and Company Furniture dealership at 209 North Broadway and the Crookston Linoleum and Paint Company at 215 North Broadway. I remember watching the contractor's (Chris Eickof & Son) heavy-duty equipment claw into the earth and remove it until just an immense hole remained. It was quite a fascination for both the kids and "sidewalk superintendents" of the town. In addition to mentioning the cost and location of the new theater, the article mentioned above also revealed that a modernistic design would be used throughout, and that included in the accommodations of the new structure would be a crying room for babies, smoking lounges, and hard of hearing aids. Also, an open stairway in the foyer would lead to a large downstairs central lounge equipped with modernistic furniture and a ladies' powder room.

All of this "modernity" may have been very attractive to the adults, but what got my attention more than anything else was the "Magic Fountain." In the foyer was a drinking fountain which went on when one simply stepped up to it and bent over to take a drink. To a curious twelve year old kid like myself who didn't like to be fooled or made a fool of by anyone or anything, this "Magic Fountain" warranted closer examination. What I eventually learned was that an electric eye was beamed in front of the drinking fountain, so when a person stepped up to it and broke the beam, water automatically gushed from it. Children who couldn't believe their newfound power put the "Magic Fountain" to the test, repeatedly, and these same bladder-filled kids had to pay the price by making repeated trips to the bathroom during the movie.

If these same children had been asked to come up with a name for this new theater, they may have dubbed it the "Watering Hole" or "Floodgate" due to their love for the "Magic Fountain." But, according to the February 24, 1940 edition of the Crookston Daily Times, the job of naming the new theater was turned over to the whole community in the form of a contest, and "1,000 entries were received with 283 different names suggested." Also, according to the same Times article, 20 people submitted the name "Gopher," and it was chosen "because it was short, easily pronounced, suitable to the decorative theme, and didn't conflict with the names of any other business firms." Each of the twenty winners received a three months complimentary ticket and a share of the $25.00 cash award, divided equally, $1.25 apiece.

Some names which were unique but not chosen for the new theater were: Beuna, Dulac, Figaro, Homeric, Malou, Somoa, Oasis, Mirage, Ducky, Uwana, Fountain of Youth, Vallhalla, Bairnaby, Cez, Laf-a-lot, Nobby, Diversepty, and High Hat.

The new "Gopher Theater" opened its doors to the public during the last week of September. Eddy Regan, a Crookston native and friend of mine, said he remembered going to a movie at the "Gopher Theater" on the Sunday Pearl Harbor was attacked, December 7, 1941. I'd like to thank Eddy for searching the internet and Sister Eileen Beutel for sending me Crookston Daily Times articles which helped me write this story.

THE WHOPPING NORTHERN PIKE

My best friend Howie Pederson and I usually fished below the "Old Dam" on the Sampson's Addition side of the Red Lake River in Crookston during the 1930's because that's where we lived and where we usually saw a little old dark-skinned man called "La-La" catch lots of big northern pike.

However, one warm summer morning, we decided to ride our bikes out to the "New Dam" which was located a few miles southeast of Crookston off State Highway #2 to try our luck there where we heard the fishing was excellent!

It was a good half hour ride, so we left right after breakfast with our rods and reels, hooks, fishing lines, and sinkers. We had wire baskets attached to the handlebars on the fronts of our bikes, so the only thing we had to hold in our hands while riding along on the shoulder of the highway was our rods and reels which we always left assembled. So, there we were, riding along as free as the breeze, talking and anticipating catching some big fish.

Now, Howie was the better fisherman of the two of us, I think, because he was always so calm and patient as he cast out his line and reeled it in smoothly without even rippling the water. Yeah, Howie was a real pro. I envied him. He always caught fish, and I seldom did. I usually got excited while I was fishing, too eager, and I wasn't the most patient ten year old in the world. I think that the fish sensed this in me by the way I reeled in my daredevil.

But this warm, summer morning was to be quite different. By the time we arrived at the New Dam, we were both hot, sweaty, and tired from the long ride but still eager to cast our lines into the swiftly flowing river below the spillway of the dam. Howie had already positioned himself near the spillway where he thought the "Big Ones" would be likely to strike. I trudged a little farther downstream where some reeds were growing near an outcropping of large boulders. Near them was a smooth and grassy mud bank against which small waves from the river lapped. I thought it'd be a safe and quiet place from which to cast and reel in my line without encountering all kinds of snags on heavy, submerged tree branches and other debris.

Howie had already got started, so as soon as I got settled, I cast out my line about a hundred feet and reeled in my red and white daredevil with the three pronged hook on the end of it. I did it too quickly. I was anxious to catch a fish, but no fish was even going to be able to catch up with my hook if I kept reeling it in that fast. The second time I cast my line out, I settled down a little, lowered the tip of my flexible fiberglass rod near the water and reeled my line in slowly, ready to snap it up quickly and set the triple hook in the mouth of any fish unlucky enough to try swallowing it. Now I was getting the rhythm and the feel of the flow of the river, and I was getting ready to settle in for the long, patient task of waiting out and outwitting the big fish that I hoped would strike at my lure that morning.

My wait was extremely short-lived! On the third cast I waited briefly for my daredevil to sink beneath the surface of the water and then began reeling my line in slowly. Within seconds I felt a tremendous tug on the nylon line as it whipped against the surface of the water and just about tore the reel from my hands. "Wow!" I thought. "I've got a "Big One!" The tip of my rod bent towards the water until it almost touched my reel. I really got excited but tried to stay calm as I backed away from the bank of the river and applied as much pressure to the spool of nylon line on my reel as I could without burning my thumb. As I tired, so did the fish, pulling the taut line deeper as I struggled to prevent it from leaving my reel too rapidly. After all, what would I do if I ran out of line? It'd just snap, I guess.

"Howie! I got one!" I yelled as I kept up the tension on the line.

"Good! Reel it in!" he shouted back as he kept on fishing. I tried reeling it in a little, but nothing doing. This baby was alive and kicking, and he wasn't ready to cash it in yet! After about a minute of the fish and me struggling against one another, I detected that the fish was beginning to give up the battle. The tension on my line weakened slightly, and I began gradually, slowly to reel it in. When I got the fish about ten feet from shore, it made a giant swish around and tried and tried heading away from me. Do you think that a fish senses that this is their final fight for survival and tries making a last surge for life? I wondered.

But I didn't wonder long. It may have been a life and death struggle for the fish. It was a matter of pride for me. This was my big chance! I'd finally caught one before Howie! Now all I had to do was land it! As I continued keeping tension on the line and began reeling it in again, I could feel the strength of the fish wane as before, but it hadn't by any means given up the fight!

Finally, when I got it right up by the edge of the river, I gave my rod a strong upright pull, and a giant northern pike broke through the surface of the water, flew into the air and landed on the bank.

This northern pike was definitely the largest fish I had ever caught! It sprang sideways into the air, trying to shake my hook from its mouth. Howie, who had run over to see what I'd caught, just stood there in amazement and whispered huskily, "Wow! What a fish!"

The two of us subdued the monster, one of us trying to hold its slippery, slimy body against the ground while the other one extracted the triple barbed hook from between the jaws of the snapping, gasping fish. Those jaws contained needle like teeth, and we both knew the damage they could do to our hands. Eventually, we got the hook out and pushed my metal tipped stringer behind the gills and through the fish's mouth. He was mine!

We kept fishing, but neither of us caught another fish all morning, so we called it quits after lunch and headed for home. At first, I didn't know how I was going to carry my fish all that way. It was about three feet long from tip to tail. What I ended up doing was tying the stringer with the fish's head under the bike seat to one side and letting the fish's tail drag on the ground. It worked. We rode slowly along the highway, and when we got to town, I could feel many townspeople's eyes on us and the big fish, and I heard expressions of amazement from them and shouts of congratulations: "Wow! You really got a big one there, Charlie! Where'd you catch him? That's a mighty nice fish, son. Bet he just about pulled you in with him." These remarks made me one proud little fisherman and eager to get home and show my parents what I'd caught.

"Oh, Charlie!" my mom asked in a surprised voice, where did you get that big fish?" I told her the New Dam and then went out in our back yard and filled a metal washtub with cold water and put the northern in it.

When my dad came home from work, I rushed to meet him and asked him to come out back to see the fish I'd caught. When he saw it he exclaimed, "That's a mighty nice northern you caught, Charlie! It'll make good eating!"

That's my dad for you, I thought, always thinking about his tummy. To be honest with you, I liked good food, too, especially freshly caught game fish. So, I immediately got to work scaling and gutting the northern pike, and we had it fried a golden brown with potatoes and vegetables that night for supper, Yummm!

THE WEED EATER

Earlier in the summer, I had caught the largest northern pike in my life when I went fishing with my friend Howie Pederson at the "New Dam." This story takes place that same summer, but at the "Old Dam" which was located about three blocks from our 416 Woodland Avenue home in Crookston.

Another big difference was that it was several days and fish after I had caught my big northern at the New Dam, and I now considered myself an older, experienced angler. After I had caught the "Big One" at the New Dam, my experience had taught me to be patient and calm after a big fish struck the hook, or I'd lose him.

Still another difference was the kind of hook I was now using. It was no longer a red and white "daredevil." One day while I was walking past the Coast to Coast store on Main Street, I noticed a shiny, silver, spoon-shaped fishing lure in the window. The fact that the lure sparkled when the sun hit it got my attention, but what I really noticed was its name, the "Weed Eater."

It was designed to troll through weeds without snagging on them. This really appealed to me because if there was on thing I hated it was reeling in my line, suddenly feeling it pull on something, thinking it was a fish, and then learning it was only a large, green clump of weeds. The "Weed Eater" would prevent that from happening. A large single hook was doubled under the silver spoon and snapped to a thin strip of red metal much like a safety pin. You could drag it through dense weeds in the water, and it would remain snapped shut, but as soon as the force of a striking fish's mouth clamped down on it, it would spring open, and voila, the fish was hooked!

The "Weed Eater" worked like a charm, but I still hadn't caught a fish with it until early one morning when I decided to try my "miracle hook" in an especially heavily-weeded area below the Old Dam where the watery current was rushing between a small island in the middle of the river and the shoreline.

I picked this particular place that morning because of all the weeds, and I wanted to find out if the "Weed Eater" truly worked as advertised. It didn't take me long to find out.

My first cast was out about sixty feet, about as far as I dared cast because of the narrow river passage between the bank and the small, brush-covered island. My cast landed purposely right in the middle of some thick, green weeds. As I held my breath and reeled in my line slowly, I thought, "This'll be the supreme test for this Weed Eater. If it can pass through these weeds without snagged, it'll be everything they say it is. It'll be too good to be true! It'll be a fisherman's dream come true!"

As I began to reel in my line slowly, smoothly, the shiny silver spoon reflected the bright sunlight through the dark green weeds and murky water, and came in to shore without a hitch. I breathed a sigh of relief. This was going to make fishing pure pleasure, even if I didn't catch anything.

I cast out a few more times, each time with the same results. It was smooth sailing. No snags! I became so engrossed in the mechanics of my new, trouble free lure that I became mesmerized by it. Once again, I cast on the other side of the weeds and was reeling the Weed Eater through them, watching it shine and complimenting myself on what a smart purchase I had made when WHAM!

A huge northern pike broke the water with my "Weed Eater" securely attached to its mouth. This action took me completely by surprise and jolted me from my dream state! I was no longer simply "weed eating!" I was fishing again! I had a big one on the end of my line!

Before I had time to react to the strike, the large northern disappeared into the weeds, and the terrific force from its pull bent the tip of my rod backwards and snapped it right in half. I panicked! Immediately, my line spooled completely out and broke from the reel.

Damn!

SKIING MISADVENTURE

It was early spring and the winter snow was beginning to melt, but the river behind our Pleasant Avenue house was still frozen. I had recently won a pair of new skis for selling newspaper subscriptions and could hardly wait until Saturday morning to try them out on the rolling golf course hills north of town. Finally, Saturday dawned, and I was out the door and on my way, but I was too eager to reach the hills to take Main Street and through town the long way across the bridge and through town when I could just as easily reach them in about one-fifth the time by simply crossing the river behind our house.

The sun was shining brightly that morning and already by eleven o'clock the snow was beginning to melt and get slushy. As I skied quickly down a gentle slope to the edge of the river and surveyed it and the inviting hills on the other side, the river looked like it would still be safe to cross, but one never knew. The sun had been shining steadily for a few days, and when that happened, the ice began melting rapidly from the bottom towards the surface, just the reverse of its freezing sequence when winter set in.

I skied very slowly out from the edge of the river and it seemed solid enough to hold my weight. However, when I got out in the middle of the river, I began getting a little scared, being only twelve years old and all alone, and began thinking about what would happen if my eighty pound body broke through the ice and nobody heard me when I called for help. No one would! I was too far from any houses for that to happen.

What was I afraid of! The ice had held me this far, hadn't it? I was getting close to the opposite bank when the ice began giving a little under my skis. I thought, "Uh oh. This ice is too soft to cross. It's rubbery!" I didn't know what to do. It would be too dangerous now to try to step out of my skis or even to turn around on them because I could feel the ice sort of bending under me when I moved at all.

In an instant I made a decision to go forward while lying stretched flat on my belly the length of my skis and pushed myself forward toward the riverbank with my outstretched arms and hands on the watery surface of the ice.

Inching forward ever so slowly, I could still feel the thin rubbery ice beneath my body wanting to give way. With a final brush of my hands backwards against the watery ice surface, I reached the riverbank and grabbed hold of some protruding branches. Slowly, cautiously, I pulled myself safely up onto the bank.

It was fun to ski the hills in the sun, but it wasn't as much fun as it would have been had I not had to live with the memory of having just about drowned in the river. You can be rest assured I took the long way home after skiing that day!

The sun had set, it began getting a little colder, and I began thinking of the hot, delicious supper that my mom would have waiting for us kids when I got home. It was a long way home, unlike the shortcut across the melting river, but I didn't care because I had made it safely, already forgotten about my morning experience, was tired from skiing all afternoon in the sun and melting snow, and just wanted to get home, jump into some dry clothes and eat.

Instead of having to carry my skis down Main Street and through town, I decided to access a trail which ran along the river. Everything was going fine until I reached a point opposite the Great Northern Depot. As I was skiing down a gentle slope, one of my skis snagged its underside on something sharp, and I was thrown forward on my hands and knees. When I got up and brushed off my pants, I noticed that they were torn at the left knee and soaked with blood. I had cut my knee on a sharp piece of glass under the snow, glass probably thrown there by hoboes who opened cans and jars of food and heated them by campfires and ate there near the river and the railroad tracks during the Great Depression of the 1930's.

There wasn't much I could do about my knee except get home as quickly as I could and just let it bleed. As I continued skiing along the trail, I began getting a little scared and thought, ""What if I faint from the loss of too much blood? What if I bleed to death!" This was getting to be too much of an adventure for one day. This morning I didn't know if I was going to make it safely across the river, and now I didn't know if I was going to make it home alive.

Tears formed in my eyes as I kept pushing my skis along the trail towards the Sampson's Addition bridge. By the time I reached it, it had gotten colder, but I was closer to home now and was pretty sure someone would see and save me if I fell and fainted. I could taste the salt from my tears as they streamed onto my lips, and I began licking them and rubbing my eyes with my mitts because I didn't want anyone to know I'd been crying.

Finally, at last, I was home! I stomped the snow from my boots and announced myself with a familiar query, "Supper ready yet, Mom?"

"Pretty soon," she answered, so clean yourself up and get ready."

I showed her what happened to my knee which she sighed over and immediately began wrapping it tightly with a clean white cloth from our "rag bag." As I sat down to supper that night, my mind kept wandering over the events of that day. "I'm lucky to be alive!" I thought.

BOY FARMER

A lot of work around Crookston was out on farms because we were, after all, located in the "Heart of the Red River Valley" where the soil was extremely rich. When I was a boy, I did a lot of weeding of onions and even rubber plants with which the government was experimenting during the beginning of World War II.

During late summer and early fall when school was sometimes let out for two weeks, I picked potatoes and bagged them in burlap sacks. There was nothing really too glamorous about this work. It was backbreaking and dirty! The wind would blow the dirt across the fields and when you quit work at night, you looked like you had just finished cleaning a chimney of its soot, black! The good thing about potato picking was if you and your partner (mine was Howie Pederson) worked hard and fast, you were able to earn lots of money, and we did because we picked over a hundred bushels a day. The bad part was that your partner and you had to tie big bundles of burlap bags around your waists while you crawled between the rows of potatoes, picking them and putting them into the wooden baskets. When they were filled, you'd both stand up and empty them into a burlap bag.

A more treacherous field job I once tried was topping beets with long, sharp, machete-like knives. I did this with my brother Bill and some other older boys near Grand Forks, North Dakota. You'd hook a beet with a sharp two inch point at the end of the blade, hold the beet in your hand, and lop off its tassel with the blade. Accuracy was vital or you might just find your hand lying in the dirt among the beets! You had to work fast because you were paid by the tons of beets you topped.

I didn't last very long at this job because I was afraid I'd hurt myself and I was afraid of the Mexicans who were working alongside us. I know that sounds silly now and even prejudiced, but when I was twelve and heard stories about Saturday night fights and knifings between the Mexicans and locals on Crookston's Second Street, I got plenty scared working right alongside them as their razor-sharp knives flashed in the sun, speedily lopping off the leafy heads of the beets. My thought was, "If they're angry at white people like me, that could be my head!" That just shows you how a child's imagination can run wild. Nothing ever happened. No one was ever attacked.

However, fear is not a very pleasant feeling with which to live, however it comes about. It penetrates one's whole being, especially when one is very young and impressionable. So, it was with some dismay that I was soon to experience it again on another farm setting during the summer of 1941 after I had turned thirteen. Having weeded onions and rubber plants, picked potatoes, and topped sugar beets, I considered myself a seasoned farm hand by now, but I was soon to learn otherwise.

It was nearing the end of summer vacation, and I'd been hanging around my dad's Second Street barbershop, bored and not knowing what to do with myself when a big red-headed farmer came into the shop, plopped himself into my dad's barber chair and bellowed, "Hi, Frank! How about a shave and a haircut!"

"You bet, Red," my dad replied enthusiastically as he went to work on "Red" Sullivan's head and face. Red and my dad began talking about how the wheat, barley, and oats were coming when Red said, "Everything's getting ready to go, but I could use a little more help out in the fields, shocking grain. That kid of yours want to come out and do a little work for me this summer?"

"Holy cow!" I thought as I pushed back in my chair and began to grow warm all over. "He's talking about me!"

Right away my dad asked, "What do you think, Charlie? Would you like to go out and work on the farm for awhile this summer and make a little extra money?"

Without thinking, I reacted spontaneously and blurted, "Yes, I'd like to!" I'd never lived on a farm before, so this sounded exciting to me.

"Okay," Red said, "when I finish up here, I've got a little shopping to do around town, and then we'll head out to the farm. You run home and get your clothes and meet me back at the barbershop in about an hour. Okay?"

"Okay!" I yelled as I dashed out the door and made a bee line for Sampson's Addition and home. When I got there, I told my mom all about what I was going to do, and she helped me get ready. I said goodbye and ran back to the barbershop. When I got there, I was all hot and sweaty. Red had already finished his town errands, and he and my dad were talking.

"Ready to go, Charlie?" Red bellowed as he rose from his chair.

"Yeah," I answered as I picked up my bundle of clothes and began following him out the door toward his pickup.

My dad waved, smiled, and said, "See you, Charlie."

I waved back and said, "Okay, Dad!" Red started driving north on Main Street, and I was feeling pretty comfortable as we passed the "Root Beer Barrel" (my favorite hamburger and root beer place) and the Crookston Agricultural School. These were familiar landmarks heading north on State Highway # 2, but when Red failed to turn west towards Grand Forks, North Dakota and kept driving straight ahead on State Highway # 75, I was lost and started becoming a little concerned. Red must have sensed my worry because he was the first to speak since we left the barbershop.

"We've got a lot of animals on the farm, Charlie," he said. "Chickens, cows, pigs, horses. I've even got a horse I'm training to be a racehorse. Just breaking him in. You may get to ride him!"

What Red didn't know was that I was petrified of horses ever since being thrown off a Shetland pony at a Crookston carnival when I was eight years old and again four years later when I tried riding an old nag bareback and was dumped into the river above the Old Dam. I hadn't been back on a horse since, and if Red Sullivan thought he was going to get me to ride his racing horse, he had another thought coming!

As we kept driving north, we passed through Warren, Minnesota, and I began wondering how much longer it was going to take. We'd already been driving about a half an hour. "His farm's a long way from home," I thought. At last, we turned off the highway onto a gravel road and the Sullivan farmhouse soon came into view. When we pulled up to the house, Red announced cheerfully, "Here we are, Charlie! Bring your stuff, and I'll tell my wife she's got a new mouth to feed!"

Reds wife was nice. She was real gentle and soft spoken compared to Red, who seemed rough and loud when he talked. She showed me my bed and the basin of water where I could wash up. "When you're done," she whispered, "come on downstairs and we'll get ready to eat."

I splashed some water on my face, and it didn't smell or taste like the water at home. At home the water came from the river and had chemicals added to it. This water was well water and just smelled and tasted different. I guess that was the key word, "different." I had only been on the farm a few minutes, and already I was feeling a little lonesome.

When I came downstairs to the kitchen, I couldn't believe my eyes. The table was loaded with food: pork chops, Jell-O, potatoes, carrots, peas, warm homemade bread, milk, two apple pies and cake. "Dig in, Charlie!" Red said. "We'll try to put a little fat on them bones of yours!" I hesitated before I started eating and thought, "What, no "Bless us oh Lord and these Thy gifts which we are about to receive from Thy bounty and goodness through Christ our Lord" like my dad always said before we started eating supper? I have to say, this was very different for me, but the food sure tasted great! And I did indeed "dig in," but there was so much food!

Shortly after we ate, the sun was going down and Red said, "C'mon out by the barn, Charlie, and I'll show you the horse I'm training." I followed Red out to the barn and watched him slip a rope over the horse's head and around its neck. Then he gradually began releasing the rope and soon had the horse trotting in circles around him in a ring. Briefly, my mind flashed back to my Shetland pony experience at the Crookston carnival.

Red's horse didn't seem too gentle, nor that it was enjoying the exercise. It bucked up and down a couple of times and snorted and whinnied its dissatisfaction, throwing its head from side to side as it ran around Red. Fear began entering my body and I thought, "No way would he ever get me to ride that animal!" Then I began wondering if my dad and he had plotted to get me out to the farm to do just that. After all, I was light, ninety-five pounds to be exact, a perfect riding weight, and Dad being from Corydon, Indiana, near the Kentucky border, was always around horses and loved to ride them. Not I! If I ever got on that horse, it'd probably buck me off and break my neck! No thanks!

After the training session, Red took the rope off the horse's head and let it run free around the corral. I got away from there fast. That animal scared me. It still seemed wild!

"Well, guess it's time to hit the hay, Charlie," Red said. "Tomorrow's gonna come around mighty early." We walked towards the house, and when we got there, I went upstairs and just lay on my bed. "Not like home," I thought. This bed was hard as a rock, and it was hot as blazes up in the small room. If I were home, I'd be sleeping upstairs with my older brother Bill, as usual, or I might be sleeping alone out on the front porch where the cool night breeze would blow through the screen and brush up against my face. Then I began thinking about what I'd given up for the rest of the summer, swimming in the pool by the library, picking gooseberries off the bushes and eating them while lying on the warm concrete and getting a tan, playing baseball with guys I liked and "Minnie" Mike down at Central Park, and playing hide-and-go seek, lost track, and post office with the girls at night in Sampson's Addition.

I undressed and got ready for bed and just covered myself with a sheet because it was still so hot and muggy, even though it was already dark outside. It was so humid my body just stuck to the sheets! I was having a difficult time getting to sleep when I heard an owl let out a screech. It was pretty normal stuff for a farm, I guess, but it startled me and I grew nervous.

I think it all began catching up with me, the smells, the sounds, the tastes, the different bed, and the being alone. My mind was twirling around and around and I finally felt myself getting sleepy when I heard this loud grinding noise coming from another bedroom. This kept me awake until I finally figured out that it must be Red grinding his teeth in his sleep. It must have been him because it was really loud and grating!

Just when it seemed I had fallen asleep, a loud jangling noise filled the air. An alarm clock was ringing loud enough to wake the dead! "Were they really going to get up at this hour?" I thought. "It's still dark outside! Someone must have made a mistake and set the clock wrong!" They didn't! It was four a.m. and I could hear Mrs. Sullivan already busy getting breakfast downstairs in the kitchen.

What a breakfast! It was just like supper! Meat, potatoes, cereal, fruit, hot biscuits, milk and coffee. All I used to have for breakfast at home was a bowl of corn flakes or a cup of hot chocolate and a couple slices of buttered toast. I ate, but I didn't eat much because my stomach was churning.

After breakfast we "men," Red, a farm boy my age who was helping out, and myself, immediately hopped into the truck and took off for a field of barley where the grain had been cut and tied into big heavy bundles which were lying on the ground. Our job was to "shock" it, that is, grab the twine with which each bundle of grain was tied and stand the bundles upright against one another, heads up, so the grain could dry in the sun. Those bundles were heavy, especially in the morning, and barley had sharp heads which scratched my arms when I picked up the bundles. Guess I should have brought a long sleeve shirt. I didn't even bring any gloves, and the shoes I was wearing were oxfords, dress shoes. Of all the dumb things! I guess I was just in too much of a hurry. Not only did my hands get red and raw and my arms sore and scratched, but thistles found their way into my shoes and made my feet feel like they were walking on pins and needles every time one of them jabbed me.

After a while I got the hang of this hard work under the hot sun and tried to keep up with Red and the farm kid he'd hired to work for him, but there was no way I could. Besides the torture I was experiencing, these guys were too strong and used to this kind of work for me to for me to come anywhere near their work output. So, even though I loved to compete, I was totally outclassed and knew it.

Before too long it was time for lunch and Mrs. Sullivan came out to the field with sandwiches and fresh, cool well water. Did I say lunch? It was only ten o' clock in the morning and we'd already been working almost five hours. I was beginning to develop an appetite with all this work, so I gobbled down the sandwiches and drank the cool water just like the other two before heading back into the field. This was backbreaking work, and doing it under the hot sun and without the right clothes made it all the more miserable, but I did get hungry and ate.

We worked until the sun started going down (I'd guess around twelve killing hours) and then Red yelled, "Okay, boys! That's enough for today! Let's call it quits and head for home!" I didn't wait for him to call me a second time. I dropped the two lead-weight bundles I had in my hands to the ground and dragged myself to the truck, dog tired. And to think I used to complain when my dad asked me to cut the lawn or shovel a little snow from the sidewalk in front of our house. Dad would never find me complaining again, ever!

After we got washed up and settled for supper, I gazed at the table which was again covered with food, a repeat of the feast we had eaten the night before. I ate more heartily this time because I had worked up an appetite and was really hungry, but my heart just wasn't in farm work. All the time I was eating I kept thinking about home, my brother Bill, swimming in the pool, playing baseball in Central Park, and just having the freedom of running around downtown Crookston.

While we were eating, I heard Red say he was going to have make another trip into Crookston in the morning to pick up a part for one of his machines. You'd better believe my ears perked up when I heard that news. I wanted to be with him! I'd had enough of farming already. I was lonely and wanted to go home.

Lying in bed that night I began thinking about how I'd tell Red I didn't want to work on the farm anymore. What if Red said, "You're here, now. You may as well stay the rest of the week." I didn't want to stay the rest of the week. I wanted to go home.

Then I began thinking, "What if Red told me I had to stay the rest of the summer until all the harvest was finished! What if I became a farm prisoner?" I began plotting what I'd do come morning. When Red went out to his truck, I'd get there before him and hide in the bed of his pickup, covering myself with an old blanket.

When morning came, Red had gotten up early, already finished his breakfast, and was heading outdoors towards his pickup when I saw him. I ran outside to stop him before he drove away. As he was getting into his pickup, I was panting and sweaty from embarrassment when I blurted, "Red, I want to go home!"

He looked at me disappointedly and said, "Okay, run in the house and get your clothes and come on down and hop in!" Just like that he said it, with no other words spoken. It was a long drive back to Crookston. We didn't say more than a few words to each other all the way home, and when he dropped me off in front of my dad's barbershop on Second Street, I thanked him, hopped out, and began walking home. I was too ashamed to go in and tell my dad what happened.

DRIVE ON ICE

Saturday mornings during the winter of 1942 I was up with the birds so I could make it on time to my job at Medved's Meat Market on North Broadway.

Besides selling meat, Medved's had a pastry department, and I was the guy in charge. Upon arriving at the market, my first job was to fill the warm, golden, deep-fried rolls which the pastry cook had just made with jelly. This was really great sport for an eighth grade boy! It was exciting to use the sharp-pointed jelly gun to puncture the rolls and inflate them. Pump, pump, pump and the roll was filled to capacity. Pump, pump and the red, juicy jelly would come seeping out its sides. Pump once again and the roll was likely to burst at which time the jelly roll maker extraordinaire would come to the rescue by licking the jelly quickly so it wouldn't get all over the floor. Of course, I'd then have to finish my job by eating the whole roll. Got milk?

Besides jelly roll making, I got to sell all of the pastry. Mr. Medved sold the meat, and his son Jimmy delivered it to people's houses. When business was slow, I helped Jimmy deliver the meat, and that's what this story is really all about, what happened one day after we had finished delivering meat out in the Carmen neighborhood south of town.

Casually, as we were riding back to the market late in the afternoon, Jimmy suggested that perhaps I could learn to drive, and that then I could make the meat deliveries all by myself. I honestly think that he was hoping that I could because he was bored with the job and wanted to be someplace more exciting like the ice arena, playing hockey with the boys.

My eyes widened as he pulled the pickup off to the side of the snow-filled country road and stopped. No other cars were around, so I guess Jimmy decided that this would be as good a place as any to learn to drive. How wrong he was!

The engine was still running when Jimmy said, "Slide over here into the driver's seat, Charlie, and we'll call this your first lesson." Cautiously, I slid behind the wheel, and Jimmy began explaining what I should do. "You see, Charlie," he said as he pushed his foot on a pedal, "you push in the clutch, put it in gear, step on the accelerator and away you go!" I nodded my head, put up a good front, and pretended I knew what he was talking about, but really I didn't because our family never owned a car, and I didn't know the first thing about driving one. I was scared, but I didn't want Jimmy to think I was because he was intent on having me learn how to drive so he could have his freedom. At least that's why I think he wanted me to learn.

So, when Jimmy said, "Okay, Charlie, let's go!" I tried to conquer my fear and just said, "Okay, I'll try it." I looked down at the clutch and eased it towards the floorboard with my left foot and at the same time tried to pull the long, angling, metal rod which was attached to the floor into first gear. After a grating noise and a little help from Jimmy, I finally made it into first gear and Jimmy yelled, "Okay, Charlie, now step on the accelerator and try putting it in second while you're moving!"

We were driving jerkily for about forty feet when Jimmy became impatient with my driving skill and commanded, "C'mon, Charlie, put the damn thing in second! Let's go!" I plunged my foot rapidly towards the clutch pedal so I could shift, but my foot hit the accelerator by mistake, and the pickup began swerving rapidly from one side of the icy, snow-covered country road to the other towards the ditch! "Jesus, Charlie!" Jimmy yelled excitedly, "take your foot off the accelerator!"

I was so scared, I couldn't do it. My leg just remained stiff. My foot seemed like it was frozen to the accelerator, and I was just too frightened to budge it. Jimmy grabbed the wheel from my hands and turned it rapidly back and forth as we went careening from one side of the snow-packed road to the other. I just sat there, stunned. I was petrified at what was happening as I heard the rear wheel spinning at a dizzying speed. "Take your goddamn foot off the gas, Charlie!" Jimmy yelled again as he kept wrestling with the wheel in a valiant attempt to keep the pickup out of the ditch.

I finally came to my senses and lifted my foot from the accelerator. At the same time, Jimmy turned off the ignition and the truck came to a skidding stop at the side of the road as he applied his foot to the brake. I breathed a heavy sigh of relief as Jimmy slid into the driver's seat and said, "I think I better drive, Charlie." My silence told him all he needed to know as we drove back to the meat market.

DANCE MAN

Do you remember your first high school dance? Mine was at Crookston's Cathedral High School in the fall of 1942, but it actually began in the living room of our Woodland Avenue home with my brother Bill who was a senior and an excellent dancer. I was a freshman and didn't have a clue, so before supper the Friday evening of our first school dance, I asked Bill to teach me how.

He was reluctant at first, but I kept begging him, and he finally relented. "O.K., Charlie," he said in a brotherly, surrendering voice. C'mon into the living room and I'll teach you the fox trot."

"Just take my hands like this," Bill said annoyingly as he pulled me near him. "I'll be the girl, and you be the boy. Now step forward with your left foot when I step back with my right one, and then step forward with your right foot when I step back with my left one, and then step to the side with your left foot when I do the same with my right one. Got it?"

"I think so," I answered happily. "It's easy!" So, Bill and I kept right, left, and side-stepping around the living room until Mom called us for supper.

That night at the small Cathedral High School gym, the first dance was an "introductory" dance designed to make the freshmen feel comfortable. A senior boy was paired with a freshman girl, and a freshman boy was paired with a senior girl. I got paired with a senior girl I'll never forget, one with whom I tried to dance the whole night away!

She was dark-complexioned, short and soft. I was lily-white, just her height, and bony. As far as I was concerned, she and I were a perfect fit, and she became a real awakening for me. I couldn't seem to get close enough to her when the music began because she smelled so good and was so soft, like a pillow.

I don't remember her name, so for the rest of this story let's just call her Lilac Pillow. I thought she and I moved smoothly as we sashayed around the dance floor. I don't know what she was thinking. After the first dance ended, I didn't leave her. I couldn't! I was too totally immersed in her perfume and softness.

When the second number began, Lilac and I continued to dance, and when I leaned my head against the side of hers and my body against her soft Angora sweater, I began growing warm all over, hot even by the time the dance ended, sweating even!

I was stuck to Lilac Pillow like glue when the third number began playing and we continued to one, two, and side step to the fox trot Bill had taught me. That's about the time my brother cut in and "rescued" Lilac Pillow from her continued torture.

"I think you better rest for awhile, Charlie," Bill said as he took Lilac's hand and led her away from me.

Reluctantly, I said, "O.K.," and walked away to one side of the gym, all my senses still very much alive and dancing with Lilac Pillow.

GANDY DANCING

Random House Webster's College Dictionary for the New Millennium in 1999 defined a "gandy dancer" as "a member of a railroad section gang that lays or maintains track."

I'd like to tell you what "gandy dancing was like for a gang of fifteen and sixteen year old Crookston kids during the summer of 1943 when World War II was being fought and there was really a shortage of men on the home front.

The Great Northern Railroad needed "gandy dancers" badly, so after our first year of high school, a gang of us guys went over to their office and applied for work. We were supposed to be at least sixteen years old, so some of us lied our age so we would be hired. The railroad didn't care. The railroad needed men to work an extra gang on the track, and I don't think they ever did check our ages. If they had, they would have discovered that many of us were only fifteen.

Our boss's nickname was "Scrapiron," "Scrappy," for short, and he was a real old, small, hunched over man with a face like tanned brown leather, but with deep creases all over it. "Scrappy" was a very gentle man for a railroad foreman.

Before we were hired, "Scrappy" lined us up and looked us over. When he came to me and asked, "Son, are you ready to go to work?" I remember just standing there as strong-looking and tall as I could and answering, "Yes sir!" I was hired on the spot and told to report to the depot the next morning at seven o'clock. I was thrilled! "Scrappy" thought I looked good enough to work for a man's pay which I learned would be fifty dollars every two weeks, and that was a lot of money in 1943, considering that a private in the Army only got twenty-one dollars a month at that time for fighting in a war.

Well, the pay turned out to be real good, but we earned it! First, we pulled out the spikes which were driven into holes on each side of a heavy iron plate which sat on the railroad tie under the rail. Heavy six foot iron crowbars with a hammer-like craw on one end were used to pull the spikes. Next, heavy iron jacks which weighed about fifty pounds each were forced under the rail, and it was hoisted about two to three inches off the ground.

This made it possible for the next procedure, pulling the old, rotten, heavily-creosoted ties out from under the rail. One worker would get inside the rails and one outside them, and with ice tongs the two men would tug at the tie until it loosened and came out. For some reason I developed a real liking for the strong tar-smelling creosote which was used as a wood preservative.

Usually, we worked in pairs when we pulled out ties and "gandy danced" which was the next step in the procedure. Bill Monroe was my partner. He and I would pull a new heavily-creosoted tie under the rails with our ice tongs and then commence "tamping" dirt and crushed rock under it until it with our shovels until it was tight against the underside of the track.

Before "dressing down" the track, the last step in the "gandy dancing" process, heavy mauls with heads that were about a foot long and an inch and a half in diameter were used to pound the spikes into the ties. That's when the fun began!

The "old hands" watched us as we tapped the spikes into the ties and then raised the mauls over our heads and took full fledged swings at them. Of course, just like when you're pounding nails into boards, if you didn't hit the spike heads flush, they'd go zinging through the air like shrapnel. Watching our feeble attempts at driving the spikes into the ties after taking five, six, and sometimes seven swings at them before being successful provided the "old hands" with lots of laughs.

Before the end of the summer, most of us could drive a spike into a tie in four or five swings. You can understand why we all stood and watched in awe while a very strong adult named Frank Sherak drove a spike into a tie with two and sometimes even one swing. The man was amazing!

The origin of the word "gandy dance" isn't known, but I think it must come from the way we had to "tamp" the ties up under the rails. Bill and I would stand on each side of a tie, facing one another. We'd stand on our left legs and together force the dirt and crushed rock under the tie with our right legs on the shovels in sort of a rocking, dancing motion. I think this was the origin of the word "gandy dance."

After "gandy dancing" all morning and most of the afternoon under the hot summer Minnesota sun, the whole crew of fifty men and boys would line the track. We'd each take a very heavy six foot iron crow bar and force it under the rail, and when "Scrappy" called out, "Yo!" a whole line of fifty men pulled their guts out until the rail moved where "Scrappy" wanted it.

After that we'd put the finishing touches on the job by smoothing the rock down from the track in a gentle slope towards the ground. And then it was time to quit and go home.

We rode to work and back to the Great Northern Railroad depot in a big grain truck which had a room built onto it which seated fifty men, twenty five on two rows in the middle and the rest on rows on each side. The smell was overpowering each day we came back. Chewing tobacco, cigarette smoke, and sweat do not do not a pleasant mixture make!

Sometimes the ride home became a little more pleasant when "Scrappy" decided to stop at a bar on the way back. The first time this happened I couldn't believe it. We all piled out of the truck and walked into a bar. "Scrappy" called out to us, "Boys, you really put in a good day's work today!" Then he faced the bartender and said, "Set 'em up!" We were all served glasses of that delicious Grain Belt Beer, and did it ever taste good after working the whole day under the hot sun.

We were sort of an odd extra gang crew, half men too old for the draft and half kids too young for it, but we all seemed to get along and learn from one another.

We worked very hard in the intense summer heat from eight in the morning until about four in the afternoon, together! It was miserable, and many of us had to take salt tablets so we wouldn't faint, but the older men kidded with us to help lighten our day, and it helped.

At one point during the first week, some of the boys who couldn't take the heat and the blistered hands, quit. My "gandy dancing " partner, Bill Monroe, hung in there, and I got to know and like him real well. You sweat in somebody's face for three months while working under the hot summer sun, and you'll get to know that person real well, too. Bill went to Central High School and I went to Cathedral High School, and we got to be the best of friends. A lot of new friendships were forged under sun that summer among young and old alike.

The fact that I survived the work helped me learn a lot about myself. In spite of being only 120 pounds and weak when I started, I learned very early that summer that I had a lot of perseverance, that I could stick with a job under some pretty severe conditions. I also learned that I was extremely shy but that I was just as shrewd at getting out of some of the more difficult jobs as the next guy.

Perhaps the biggest plus which resulted from a summer of "gandy dancing" was a new self image, a new sense of confidence which I had lacked at the beginning of my freshman year at Cathedral High School. I liked the feeling of being in more control of my body and of being stronger. I also like the independent feeling of having lots of my own money to spend. Of course, I had had money of my own before from selling the Crookston Daily Times on the streets and from delivering the Minneapolis Star Journal, the Saint Paul Pioneer Press, and the Grand Forks Herald, but I had never had anything like this much money coming in on a regular basis, and it made quite an impact on my style of living. Now I was able to buy all of my school clothes at Penny's, C.O.D., Ruetell's or wherever I wanted, play pool at The Playhouse whenever I wanted, and fill up on as many "Little Dicks" or "Big Dicks" after school at Schreiter's Drug Store as I wanted.

It seemed that life was just beginning to get started for me during he summer of 1943, and now I was ready to continue its dance, and it made me very happy!

DAD

The river trail was a short cut between downtown Crookston and our house at 416 Woodland Avenue in Sampson's Addition. To get to it I walked through the Great Northern Railroad depot, across the tracks, and then along the trail and behind the Crookston Steam Laundry to the bridge and home. As I reached the laundry, there was a neat little hill I always ran down, and in the winter it got slippery, and I'd usually run and slide down it. Well, that's what this story is all about, that little hill.

When World War II started, my dad and Uncle Jim closed their barbershop on Second Street and took different jobs. Uncle Jim went to Duluth to work in the blast furnaces, and Dad became a bartender at the Veterans of Foreign Wars Club which was located above Meng and Garviik's restaurant right next to the Great Northern Railroad depot. This job was a perfect fit for Dad because he was the V.F.W. service officer all the time he was barbering, and his life was very involved with World War I vets. This new job was a good fit for me, too, because on the way home from an evening of pool at the Playhouse, I'd often walk to the V.F.W. Club at about closing time so I could sip a beer with Dad and walk home with him.

One particular evening I'd like to tell you about was a cold winter one with new fallen snow on the ground, so naturally Dad and I decided to take the shortcut home, the river trail. It only saved us about a block, but when it's freezing outside, any distance saved is helpful.

As we were walking along the trail and talking to one another, our only light came from a bright yellow moon set in an ink black sky. While we were walking along, it dawned on me how lucky I was to have a dad I liked as a friend, a dad I could even joke around with and sometimes even tease into a playful sparring match.

Unfortunately, on this cold winter evening, I did something which ruptured our friendly father-son relationship for a moment. As we approached the Crookston Steam Laundry, I took a run ahead of Dad and slid down the hill which had become a little icy and covered with new-fallen snow during the night. A fifteen year old could do that. Dad, on the other hand, was more cautious. He was fifty-four years old and no longer had the balance or daring do of a kid. So, when he approached the hill, he sort of shuffled his feet one ahead of the other and kept them both on the ground at all times so he wouldn't slip and go head over teakettle.

"C'mon, Dad! You can make it!" I yelled as he began slowly down the treacherous little icy hill.

Suddenly, both my dad's feet slipped from under him, and I saw his legs and arms fly into the air. With a pained groan he landed on his butt and back at the bottom of the river trail hill. He just sat there, stunned, and I began laughing because I thought my dad looked so funny just sitting there, not moving. What I had forgotten, unfortunately for me, was my dad's Irish temper!

As he got to his feet, I heard him say, "So you think that's funny, do you, Charlie?" And that's when I felt the sudden impact of a fist meeting my jaw. It set me on my own butt, right in the cold snow.

I couldn't get mad at Dad for hitting me. I had it coming for laughing at his misfortune. I just sat there for awhile, chuckling to myself. As I rose slowly to my feet, I immediately apologized to Dad for laughing at him. I slung my arm around his shoulders in a friendly fashion, and we continued talking and walking towards home, the incident forgotten.

MINNEAPOLIS, SUMMER OF '45

Where were you on August 6, 1945 when the atomic bomb was dropped on Hiroshima, Japan, effectively ending World War II? I was washing my clothes in the basement of the Nordic Hotel in downtown Minneapolis. It was late afternoon, and people were hugging, kissing, and shouting, "The war is over! The war is over!" When I walked the two blocks from the hotel down to Hennepin Avenue, the same scene was being played out as ecstatic people flooded the street and brought all traffic to a standstill. It was exciting to be in Minneapolis that summer!

I was seventeen, had just finished my junior year at Cathedral High School, and wanted to get away from Crookston for awhile and be with my older brother Bill in Minneapolis where he was living downtown at the Nordic Hotel (paying $7.00 a week for rent) and working for Minneapolis Honeywell Regulator Company. The train ride to the twin cities was uneventful except for a Crookston boy offering me a cigarette and encouraging me to inhale. I didn't smoke, and when he offered me a second cigarette and I inhaled it, deeply, I felt like I was floating about three feet in the air! That was the last time I smoked! When we arrived at the depot and I saw all the people milling around, I got very nervous because my brother wasn't there to meet me. Luckily, I met an older woman from Crookston on the train, and she gave me directions to the Nordic Hotel.

My first two days of job hunting were disheartening, but on the third day when I was just about ready to pack my bags and head home, I struck it rich! I was walking to the Honeywell plant to meet my brother after work when I noticed a fruit and vegetable warehouse where a lot of men were working. As a last gasp effort to find work, I decided to stop and ask the foreman on the dock if they were doing any hiring, and he said, "Yes, we certainly are!" My heart just about skipped a beat when he asked, "Do you have a social security card?"

"I have one, but I left it at home," I replied.

"Where's home?" he asked.

"Crookston," I said.

"Well, that's okay," he said nervously. "Just send home for it, and when you get it, bring it to the office. In the meantime, go and fill out an application and a time card. You start work tomorrow morning at six."

When I met my brother Bill after work at Honeywell, I was so happy inside I could barely control myself because I wasn't going to have to go home a failure, after all! "Bill," I blurted, "I got a job, and it's only a couple of blocks from your place!"

"Good going, Charlie," he said, "now you'll be able to split the rent at the hotel with me."

As we walked past Gamble-Robinson, I pointed to it and said, "That's it right there. It's a fruit and vegetable warehouse."

I was up at five o'clock the next morning, ready and rarin' to go. Gamble-Robinson was only a little over a mile from our hotel, so I walked down Hennepin Avenue to a White House for a little breakfast and then ran the rest of the way to the warehouse. When I got there, a time card already had my name on it, so I punched in and went to work with Minneapolis high school boys who had been hired with me. We unloaded boxcars of big bunches of green bananas that were four to five feet high. A little Italian guy whose name was Jimmy would tie a rope around the top of each stalk, and then one of the stronger boys would heave these stalks of bananas onto our burlap-bag-covered shoulders. We'd carry the bananas from the boxcar to the dock where the rope was attached to a conveyor belt and the bananas were taken down to a ripening room.

It was fun when we unloaded watermelon because we'd form a line and slide them from the hands of one worker to the next, and when we wanted to eat one, a boy in the line would simply drop it on the concrete floor, it would burst open, and we'd all have a deliciously sweet, watery watermelon feast! The same held for the bananas mentioned above. Whenever we wanted to eat one, we simply whacked a ripe one off a bunch, and nobody cared!

We also unloaded big crates of iceberg lettuce and carrots packed in ice and boxes of peaches, plums, apples, and pears. The dry goods were the heaviest, the hundred pound sacks of sugar and flour, and the heavy cardboard boxes filled with canned goods. Unloading sacks of potatoes was the most fun because after wheeling them to a certain location on the warehouse floor, I'd throw blocks into a pile of them to straighten the pile and to prepare for the fall football season! We used two-wheeler hand trucks to move everything into the storage bins because they didn't have fork lifts and pallets in those days. It was always a challenge to stack boxes of oranges and cantaloupe eight high on the main warehouse floor where they could be easily seen by the buyers. Sometimes a stack would wobble and topple, and there would be fruit flying all over the place. By the time the summer was over, I had sprouted muscles all over my body, and not only from this work.

We got to eat all the fresh fruit and vegetables we wanted, and I did, so when I got home to the hotel at about 3:00 p.m., I still had plenty of energy, so I did exercises in the hotel room, 100 push-ups, jumping jacks, sit-ups, etc. The warehouse work, added exercise, and almost daily swimming at Lake Calhoun and Lake Nakomis made for a good mix of work and play during my summer stay in Minneapolis.

After swimming in the lakes and the long streetcar rides back downtown, I became too tired to do anything else, so I began playing pool at the Minneapolis Recreation Center which was a large two story pool hall on Hennepin Avenue. Four men played at each pool table, and after the owner watched me play a few times, he hired me as a "houseman" to fill in at a table that had only three players. The two losers always paid for the game, and because the owner was "paying me" fifty cents an hour to play pool for the house, I was expected to win with whomever happened to be my partner. At last my Crookston "Playhouse" training was paying off!

Other entertainment during the summer involved Crookston friends visiting with us and having fun together. Les Martin stopped on his way back from Coast Guard training in New York, and we sipped a few beers together, I met Rosita and Betty Ellingson one evening and took them canoeing out at Lake Calhoun, and my high school sweetheart, Pauline Bombardier, was visiting friends in Minneapolis, and we went swimming at Lake Calhoun with my brother and his girlfriend, Pearl Carlson (whom he later married), and dancing at the "Prom Ballroom" in Saint Paul. All in all, that just about sums up my summer of 1945, perhaps one of the most rewarding summers of my life because it made me healthy, happy, busy, tired, in the bucks, and aware of a new way of life!

When the end of summer arrived, I was sort of sad to leave Minneapolis. I had met and made new Minneapolis high school friends at work and had developed a lot of confidence in myself. I had attended St. Olaf Catholic Church (which was a block from our hotel) and learned a lot from the Sunday sermons and the booklets they made available. I became very comfortable living in Minneapolis and liked the ease with which I could get around the city on the streetcars, and I loved living with my brother and the freedom it allowed me, to be me!

But, good things seldom last forever, and the end of my summer came when a group of classmates traveled to Minneapolis in late August and met me at work on my last day at Gamble-Robinson. I picked up my last check, whacked off a big bunch of ripe bananas to share with the guys, and walked out the door! The next day, all of us and Father William "Bill" Keefe who had accompanied the boys to Minneapolis, took the Great Northern train home to Crookston to begin our senior year at Cathedral High School.

THE UNDEFEATED SEASON

Our undefeated football season of 1945 really began in the fall of 1942 when my brother, Bill, who was a senior, encouraged me to go out for the Cathedral High School team. I was going to be a freshman and wanted to belong, so I did.

It started out being a lot of fun, putting on a uniform, running and doing exercises together, and learning plays, but the fun soon turned to pain and aches when we began driving our shoulders into the blocking dummies and one another. When that happened, I didn't know if I was going to like football very much, especially when we began having "live" blocking and tackling and had to run head on against big juniors and seniors and get trampled.

I didn't give up because my brother was on the team and also because it was sort of fun when we got to travel to other towns to play their teams, even though most of the freshmen were bench warmers. I especially remember one game out of town which was played at Grafton, North Dakota.

It was the last game of the season, about the first or second week in November. It was snowing, the wind was blowing, and it was extremely cold. "Spanky" Sullivan and I were sitting on the bench. Our feet were freezing, and we weren't about to get put into the game, so we decided to go sit in a nearby car and watch from it so we could stay warm. It was pretty nice until our coach Don Norman saw us.

He came over to the car, ripped open the door and yelled, "What the hell do you two think you're doing!" Sheepishly, we got out of the car, walked back to the bench, and watched our freezing team lose miserably to Grafton in the snow.

The only other embarrassing thing about Cathedral High School football for me was getting used to a small gang shower crammed with about twenty bodies at a time, all vying to squeeze under a limited number of shower heads. But, I survived, and I think I became a better person because of it. It built character. I became more determined to succeed, more able to put up with a little pain, and was happy to be with a group of boys who were all working toward the same goal.

When tenth grade began, I was looking forward to football. I had just finished working as a section hand on the Great Northern Railroad all summer and had put on a little weight and grown a little stronger, so I thought football was going to treat me more kindly. It did.

When we started the new season, everything was routine, and I even learned to like head-on blocking and tackling. This is why. One day during the first week of practice, our coach who was still Don Norman said, "O.K., let's line up for some head-on blocking."

I thought, "Oh no, this again!" But as players ran from each line and knocked one another down, I decided to do something I had never done before, leave my feet when I threw a block. The guy I was going to have to block was Les Martin. He was a real nice guy, but he was a senior and a fullback. When our turn came, I ran as fast as I could towards him, and right before I reached him, I threw my body across his mid-section and sliced him in half. He flew in the air over me and landed hard on the ground.

Everyone sort of oohed and aahed, and Les himself said, "Nice block, Charlie!"

I thought, "Hey, that didn't hurt at all. As a matter of fact, it felt sort of good!"

Coach Norman was watching us closely and giving the team hints on how to throw better blocks, but when he saw me block Les Martin, he yelled, "Wow! Did you guys see that? Now that's the way a block should be thrown!" When Don Norman said that about me, I think I was the happiest guy on the team. Everyone loved the man because he was such a great coach and human being. He really had a sense of humor, too. Don yelled, "Charlie, you and Les line up against one another again. I want you to show the team how to throw a block."

Les and I ran back and once again I tore into him, and he really flew up in the air this time. When he landed on the ground with a thud, I heard him mutter, "Geez, Charlie, take it easy, will ya!" I couldn't believe what I was hearing. A senior was asking me to take it easy on him. The rest of the year went pretty well for me. I got to play left guard on a pretty regular basis, well enough to earn a letter that year, and I was learning to like football.

During my junior year football was still an important part of my school life. I weighed about 150 pounds and was about 5' 10" tall. I still played left guard, but now I was first string. Again I worked all summer as a section hand on the railroad and became stronger. Don Norman was still our coach, and we were all familiar with the plays and with playing together, so we had a winning season. We lost a couple of games, but we won nine. The next season, my last, would turn out to be the best of all because Cathedral High School ended it undefeated.

Instead of working for the railroad as a section hand during the summer of 1945, I decided to go to Minneapolis and look for work. My brother Bill said I could stay with him at a downtown hotel (the Nordic) where he had a room. He paid seven dollars a week for it, and I got a job and split the rent with him. The job I got was as a warehouseman at Gamble and Robinson, a fruit and vegetable warehouse.

Suffice it to say that the summer of 1945 was successful for me. I made good money, ate tons of free fruits and vegetables, and worked like a horse but loved every minute of it. When I left Minneapolis for home that summer, I was in the best physical condition in which I had ever been. When football practice began, I was more than ready.

When we did pushups, they were easy because when I'd come home from work each day in Minneapolis, I had so much energy that I'd exercise in the hotel room, and part of that exercise routine included doing 100 pushups nonstop. Besides gaining ten pounds and becoming stronger than ever before during that summer, I developed a lot of speed.

Everything was looking bright and rosy except for the fact that our old coach, Don Norman, was no longer with the team. He had joined the Navy, and we were coached by Rev. William Keefe and Pete Sullivan. We ran the same plays and kept the same offense and defense we had the three previous years, so everything was familiar.

The only problem was that the coaches didn't know what position I should play. Soon it was decided. Our center from last year, Bill Sumpman, had graduated and gone into the service, and we needed a center, and I became it. It turned out to be a great position because I had my hands on the ball during every play when we were on the offense, and on the defense I got to back up the line and make tackles and interceptions. It was 100 per cent action, just what I wanted!

Our first game was a night game with East Grand Forks. We'd never played a night game before, and keeping track of the players and the ball just weren't the same for me. Near the end of the game we were trailing 6-0. We were going to lose our first game if something didn't happen in a hurry, and it did. "Vernie" Ogaard, one of our ends, ran a criss cross pattern and Johnny Noah, our quarterback, bulleted a pass right into his arms. "Vernie" was fast, a real sprinter, and he dashed like a deer into the end zone. Only a few minutes remained when Johnny Noah booted the extra point to make the score 7-6 in favor of Cathedral High School, and our team caught fire! East Grand Forks tried to score during the remaining minutes of the game, but we held them and chalked up our first victory of the season.

We played our second game at home in Central Park against Grafton, North Dakota, the same team "Spanky" Sullivan and I had watched beat us in the cold and snow (as we sat keeping warm in a car) three years before. We hadn't played them since. Now, "Spanky" and I were seniors and ready for battle.

It was a beautiful, sunny, fall afternoon, and a large number of Crookston's football fans had turned out to see us play. My mom and dad even came to see us play, a first for both of them.

The Grafton team looked just as spirited as they were three years ago when they had beat us in the snow. I guess they remembered having pummeled us before, and they were out for a repeat performance.

We kicked off, and Johnny Noah booted the ball almost to the end zone. What a leg! What an athlete! A Grafton back caught the ball, tucked it in, and began streaking down the right side of the field. I was the first player to reach him, and right as I was about to tackle him, a Grafton player threw a fierce block into me that made me do a complete somersault and come down with a jolt on my butt. The crowd roared, and I remember just sitting there a few seconds to regain my senses before getting to my feet. "Wow! These guys are really out for blood!" was my thought as I ran over to the line of scrimmage for the next play.

The game turned out to be an afternoon of struggle, of real hard, clean football, just the way the game is supposed to be played. We won the game 12-0, and it gave our team a lot of confidence to have the first two wins under our belt.

Our third game was away, and it looked like it was going to be a catastrophe because a couple of our senior starters got hurt and had to be taken out of the game. We were playing Mayville, North Dakota, and their players were so big that at half time rumors began circulating that they were using college players from Mayville State College to play against us. I never found out if it was true, but those guys sure looked bigger and older than high schoolers.

Well, the game went back and forth with each team battling for their scores, and with some of our players being taken out, hurt and injured. Somehow, we managed to survive and were ahead of Mayville 25-21 with only a few minutes remaining near the end of the game. Mayville had the ball, and they tried a long, desperation pass. I tried running back, but their end whizzed right past me. The quarterback let the football fly, and as I was running back, I could see that it wasn't going to be far enough to reach their end, so I ran forward, took a flying leap into the air and caught it in mid-air with my hands.

From the sidelines I could hear our team and Father Keefe shouting, "Run, Charlie, run!" Believe me, I did. I was about seventy yards from our goal line when I caught the ball, and I took off for it straight down the center of the field. All I could hear was the roar. I didn't even think of making a score. When I was about thirty yards from the goal, a Mayville player smeared me.

After that interception, it was all history for game three. Johnny Noah threw the ball into the end zone for six points, and we were leading 31-21 with only a couple of seconds remaining. We converted the extra point, and the hard fought game ended 32-21.

I had never experienced anything quite like this game. We were taunted and heckled by the Mayville linemen during the game because we were Catholics. This had never happened before, and I think it was one of the reasons our team got fired up enough to beat Mayville. This was definitely a turning point game for us.

Entering our fourth game against the local Crookston Agricultural School, we were a seasoned machine, a speedy, spirited team of guys who had played together for four years. We were a team that been coached for our first three years by Don Norman, and now in our final year, his hard work and love for us was finally paying off. My only regret was that he wasn't around to reap the fruits of his labors, to see that what he had done had paid off in a string of well-earned victories against worthy opponents.

The Crookston Agricultural School "Aggies" put up a fair fight, but they were no match for the Cathedral Blue Wave at this point in our high school football careers. We beat them 31-7 without too much effort. The points seemed to come so easy! We'd run a couple of plays for twenty or thirty yards and then reel off a long pass. There was just no way we were going to be beaten at that point in the season. Our first three games were the toughest, and the rest were easy.

Our fifth game against Warren ended 40-0. We beat Red Lake Falls 33-0, and our last game against St. James of Grand Forks, North Dakota was won by a score of 40-0, and that ended the season, undefeated!

Buddy Salem, Bill Carter, Spanky Sullivan, Charlie Dowdle, Duane Capistran, Mike Conneran, and Vernie Ogaard were linemen, and Buddy Schraeder, Louie Lones, Morrie Theroux, and Johnny Noah were backs. We all shared in the glory of the undefeated team of 1945.

YOU'RE IN THE NAVY NOW

Schreiter's Drug Store on Broadway was a popular "hangout" for many Cathedral High School teenage boys and girls because it had a great soda fountain. Cherry and lemon cokes for a nickel and "Little Dicks" (sundaes) for a nickel and "Big Dicks" (sundaes) for a dime were the teenage favorites. If you really wanted to pig out, you ordered a chocolate, marshmallow, and caramel sundae with lots of nuts for fifteen cents, or even a chocolate or strawberry sundae. They were all good and helped to make Schreiter's Drug Store just a real comfortable place to meet other kids and exchange small talk.

That's about what Ray O'Claire and I were doing after school one cold winter afternoon in early January when he sat down next to me and said, "Hey, Charlie, guess what I'm going to do. I'm going to join the Navy!"

I couldn't quite believe what I'd heard and replied, "You're kidding!"

"No," Ray said. "I'm serious. I found out I could do just what I've been doing in the drugstore if I become a medic. I forgot to mention that Ray had a part time job working at Schreiter's Drug Store, and what he had said about doing the same kind of work really got my attention because I always used to hang around Wallace's Drug Store when I was little just because I liked the smell of the pharmaceuticals and watching the pharmacists fill prescriptions. The next thing Ray said just about put me in shock when he surprised me by saying, "Why don't you join with me!"

How could he even think of such a thing? World War II had just ended the previous summer of 1945 with the bombing of Hiroshima and Nagasaki on August 6th and 9th; I was doing better in school than ever before, and I just loved physics and my teacher Sister Cyprian; and ice hockey had just begun, and Morrie Theroux and I were playing first string defense. And Ray wanted me to leave all of that!

As I was leaving him, I said, "Listen, Ray, this is something I'm going to have to talk over with my folks."

"Don't wait too long," he said. "I'm gonna quit school and join up next week."

That night at the supper table I brought up the idea to get my parents' reaction. I was seventeen, and my parents would have to sign the necessary papers before I could enter the service. My dad, who always talked about the Army in World War I, surprised me when he said, "I think it sounds like a good idea, Charlie." Did he want to get rid of me? Why was he so eager with his assent?

My mother was more questioning and hesitant. "What will you gain from quitting school?" she asked.

"Gee, Mom," I said, "if I sign up now, I'll only have to be in for two years, and I'll have a choice of the services, but if I wait until this summer, I'll be drafted into the Army." What my mom didn't know was that when I left Ray O'Claire, I had already begun convincing myself that joining the Navy now was the thing to do. It sounded exciting, and I'd be away from my mom's nagging, and I'd be able to experience "sweet freedom."

My dad said smilingly, "If you get into the Army, Charlie, you'll have a lot of walking to do, and you'll get to sleep in the mud one in awhile, too." Dad knew as he was in the infantry. The more he talked, the more convincing he became, and the Navy began to appeal more to my mom, too.

I struck while the iron was hot and said, "My friend Ray O'Claire, who works at Schreiter's Drug Store, said he's going to sign up for the Navy next week, and he's going to be doing the same kind of work that he's been doing in the drugstore, and besides that, we can get four years of college all paid for by the government if we sign up now."

My parents' eyes gleamed when they heard this because doctors were highly regarded in Crookston which at the time was a very medically-oriented community, and I guess they thought I'd become a doctor. So, without too much hesitation, they said it sounded o.k., but they wanted to think about it. The next day when I told them I'd graduate from high school while in the service, they agreed to sign the necessary papers.

I stopped at Schreiter's Drug Store that night and broke the happy news to Ray by blurting, "My folks aid it was o.k. I'm with you, buddy!"

Then the real fun began. Ray shouted, "Great, Charlie!" and he slapped me on the back. Two other friends of ours, Joe McNamee and Bobby Simmons, moved over by us and asked what was so great. We told them we were quitting school and joining the Navy, now! It became contagious. They were tired of school, too, so when they heard our plans, they said they'd join with us, just like that!

That same week a chief in the Navy came to each of our homes and had our parents sign the necessary papers for us to join up. The next week the four of us had to go to Grand Forks, North Dakota to take preliminary tests. We all passed, and Ray and I both told them we wanted to be medics.

The week after that all four of us found ourselves boarding the train for our more extensive physicals and swearing in at Fort Snelling in St. Paul, Minnesota. Ray just about didn't make it because his blood pressure was so high, but they sent him out and said they'd take it again in a little while. We tried to calm Ray down, and when he went to have it taken the second time, he made it. How ironic that would have been, I thought, if the guy who had talked me into joining the Navy hadn't been allowed to join up himself.

A couple of doctors interviewed Ray and me, and we signed the papers to become medics. We were sworn in the same day. When we signed the dated papers, I couldn't believe it! It was February 1, 1946, my eighteenth birthday! "Hey, you guys, " I yelled, "today's my birthday!" They just laughed and couldn't believe it.

Well, the Navy loaded us all on a train and sent us to Green Bay, Wisconsin and "boot camp" at Great Lakes Naval Training Station. From there we all got separated.

Ray O'Claire ended up being a medic at Guantanamo Bay, Cuba. I got trained to mix drugs and fill prescriptions at the U.S. Naval Academy at Annapolis, Maryland, and ended up working with doctors at Annapolis for two years as a Pharmacist Mate Third Class. It was fascinating work, mixing drugs and filling prescriptions, which I was surprised they let an eighteen-year-old kid do.

I never learned where Bobby and Joe went, but I got to go into Washington, D.C., New York, Philadelphia, or Baltimore whenever I wanted, and this was quite a trip for a small town boy like myself, and I even got my four years of free college as promised by Uncle Sam.

When I went home for my first-ever high school reunion in Crookston in the summer of 2002, I learned that all three of my former high school buddies had passed away.

COINCIDENCE

It was not a coincidence that Dennis "Spanky" Sullivan and I attended elementary school at the Saint Joseph's Home and high school at Cathedral together. Nor was it a coincidence that we both played football for Cathedral. We were both Catholic, and it was expected that we'd attend the local parochial schools, and Cathedral High School was so small that just about everyone was expected to go out for the football team, or the school just might not have one! Spanky played right guard and I played left guard until our senior year when I was shifted to center. During that year I think that both of us were at the pique of our virility! Each day at noon before being dismissed to go home for "dinner" (lunch), we'd stand and Sister Cyprian would lead us in a prayer. Spanky and I would be standing next to one another, our hands solemnly folded, our knees slightly bent, and our butts sticking out behind so our classmates wouldn't notice the protrusions in the front of our pants as Sister Cyprian began the prayer, "Angel of God, my Guardian dear, to whom His love commits me here." Spanky would then look at me and I at him, both of us blushing as our male hormones continued to rage and Sister Cyprian continued the prayer, "Ever this day be at my side, to light, to guard, to rule, to guide." At this point, Spanky and I were just bursting to get outside and begin walking home as the prayer ended. "From sinful stain oh keep me free, and in death's sorrow my helper be."

But it's not what happened at Cathedral High School with

Spanky and me that was coincidental. Rather, it's what happened after graduation in 1946.

I had quit high school after the first semester of my senior year and joined the Navy with three of my classmates, Ray O'Claire, Bobby Simmons, and Joe McNamee. We all went to "boot camp" at Great Lakes Naval Training Center and were all separated after "boots." Spanky waited until after graduation, and then he, too, joined the Navy.

In the meantime, I had trained as a Pharmacist Mate and was stationed at Annapolis, Maryland when I had a chance meeting with Spanky aboard an aircraft carrier one day in 1947. I was busy in my lab/pharmacy early one morning when my boss, Commander Mel Snowden said, "Dowdle, they're practicing firing the catapult on the Block Island (a "baby" aircraft carrier), and they need a medic down there in case anyone gets hurt! I want you to go down there this morning." Of course, I left immediately, boarded the ship, and went below deck to observe the action! Boy, did I get an eyeful!

Sailors dressed in blue, greasy dungarees and shirts moved about like ants at work as they prepared to fire the catapult! This was serious business! It wasn't like days of old when a catapult was an ancient military engine used to hurl spears, stones, arrows, and large weights against an enemy's defenses. This device was a complicated piece of machinery used to launch an airplane from the deck of an aircraft carrier! As pressure was generated and the steam-driven piston that would propel an airplane down the deck until it reached flying speed was about to be unleashed, I noticed among the scrambling sailors, an old friend of mine, Dennis "Spanky" Sullivan!

I couldn't believe my eyes! I just sat and watched Spanky in action until the training exercise was completed that morning, and then I casually walked up to him and said, "Hi, Spank!"

"Charlie Dowdle! What in the hell are you doing here?" he asked.

"Making sure someone is here to take care of you in case you get hurt!" I replied. We didn't have much time to talk, but we agreed to go to Washington, D.C. on a weekend together as soon as he got liberty. It wasn't long before that time came, and we were off. When we got to Washington, we took a streetcar out to Georgetown University to visit one of our classmates, John DeWaard, but he was gone, so we went back downtown, stopped at a bar, and drank a couple of beers.

"How sweet it is!" I thought as we left the bar in the evening and prepared to go dancing. Here I was in Washington, D.C. with my Cathedral High School friend, Spanky Sullivan. He told me that the Ellingson sisters, Rosita and Betty, were going to be singing in a contest that evening at the Y.W.C.A. where they also had dancing, so that's where we went. The Ellingsons had also gone to Cathedral High School, but they were a little older than us. I couldn't believe my luck!

After dancing most of the night away on three different floors, the top one being the roof under the stars, we stopped for the entertainment. Before long, out came Rosita and Betty who sang their hearts out, and the audience applauded and cheered wildly for them! After talking to them for awhile, we left, stopped to have a couple more beers, and headed back to the base.

When we got back to Annapolis, we entered the Naval Academy gate and walked along the seawall to an open boat which would ferry us across the Severn River to my barracks and Spanky's ship. The boat came, and I ran and jumped into it! Spanky was behind me and had to run and dive to make it! He did! Don't ask!

MINAKWA GOLF AND COUNTRY CLUB

During the summer of 1949, my fiancée, Marilyn Kirkwood, and I came home to Crookston and lived with our parents. Marilyn's father, W.J. Kirkwood, died suddenly of a coronary attack in April, 1949 at the age of 58 while motoring to Minneapolis with his wife, Beth, and Marilyn quit her medical stenography job in Minneapolis to come home and help her mother settle the estate. "It," Marilyn said, "created a great deal of business closure problems for my mother." I followed Marilyn home from College of St. Thomas in St. Paul at the end of the school year.

While looking for work, Don McKenzie, one of Crookston's premier golfers at the time, asked Bill Sullivan and me if we'd like to manage the Minakwa Golf and Country Club during the summer. We both jumped at the chance, and the job proved to be well worth our while.

Because I didn't have a car, I walked out to the course each day with my younger brother, Jerry, who became a caddy. Bill and I would play nine holes each morning and take a caddy with us so we could teach them the "finer points" of their job. No, they didn't get paid while learning!

I was eager to earn all the money I could because I wanted to buy an engagement ring for Marilyn by the end of the summer, so while I wasn't being a bartender or collecting green fees, I'd do odd jobs for members like waterproofing their shoes and rewrapping the heads of their woods (drivers, brassies, and spoons) with fishing line and shellac. Of course, I'd charge for this service!

Another way I had of earning money was serving drinks to members on the nights when they had dinners at the screened in dining room of the clubhouse. Don McKenzie would mix them and I'd run up the stairs to the dining room and serve them. The tips were great!

I don't want this golf course job to sound like it was all work, so I'll tell you that when the dining room wasn't being used on Saturday nights, Bill and Dee and Marilyn and I would have our friends out there to play games, sip a few drinks, talk, and dance the balmy nights away under the stars. It was pleasant, relaxing, and mosquito free because of the screened in dining room, and a good time was always had by all!

Near the end of the summer, I had amassed quite a bankroll, so Marilyn and I visited with Walt Johnson and picked out an engagement ring for her. Walt said there were larger diamonds that were flawed and didn't cost as much, but I told him I wanted one as perfect as they came, to match my wife, and that's what we bought!

At the end of August before the caddies went back to school, Bill Sullivan and I held an elimination caddy tournament as our way of thanking the caddies for all the good work they had done during the hot and humid summer days. My brother Jerry had developed into a pretty good little golfer, and at the end of the tournament, Bruce Teal and he were the only two boys not eliminated. So, a nine hole playoff was held!

All of the other caddies formed the "gallery" which was rooting for Bruce! I, of course, wanted my little brother to win, but had to remain silent and impartial throughout the entire playoff. Those little guys, ten year olds, would drive the ball straight down the fairway 150-200 yards every time they hit it. At the end of nine, the tension grew because the score was tied, and the champs had to play an extra hole to see who would win the trophy! Then both boys parred the number one hole and had to continue to the number two hole to determine a winner!

Their drives were right down the middle and two hundred yards out. My brother's second shot rolled across the green and over a hump which he would have to negotiate on his way back to the cup. Bruce's second shot landed twenty yards short of the green, and the young gallery began tasting victory for him and yelling, "C'mon, Bruce! You can do it! Just chip it up by the pin for an easy sink and a par!"

Bruce was away, so he shot first, and his ball landed four feet from the cup! The gallery broke the silence with wild screams and congratulations! "That a way, Bruce," one boy yelled. "Now you got him!" Jerry didn't know what club would be best to use to get over the hump, but after pondering his lie, decided on an eight iron. It proved to be a wise choice! His chip shot cleared the hump, rolled down a sloping green, and stopped six feet from the cup!

Now both boys had a good chance to par the hole. Silence filled the air as Jerry approached his ball and placed his putter gently behind it. Slowly, he drew back his putter and kissed the ball with it, a soft, whispered kiss, and his ball sank for a par four! Now it was up to Bruce. Four feet from the cup was an easy putt for him, putts which he sank regularly. However, this wasn't to be his day. His ball headed straight for the cup and then rimmed it for a five! The gallery let out a groan, and my brother Jerry won the trophy! For coming in second, Bruce won a new putter.

THE HEALERS

Boasting three hospitals (Bethesda, Saint Vincent, Saint Francis), two clinics (Crookston, Northwest), a tuberculosis sanatorium, and an abundance of highly skilled doctors, dentists, and nurses during the 1930's, 40's, and 50's, Crookston was noted for being a premier Red River Valley medical community. The first "line of defense" against disease and infection fell to Mrs. Lowe, Polk County Health Nurse, who visited our classroom on a regular basis to examine us. She was a matronly woman, tall and sturdy, who always wore her gray hair in a bun and came dressed in low-heeled, black, comfortable shoes and a blue dress with a red cross on her breast. As she set up her equipment on the teacher's desk in the front of the room and sat down in a straight back chair, facing us, she would announce, "All right, children, we're ready to begin, so please take off your shoes and line up on this side of the room." This was very embarrassing for me sometimes because I had holes in my socks and my big toes would stick out! Next, Mrs. Lowe would have us approach her one at a time to be weighed, measured, and inspected for sore throats, ear infections, and other common diseases like mumps, measles, and chicken pox. If we had one of the latter mentioned or any other serious communicable disease, we would be sent home immediately and be quarantined to prevent the spread of the disease. The same held true for children and adults who had contacted tuberculosis, only they had to be confined to the sanatorium under the care of Dr. Paradis until a cure had been effected and they had regained their health. It was no fun being isolated, but that's the way it was for children and adults alike in those days.

Dr. Nelson was our family physician, and when he retired, Dr. Reff, but the only thing I can remember my brother Bill or I going to them for was to be vaccinated and to get our shots! What we needed as a result of our activities was surgeons!

Bill was first when he fell from the top of a boxcar (while playing tag) onto a pile of glass below and chipped a piece of flesh the size of an egg from his thigh! Hello, Dr. M.O. Oppegard! Bill was second, too. He was catching an American Legion baseball game in Central Park when a fastball thrown by his pitcher buddy, Jim Laurent, came in low, hit him in the testicles, and ruptured him! I remember my brother hitting the dirt and just writhing with pain! He lived with this injury for some time, and often he'd be lying on the couch and I'd hear him moaning. He said it felt just like someone kicking you down there or like it feels when you're riding your bike and you slip and fall on the horizontal bar. I felt so bad for my brother, but there was nothing I could do to comfort him! Finally, the intermittent pain grew so intense after a year that Dad took Bill to see Dr. M.O. Oppegard a second time.

Dr. Oppegard said Bill needed surgery because one of his testicles had grown up near his stomach and would have to be removed! It was, successfully, and when Bill was released from St. Vincent's Hospital, we wheeled him home to Sampson's Addition in a wagon because we didn't have a car. Years later when he was working for Minneapolis Honeywell Regulator Company in Minneapolis, Bill was discussing his condition with a supposedly knowledgeable fellow worker who told him he'd never be able to have children. I discussed this with my brother and told him that this guy didn't know what he was talking about and that if he really wanted the truth, he should go and see a doctor. He did, and later when he got married to a lovely woman, they had four daughters and a son!

Unlike my brother Bill, I never needed the services of Dr. M.O. Oppegard for surgery, but when I was twenty-four and on my first teaching assignment at Karlsruhe, North Dakota, I came home during Christmas vacation and Dr. C.L. Oppegard performed a tonsillectomy on me at St. Francis Hospital. I was admitted the evening of the day after I got home, and my tonsils were removed at six o'clock the next morning. I walked down to the operating room and Dr. Oppegard and a sister/nurse were already waiting for me. "Good morning, Mr. Dowdle!" Dr. Oppegard said cheerfully. "How are you feeling this morning?"

"Okay," I said.

"Well, you're going to feel a lot better after we get those diseased tonsils out," he countered. Then the nurse had me sit in a chair that looked just like a dentist's chair, and Dr. Oppegard approached me with a syringe and said, "Okay, Mr. Dowdle, if you'll just open your mouth wide for me, we'll deaden the area around your tonsils a little and be ready to go." So far, so good, I thought, until I saw Dr. Oppegard pick up a forceps and a pair of scissors.

"All right, Mr. Dowdle," he said seriously and without hesitation, "if you'll open wide again, we'll go in for the first one." I did, and then I heard a snip, snip, snip, and Dr. Oppegard held my pus-pocketed tonsil in front of me to see and said, "These babies really had to come out! Are you okay?"

All I could answer with was "ah, ah, ah," because my throat was numbed. Then I opened again, and quick as a flash my second tonsil was removed. The last thing I remember was hearing the nurse saying, "Doctor, I think he's going," and I fainted! At noon I was released and drove to the Times Apartments where my wife Marilyn and I were staying with her mother Beth Kirkwood during Christmas vacation. It was a great place to recover because I got lots of TLC from two women who served me delicious milkshakes for a solid week. At first the milkshakes slid down painlessly, but when the scabs formed and began sloughing off, each swallow felt like it was mixed with sharp tacks!

The last time I saw a Crookston doctor was in 1954. I had ruptured a disc in the lumbar area of my back during the summer of 1949 while unloading hundred pound sacks of sugar at a Minneapolis warehouse. It was hot and humid, and when I failed to bend my knees for just one sack, I could feel the disc pop and the pain begin! I lived with that pain and caused it to become more intense when I took a summer job on a railroad extra gang in Perham, Minnesota.

That's when Mrs. Kirkwood, who was working at the Crookston Clinic at the time, called and said that an osteopathic physician and surgeon, Dr. John McDonald, was doing wonderful things for people who had back problems. It didn't take long before I made an appointment with Dr. McDonald and came home to be treated by him.

I was waiting in an examination room when the doctor entered, talked to me briefly about my injury, and had me lie on my back on the examining table. "What I want you to do," he said, "is to bend your left leg at the knee, rest the bottom of your foot on the table, and just let your right leg lie flat." I had been in pain for so long, pain that was just excruciating like a constant toothache in your back, that I followed his instructions precisely.

"Now, what you're going to have to try to do, Mr. Dowdle, is relax a little or this isn't going to work. Boy! Did I ever try to relax! I closed my eyes and began imagining beautiful outdoor scenery as Dr. McDonald placed one hand on the outside of my bent knee and the other on the inside of my thigh and pushed them forcefully in opposite directions. All I felt was a whack and Dr. McDonald saying, "Okay, stand up now and let's see what happens. When I stood, it felt like pins and needles were traveling all over my left leg and foot, and the pain was miraculously gone! I couldn't believe it! I thanked the man and could have kissed his feet I was so deliriously happy!

That's the last time I was ever treated for any ailment in Crookston, but I certainly have fond memories of all of the health providers who cared for us and helped to make us whole.

THE CATCH

In July of 1988 when my brother Bill and his wife Pearl flew out from Minneapolis to visit with my wife Marty and me in Santa Rosa, California, we had one goal in mind. Show them a good time!

"How'd you two like to go ocean fishing," I asked.

Bill's eyes smiled as he looked at me. "Are you kidding!" he said. "I'd love it!"

"Oh, ya," Pearl chimed in in her soft Swedish accent. "That'd be fun, Charlie."

Of course, I knew they'd both like to go fishing. Bill and I always fished Crookston's Red Lake River for walleyes and northern pike from the Sampson's Addition bridge when we were kids, and Pearl liked fishing just as much as he. They both fished Minnesota's lakes often during their vacations.

"Okay," I said, "get a good night's sleep tonight because we leave here at six o' clock tomorrow morning for Bodega Bay."

What Bill and Pearl didn't know was that I had made reservations on a party boat, the Sea Angler, a long time ago, when we first learned they were coming to visit. Marty decided to stay home because she gets queasy on the water.

Bodega Bay was socked in with fog when we arrived at the Sea Angler. Men were milling around the boat, preparing to board, and the captain and crew were making her ready. There were fifty fishermen, and Pearl was the only woman among us. It didn't seem to bother her, but I could sense that some of the men didn't appreciate having their territory invaded by a woman.

As the boat headed out to sea, rods and reels were handed out to those who didn't bring their own, and, as was the custom, two dollars was collected from each person. Whoever caught the heaviest fish would also win a hundred dollar jackpot! Bill, being an avid and skilled fisherman and a real competitor, thought this was going to be great fun!

And it was! "Okay," the Sea Angler's captain announced, "we're going to drop anchor here and see what happens." Bingo! It happened! My brother's rod doubled over and his line whistled out as he reached for the star drag to increase the tension.

The other fishermen moved aside to give him plenty of room and to allow the crewmen to net the fish when he got it near the boat. It was a beauty, the first catch of the day, a thirteen pound king salmon! Boy! Did Bill beam! He couldn't believe his luck. Nor could I. Nor could Pearl.

We fished all morning, moving from one spot to another, dropping our lines and then reeling them in whenever we moved. Several other men caught salmon during the morning, some of them bigger than Bill's.

Before long it was noon and time for lunch. "Okay," the captain announced, "let's eat, fish for a couple more hours and then head in. Let's see what you can do. Good luck!"

So far, Pearl and I had been skunked, and it looked like that might be the way our day would end because neither of us had gotten so much as a nibble all morning. It was disheartening! I wanted to catch a fish, and I wanted her to catch one, too.

Shortly after lunch when we started fishing again, the salmon began hitting like crazy, and men began bringing them in to the left and right of us. They were coming in so fast that the netting crew couldn't keep up with them. I was hoping that I was going to be next, but nothing happened.

Suddenly, Pearl's rod doubled over, and she gasped, "Oh, Charlie, I think I got one!" Quietly, the men around her just stared and backed away, wanting to see, I suppose, what she was going to do with it. Pearl was calm, but I got excited and tried to help her by turning the star drag on her reel. I turned it the wrong way, and one of the boat's crewmen who had moved near us with a net, looked at me angrily and barked, "What the hell are you doing! You just about caused her to lose that fish!" I backed away in a hurry, embarrassed, and it was all Pearl from then on. She played that salmon like a pro, steadily and patiently, and when it was netted and brought on deck, it looked huge! Bill couldn't believe his eyes.

Soon it was time to quit, the boat headed back to Bodega Bay, and the fish began being weighed and distributed. Even now, sixteen years after "the catch," when I recall and write about this scene, I begin laughing to myself, and tears of happiness come to my eyes. Pearl's king salmon weighed thirty-nine pounds and was the biggest catch of the day, so she also won the hundred dollar pot!

I overheard a couple of men, old fishing curmudgeons, grumbling about Pearl's catch as we left the boat. "Wish she'd stayed in Minnesota to catch her fish," one grumped. I couldn't believe my ears!

On our way home, Bill had me stop in Bodega Bay to have both fish filleted and wrapped in packages. We had fifteen packages of fish in all. There were so many of them that we couldn't stop laughing about it all the way home. Tears of joy flooded our eyes we were so happy. Bill and I were slap happy! Pearl was quiet, smiling, and amused by us. "What's the matter with you guys? You're silly," she said. She said she felt bad about me not catching anything, but I could have cared less, I was so happy for her.

When we got near Sebastopol, I had a brainstorm. "Let's fool Marty," I blurted. "Let's tell her we didn't catch anything and stopped in Bodega Bay to buy some salmon for our dinner."

Pearl said, "Oh, I don't know if that's such a good idea, Charlie." But Bill and I talked her into it, and she went along with the plan.

When we pulled into the garage, Bill took a package of salmon from the trunk, and when he met Marty in the kitchen, he said, "We didn't catch anything, so we stopped and bought some salmon for dinner."

"Oh, that'll be fine," Marty said. "Did you have a good time?"

With a mischievous glance at her, he answered, "We sure did!" Then I opened the door and marched in with a package of salmon in each hand, followed by Pearl, and we kept the packages coming until all fifteen of them were on the kitchen counter. Marty looked a little bewildered until we all stopped laughing long enough to tell her what really happened.

BILL DOWDLE

❖·❖·❖

My name is Chuck Dowdle. I'd like to say a few words about the brother I admired and loved and who will always be with me. I can just hear Bill saying, "Charlie, Charlie. Let's not go overboard now."

First, let me give you a little family background. We're from Crookston. Bill was the eldest of five children. I was second, my sister Betty was third, my sister Cathy who died at an early age of Parkinson's disease was fourth, and my brother Jerry was fifth. Our dad died of a heart attack at age 73 and our mom lived into her 90's.

Bill was a lot like Dad. He loved life; he enjoyed a good time; and he loved people. When he was in the hospital he said, "I sure wish I could go quickly like Dad did."

I got to know my brother real well when we were growing up. We shared the same bedroom for about fifteen years. We shared brotherly secrets and experiences. We shared a paper route and delivered during sun, rain, and freezing blizzards in the early hours of the morning. When Bill was a senior at Cathedral High School and I was a freshman going to my first school dance, I didn't know how to dance, so Bill taught me the fox trot, reluctantly. It seemed that Bill was always looking out for me in a sensitive and nurturing way.

He taught me how to fish the river. He introduced me to sports, which he loved, especially ice hockey and baseball. He captained his high school hockey team and caught for the home town American Legion team. We used to go outside in the winter with Mom's pillows stuffed in our pants and take turns shooting pucks at one another. Bill even played football when he was a senior. He played end. Can you imagine a 5' 7" 120 pound end!

For a short time after graduation, Bill worked for the Great Northern Railroad, firing a passenger train which ran between Grand Forks and Seattle. He hated it, and that's when he decided to go to Minneapolis and look for a job. I remember seeing him off at the Greyhound Bus stop. I had saved up some silver dollars to give him as a going away present because when he left, it was like part of me went, too. Bill got a job with Honeywell Regulator Company and he worked with them for forty-two years. He took early retirement when he turned sixty-two, and he died two years later at sixty-four.

I'd like to tell you people how Bill died, because I think he lived like he died, filled with courage, faith, and love.

Pearl, his wife, said, ""On Monday of last week the doctor was going to come into Bill's room and tell the family the results of some tests, and Bill wanted the whole family to be there. I think Bill knew what the results were going to be because after all of us were in the hospital room he said to Pearl, "Close the door, Honey. We don't know what the doctor's going to tell us, how much time I have left, but I want to spend it with my wonderful family, and I want to tell you all how much I love you, including the sons-in-law and the grandchildren. And I just wanted to tell you to love everybody and to tell you to love your spouses as much as I love your mother." Then everybody began crying and telling Bill how much they loved him, and Bill said, "That's all right. It's good to cry. Now lighten up!"

My wife "Marty" (nee Marilyn Kirkwood) and I entered Bill's room for the first time last Thursday morning as a cancer specialist was just beginning to explain to Bill and the entire family that his chances of surviving were extremely slim. Bill took this news fearlessly and calmly. My wife and I visited with Bill and Pearl all day, and my brother and I got to talk about all the good times we had had together, and I got to tell him how much I loved him.

Pearl, who had been sleeping by Bill's side since he entered the hospital, called us early Friday morning and said that Bill's blood pressure and pulse had dropped. The whole family got there before Bill gave up his life at around eleven a.m. It seemed like he was just struggling to wait until they all arrived. As he repeatedly made the sign of the cross, his dying words were, "Can't take it anymore! Bye, bye! I love you!" And then Bill stared at the ceiling as if seeing a vision, and died.

I'd like to end by speaking directly to my brother. You folks can just listen in.

"Don't worry about Pearl and the kids, Bill. She and they are following right in your footsteps. You'd be proud of them. After you died Friday, the whole family went to Hillside Cemetery and purchased two lots, one for you, one for her, side by side, and right next to Pearl's mom and dad whom you loved so much. I remember how you fell in love with the whole Carlson family when you met Pearl. You put faith in Pearl and the kids to carry out your well-laid plans, Bill, and they're doing your bidding to a "T." Bill, you taught me what it means to be a man when you lay dying and asked God's forgiveness for any hurt you may have caused anyone. Not to worry, Brother. You were too gentle, kind, sensitive, and thoughtful to hurt people. Father Jim Studer, the priest who gave you the blessing of the sick and dying, said he'd never seen a greater demonstration of faith in a dying man in his life. You're home free, Brother!

Lastly, Bill, let's talk a little about love. Do you remember when you wanted to go on a double date with me because you had met this real neat gal from Columbia Heights? You wanted me to check her out. I didn't know who to go with, and you said, 'How about that Kirkwood girl you went to high school with; she lives in Minneapolis.' Those two gals became our wives. We sure knew how to pick 'em, Brother! Bill, it has to be true that 'Home is where the heart is' because the love that your family is showing for one another right now is extremely touching. I think you taught us all a good lesson about how to go about understanding and caring for people. Your whole family seems to have developed your touch, Bill. They love one another!

I think you knew all along you were going, Bill. You just waited so all of us could be here with you. Your spirit lives, Brother. Thanks a lot for showing us the way. We love you!"

MARILYN KIRKWOOD

On Sunday, August 20, 2000 at 11:40 a.m., the love of my life, my wife Marilyn "Marty" Kirkwood Dowdle, my buddy and best friend, died of ovarian cancer. As she took her last soft breaths, I held her hand and told her how much I loved her. She died peacefully with no pain, no nausea, and a smile on her face.

Earlier that same morning she had been going through hell! She was receiving demerol via a computerized pump, and I was pumping an extra shot of it into her body every ten minutes, but it wasn't doing the trick, so when one of my daughters came in and saw this, she immediately called Home Hospice, and Patty Shribbs, an angel as far as I'm concerned, came to the house immediately and asked me if I wanted to give Marty nemutal suppositories to relieve the pain. I told her I definitely wanted the pain gone, so she gave Marty two nemutal suppositories, and the pain left her. It was a bittersweet moment for me because I was glad to have my wife free of pain and nausea, but I was already beginning to feel a sense of loss that I knew I was going to begin living.

It's terrible! That evening I put on one of our favorite songs, "All the Way," sung by Frank Sinatra, and I started dancing around the living room as if Marty were in my arms, and I, hyperventilating and crying uncontrollably all the time. For those of you who have been there, you know what I mean. Why, I'm crying like a baby right now as I write this, but I don't care. I want all my tears to flow out naturally for the person I loved more than anyone else in life.

My daughters run a close second because I don't know what I would have done without them, all five of them. The day after Marty was told she had cancer, our daughter Ally arrived early the next morning from Eugene, Oregon to be with Mom. She drove the ten hours straight to Rohnert Park, California as soon as she heard about it.

Ally also drove us to Sacramento to consult with a gynecologist/oncologist/surgeon. He told Marty she had three options: 1) Do nothing; 2) Inject the liver which was already three times its normal size; or 3) Have surgery. Marty prayed about it all that night and opted for surgery. We were all pretty happy with her decision, hoping that the surgery would be successful and that we'd have our wife and mother back. That's not the way it happened.

After a week in the hospital in Sacramento, my daughter Ally and I, taking turns staying with Marty in her room and driving back and forth from our motel, were finally able to bring her home. She had a duragesic patch for pain and composine for nausea. As it turned out, neither was very effective. Also, Marty's incision began leaking badly.

For a solid week, every hour on the hour, I was changing a Depends and a soaking hand towel from the incision leakage. Besides that, Marty kept saying, "All I want to do is die! Just help me die!" Believe me, if she had had the necessary pills at that time, she would have taken them, and I would have assisted her. Marty and I both believe in the right to die without unnecessary pain when you're terminal, and she was. The doctor pegged it at less than six months. Marty lived a month after surgery.

During that month a little humor entered our house. Once was the second week, the week Marty was at home after surgery. One of the two drugs she was taking caused her to hallucinate. She said she heard Tex Beneke playing and saw Spanish dancers. We both had a good laugh. She also had a good laugh the week before she went into surgery when I came home with all my hair cut off. I thought if she was going to have surgery and then maybe some chemotherapy and end up losing all her hair, I wanted to look like her. It provided us all with some welcome relief from what was about to happen.

Marty could have tried chemotherapy after the surgery, but she was assured there was no way the cancer was going to be cured, so she chose not to have it. She was already weak from the surgery, and she can stand pain more than she can stand being nauseous, so she was very definite about having no chemotherapy.

I had to readmit Marty to Kaiser in Santa Rosa after she was home with me for a week because the meds and incision were out of control. While she was in the hospital, one daughter began probing about why she didn't want chemo, and Marty told her, "I'm not having any chemotherapy, so if that's a problem with you, you'll just have to deal with it in your own way." I just stood there in awe and wondered where this woman who had already been through so much got the strength to confront her daughter in such a calm, firm manner when she was so sick. I sing the praises of my wife! I sing the praises of women in general! They're the saints of this world as far as I'm concerned.

I know my wife was. She always put everyone else before herself. Why, she was helping her sister pack and move into the Altamont Apartments in Rohnert Park, California when she had a huge pelvic mass in her belly. Marty was the inveterate volunteer. When the Sonoma County Volunteer Bureau was formed in Santa Rosa under Sheila Albert's direction, Marty became Sheila's secretary and stayed with her for eight years. After that she spent many years at the front reception desk at Memorial Hospital. She was always badgering me to get out there and volunteer. Now, I think I will.

So, there you have it. Surgery in Sacramento one week, all hell breaking loose at home the second week, back in the hospital the third week, and home again the fourth week.

Let me tell you a little about the fourth week because it was beautiful! All the girls got to have some extremely intimate talks with their mom. I'd say talks that were life changing for them. Marty was so thankful that she got to say goodbye to each of us in this way, and so were we. We all treasured those moments. During one of them, I overheard her tell one daughter, "Don't sweat the small stuff," and another daughter, "You look so sad, I could just hug you every time I see you." She did.

We also treasured the way we sent her off, celebrating her life! She was cremated and her ashes were spread outside at the Rose Garden at the Santa Rosa Memorial Park on Franklin Avenue in Santa Rosa, California. On Sunday, August 27, 2000, one week after Marty died, my five daughters and I took a white limousine to the cemetery and visited there. Other relatives followed in their cars. While we were all standing around the Rose Garden, I read a poem titled "I'm Free" which captured the way Marty felt about death. I'd like to share it with you:

"I'm Free"

Don't grieve for me, for now I'm free
I'm following the path God laid out for me
I took His hand when I heard Him call
I turned my back and left it all.

I could not stay another day
To laugh, to love, to work or play
Tasks left undone must stay that way
I found that place at the close of day.

If my parting has left a void
Then fill it with remembered joy.
A friendship shared, a laugh, a kiss
Ah yes, these things, I too, will miss.

> Be not burdened with times of sorrow
> I wish you the sunshine of tomorrow
> My life's been full, I savored much
> Good friends, good times, a loved one's touch.
>
> Perhaps my time seemed all too brief
> Don't lengthen it now with undue grief
> Lift up your heart and share it with me
> God wanted me now, He set me free.
>
> Author Unknown

One son-in-law said, "All the time I've known Marty, I've never heard her say one negative thing about another person." He was so right. That was my wife through and through, always thoughtful, gentle, sensitive, and kind to others. Another son-in-law said, "I remember the worst she could say about our baby when he was crying up a storm and she was walking with him and cuddling him, trying to comfort him was, "He's a little tiger. He's a real puzzle." Believe me, folks, Marty's going to be a hard act to follow.

After visiting the cemetery, we all drove out to Armstrong Redwood Grove at Guerneville, California and walked Marty's and my favorite trail. Then we all drove home, had lunch, and just talked over the many good times we all had had together with her. We really celebrated her life! That's the way she wanted it, and I tried to carry out her wishes to a "T." I did my best, honey.

When Marty and I were talking about God during her last week at home, she said, "Chuck, my God is a non-judgmental, compassionate, and merciful God." The way Marty thought was the she lived. I loved that woman!

PHARMACISTS

During the 1930's and 40's, Crookston, Minnesota was a thriving medical community which boasted three drugstores, all located on South Broadway within a couple hundred feet of one another. Wallace's, on the corner of Second and Broadway, was owned by Sam Wallace and later by Bill Eagle, Daniels', a half block south of Wallace's and next to the alley was owned by Sherm Daniels, and Schreiter's, a half a block south of Daniels' was owned by Norm Schreiter. All of these men were energetic pharmacists whose businesses teemed with action, sometimes near the fronts of their stores where the soda fountains, toiletries, cosmetics, stationery, etc., were located, and always near the backs of their stores where they were kept busy filling doctors' prescriptions.

My first memory of ever visiting the back of a drugstore was one sultry, summer, Saturday afternoon in 1933 when I was just a young boy visiting with my Uncle Jim and dad at their Dowdle Brothers Barbershop on Second Street across from the Wayne Hotel. My dad, who had been sitting in his barber chair, hopped down and said, "C'mon, Charlie. Let's go for a little walk over to Daniels' Drugstore. I want to get some medicine."

As we walked out the door and up Second Street towards Broadway, Dad took out his handkerchief, wiped his forehead, and said, "Sure is a scorcher today, isn't she Charlie!"

I said, "Yeah," and just kept trudging quietly alongside him.

Within minutes we arrived at Daniels' Drugstore where Mr. Viau, a short, dark-complexioned pharmacist employee of Mr.

Daniels greeted us. "Hi, Frank!" he said. "What can I do for you today?"

"Hi, Louis!" my dad answered. "Is Sherm in the back?"

"He sure is," replied Mr. Viau. I liked Mr. Viau because he was always kind, gentle and helpful, just like all the other pharmacists in town. Mr. Viau's son Bobby and his two good-looking daughters (Virginia and Lorraine) were older than I, but we played together once in awhile anyway because we were Sampson Addition neighbors.

As my dad started walking towards the back of the store, he waved his hand to me and said, "C'mon, Charlie. Let's go back and talk to Sherm."

When we reached the back of the store, three other men and Mr. Daniels were all talking, laughing, and sipping "medicine" from paper cups. "C'mon in and join us, Frank," Mr. Daniels urged as he began pouring Dad a paper cup of "medicine." Then he saw me, and this roly-poly, joyful pharmacist squealed, "There's Charlie! How have you been, Charlie?"

I didn't say anything. Just stood there and listened to the men jabbering. Then Mr. Daniels reached into the cooler for a frosty bottle of Pepsi which he handed me, and I began sipping, too.

Of course, when I got older, I realized that what those men had been sipping from paper cups during the summer of 1933 was "medicine" all right, but it was still illegal "medicine" until the states ratified the 21st Amendment to the Constitution and national prohibition was ended on December 5, 1933.

When I was around ten years old, I used to like to hang around Wallace's and watch the pharmacists mix their drugs and fill prescriptions in the back of the store. They didn't seem to mind because Joe Zimmer and Bill Eagle, the pharmacists, never shooed me away. As a matter of fact, Mr. Eagle who was always kind and courteous to me, encouraged me to watch, thinking perhaps that I myself might some day become a pharmacist.

I liked the smell of the chemicals and bought my lined school paper at Wallace's because it was located in the back of the store and always smelled like pharmaceuticals. In addition to the paper, Wallace's always sold beautiful fountain pens, so I bought my pens and ink there, too.

Sal Hall and Bud Ewert weren't pharmacists, but they were Wallace's employees and were always very kind and helpful just like the pharmacists. Sal was a short man, ruddy-complexioned with brown wavy hair, and very quick and businesslike. Bud was a tall, slender man, more pale faced than Sal, blond and balding, and more casual. He always showed me one of his magic tricks whenever he waited on me, and he would smile at my awestruck face as he would twist his hands together and make money disappear before my very eyes.

Another thing I liked about Wallace's was the long soda fountain and booths which stretched almost to the back of the store. On Saturday afternoons during the fall football season, Mr. Eagle would place a radio in one of the booths, and clutches of kids like myself would huddle around and listen to men like Harold Van Every and Ed Widseth star for the Minnesota Golden Gophers against one of their Big Ten opponents.

When I became a ninth grader at Cathedral High School, I usually stopped at Schreiter's Drugstore after football practice to have an appetizer like a cherry coke, lemon coke, soda, sundae, or malted milkshake before heading home for supper. The soda fountain was manned by Myrtle Teal, a cheery teenage redhead with whom all the boys liked to flirt, and which made stopping at Schreiter's all the more pleasurable. Mr. Schreiter, a short, quick-moving, witty man, would hail us by our first names when we came into his store and always make us teenagers feel welcome which simply added another layer of pleasure to the total experience.

By the time I was a senior (1945), World War II had ended, but I was still stopping at Schreiter's, not so much to eat ice cream now or to flirt with "Myrt," but to talk with my buddy Ray O'Claire who worked there part-time. Ray and I had become quite close, so one cold afternoon after school in January when we were sitting at the soda fountain and he said, "Hey, Charlie, guess what I'm going to do. I'm going to join the Navy!" I was surprised, but I was also very interested because all of us were going to be drafted into the Army after graduation. Then when Ray said, "I found out you could do the same kind of work a pharmacist does if you sign up to be a Hospital Corpsman," that clinched it for me. I wanted to do what Ray was going to do!

Unfortunately, Ray never got to do the work of a pharmacist after Hospital Corps School, but I did. After "boot camp" at Great Lakes Naval Training Center and Hospital Corps School at Bainbridge, Maryland, I became a Hospital Apprentice 1st Class and was sent to the United States Naval Hospital at Annapolis, Maryland. It was quite impressive because it was right on the Naval Academy grounds, but the work scared me because I was totally unprepared to work a forty bed ward all alone at night with "vets" who had contacted malaria or been shell-shocked during the war. I put in for sea duty the very first week and was transferred after only twelve days to an outpatient dispensary which was also on the Naval Academy grounds.

I couldn't believe it! This place treated only the wives of officers and enlisted men, and my job was to learn how to mix medicines and fill prescriptions, the very kind of work Ray O'Claire said we'd be doing! The Chief Pharmacist Mate who trained me treated me just like a son. "You just follow me around and watch what I do for awhile, Charlie," he drawled in his heavy Tennessee accent, "and you'll pick up this work real fast," and I did, but I had one real close call.

I had filled a woman's prescription for an eye medicine, and shortly after she left, it dawned on me that I may have made a mistake in measuring the amount of powder that went into the medicine. I raced out the door after her and caught up with her about a half a block from the dispensary and asked her to come back so I could check. As it turned out, I hadn't made a mistake, but it was a scary moment for me because I was harboring thoughts of causing the woman to go blind.

After several months the dispensary closed, and I was transferred across the Severn River from the Naval Academy to a dispensary which treated sailors and marines. My job was to run the pharmacy and fill prescriptions for four flight surgeons and two dentists. Mixing cough medicines like Brown's Mixture and Elixir of Terpinhydrate was a snap, but when I mixed an anesthetic and then watched it being used in surgery, that was a different story! I just prayed that I'd done everything right.

Before too long I was promoted to Pharmacist Mate Third Class and my two year hitch was just about to end. My boss, Commander Snowden, was being transferred to a new aircraft carrier, the Coral Sea, and he said he'd make me a Pharmacist Mate Second Class if I signed up for four more years and went with him. I declined and was soon packed and ready to head home, but before I left, I mixed one last medicine, a five pound jar of Vicks Vapor Rub for my dad. He loved the stuff!

On November 28, 1947, Thanksgiving Day, I was mustered out and given a total cash payment of $283.61 upon discharge. Fortunately for me, many officers had flown into Washington, D.C. at that time to attend the traditional Army-Navy football game, and I was able to catch a free "hop" to Chicago. From there I took the train to Minneapolis, and from Minneapolis the Great Northern to Crookston. It took me sixteen hours to get from Washington, D.C. to Minneapolis and another sixteen to get to Crookston because it was blizzarding and the train traveled slowly and had to make a couple of unscheduled stops. That was okay with me because as I gazed out the window at the flurrying snow, I began reflecting on what had happened in my life during the past two years and what I was going to do with it in the future now that I was coming home.

TEACHERS

Recently, I began thinking about all the different teachers I had and why I remembered some and not others. When I attended elementary school at the Saint Joseph's Home in Crookston from 1934 until 1942, I had eight nuns for teachers, but I remember only Sisters Elizabeth, Amata, Carmel, and Lamberta. I can picture those four nuns as clearly in my mind today as when they taught me.

Sister Elizabeth taught kindergarten and first grade, and she was always gentle, kind, thoughtful, and demonstrated a lot of enthusiasm for her work. She showed me how to color pictures within the lines in kindergarten and how to read stories and write in manuscript in first grade. Her face was very pale and stood out against her black habit which swished as she moved from one student to another.

Sister Amata was darker complexioned than Sister Elizabeth, and she had a dark brown mole on one cheek. We kids noticed every little thing about our teachers. Sister Amata taught second and third grades, and like Sister Elizabeth she was kind, gentle, and loved to teach children.

Sister Carmel was an extremely happy, energetic, outdoors person who organized sleigh rides for us in the winter and took us tobogganing down the hills behind the Mount Saint Benedict Convent. She was a good-looking woman who had a zest for life, and I think I fell in love with her in the fifth or sixth grade.

In the eighth grade I had Sister Lamberta who dedicated all her energy to her classroom work. I especially remember a long and detailed project which involved making visuals for every aspect of the Roman Catholic Mass. Sister Lamberta was tall and slender and moved quickly around the classroom in her attempt to help us all get ready for our big move to the ninth grade at Cathedral High School.

I think I remember those four elementary school teachers best because they loved their work, loved kids, and didn't use fear or threats to accomplish their goals. I don't know if the other four elementary school teachers did because I can't picture them nor remember their names, but what I do remember is being disciplined by having to hold the palms of my hands out and having them whacked hard several times with a ruler. It felt just like a bee stinging every time the ruler struck the palms of my hands. Sometimes whole rows got it, but I don't remember who dished out the punishment.

In the ninth grade at Cathedral High School I had Sister Adelaide for general math, and when she walked up and down the rows of desks while watching us do our problems, I kept my nose to the grindstone because I was intimidated by her! I mastered my math because I was afraid if I didn't I'd get clobbered, and Sister Adelaide was just husky enough to do it, though she never did.

Another high school teacher I remember was Sister Patricia who taught eleventh grade English. We were studying Friedrich Wilhelm Nietzche's "Thus Spake Zarathustra" one day, and Sister Patricia said that this German philosopher taught that men could become "supermen," blond, blue-eyed, beast types, and then she cast her gaze at me, and I just smiled innocently back at her, thinking she had just paid me a compliment because I was blond, blue-eyed, and my mother was of German ancestry. Little did I realize what she really meant!

The only subject I flunked in high school was geometry which was taught by Sister Mary John. She went so fast that I was lost after the first week and simply gave up and faked it for the rest of the year. I felt dumb when I raised my hand and tried to ask a question, so I stopped doing that, too.

My first and only male teacher at Cathedral High School was a brilliant man who taught me a lot, and I'd really be remiss if I didn't mention him, our football and ice hockey coach, Don Norman. He encouraged us, trained us in the basics, and constantly kidded us in an attempt to get us to do our best. He worked our bodies to the bone during football practice and challenged our brains at night with "chalk talks." When he took us to Winnipeg to play ice hockey against the Canadians, he was always supportive, even when we lost. My graduating class, the Class of 1946, was coached for three years by Don before he went into the Navy, but his absence didn't matter because he had taught us so well. I loved and respected Don Norman for being such a caring man and such a great coach! My only regret is that he wasn't around to enjoy the fruits of his labors when we had an undefeated football season during our senior year.

Sister Cyprian, our homeroom teacher, was another outstanding teacher! She taught general science, biology, chemistry, and physics and was a well-spring of patience and understanding. She was a teacher's teacher, a person who mastered her subject matter, was organized, understood kids, and loved to see them learn. She also had excellent classroom discipline and wasn't afraid to display a sense of humor, even going so far as to let Johnny Noah get up in front of the class and sing a few verses from "The Old Chisholm Trail" cowboy song every once in awhile. The class would laugh until tears came into their eyes. It was great fun!

When she taught biology and began talking about blood and dissecting, I always grew uneasy, and my belt seemed to tighten uncomfortably around my waist. Little did I realize that Sister Cyprian had the same problem. One day before we began to dissect frogs, she cautioned us not to come to her if we cut ourselves. Well, one student did just that, and Sister Cyprian went outside, fainted, and hit her head! Like me, I guess she got very squeamish at the sight of blood.

I think I enjoyed physic during my senior year more than any other class because there were only four of us in it (Franny Morrisey, Joe McNamee, Bobby Simmons, and I), and I loved the subject matter, especially the daily problem-solving challenges. Each evening after I'd come home from playing pool at the Playhouse and our house was nice and quiet, I'd begin doing my physics homework and stay up sometimes until one or two in the morning and enjoy every minute of it! I respected Sister Cyprian so much that when I got to school each day for her physics class I wanted her to be happy with the work I'd done, and she was. A nickel's worth of praise from her, got a dollar's worth of effort from me. She would have gotten my vote for "Teacher of the Year!"

When it comes right down to it, I guess what I liked most about the teachers I remembered was that they cared for us and loved to see us learn.

THE BETHESDA HOSPITAL

In 1941 when I was a thirteen year old boy delivering newspapers to my Sampson's Addition customers in Crookston, the last stop on my route was the Bethesda Hospital where Ruby Gregerson, the head nurse and director of the School of Practical Nursing, gave me permission to sell papers to the patients. They were eager to see me when I entered their rooms and would usually say, "Just take the money you need out of my drawer," if they wanted to buy a paper. This became a lucrative way to end my route each day, and it all began early one summer morning when I gathered up enough courage to walk across the street from our 416 Woodland Avenue home and talk with Mrs. Gregerson.

I got real nervous when I saw her walking briskly down the hall in her crisp, white uniform towards the admissions desk. She was obviously very busy with her patients and staff when she met me. "What can I do for you?" she asked.

"I was wondering," I said shyly, "if it would be alright to sell papers to the patients."

Mrs. Gregerson thought for a moment and then asked, "Aren't you the Dowdle boy from across the street?"

"Yes, maam," I answered.

"Well, I think it would be alright as long as you did it quietly and didn't enter any rooms you're not supposed to. Some patients might enjoy reading the papers while they're getting well," she said.

"Thanks a lot, Mrs. Gregerson," I said as I turned to leave.

I was surprised at the welcome I received when I entered

the patients' rooms the next morning and asked if they wanted to buy a Minneapolis Tribune, St. Paul Pioneer Press, or Grand Forks Herald. And I was warmed by the cordial greeting Mrs. Gregerson gave me when we met in the hallway. I sold lots of papers that day and each day thereafter, and my friendship with Mrs. Gregerson grew.

One day I walked into a patient's room, and the man was hiccupping so frequently he could barely talk, and after he bought a paper, he made a strange request. He asked if I'd run down to Daniels' Drugstore and buy him a quart of plain soda water. "I'll give you a quarter if you do," the man said, so I was all for it! "Remember, just plain soda water," he repeated as I began to leave. "I think that's what I need to cure these hiccups."

Well, I was a boy on a mission! I raced downtown to Daniels' Drugstore licketysplit and was back at the hospital in no time flat with the man's soda water. I didn't stick around to watch him drink it because I was a little afraid of what might happen. I think the soda water must have helped cure his hiccups though because he was already discharged when I came around to sell him a paper the next morning.

After a couple months I became a regular fixture at Bethesda, so much so that the nurses and nurse trainees greeted me by my first name whenever they'd see me, as did some of the patients who had been hospitalized for a long time. It was a win-win situation for me, helping me earn money and at the same time making patients happy.

When November arrived and the first snow started flying, my newspaper manager, John Scully, told the carriers that there was going to be a subscription selling contest with lots of prizes. Then John announced a blockbuster prize! "The carrier who sells the most subscriptions," he whispered quietly but dramatically as he withdrew a new eight millimeter movie camera from its box, "will receive this plus his other prizes!"

When I saw that camera, I wanted it badly! The first person I approached to sell a subscription to that day was Mrs. Gregerson.

She listened patiently to my sales talk and agreed to take a subscription to the Minneapolis Tribune. Then she asked if I'd like to come down to the dining room when the nurses were eating their supper and ask them if they'd like to buy subscriptions, also. I was flabbergasted but happy to do so!

While the nurses and nurse trainees were all eating, Mrs. Gregerson stood and said, "Most of you know Charlie Dowdle, the boy who sells papers to the patients each morning. Well, he has something to say to you."

I was scared stiff! This was the first speech I'd ever given! As I stood there trembling, my voice barely audible, I explained as best I could about the contest. When I asked if any of them wanted to buy subscriptions, numerous hands waved in the air, and I was overwhelmed!

In addition to the nurses, I sold subscriptions to many of the townspeople, and when the time came in December to count our totals, I was praying that I'd sold enough to win that camera, but I didn't! My cousin, Bill Carter, beat me by one subscription. I was heartbroken, but I did win three pairs of skis, a half dozen pairs of sheepskin-lined soft leather mittens, and other prizes I was able to give to my family for Christmas, so I was happy!

I continued delivering papers until the end of the eighth grade in 1942. Mrs. Gregerson and I didn't see each other very often after that, but we remained good friends.

When I got out of the Navy in November of 1947, I walked across the street to the hospital to see if Mrs. Gregerson was still there, and she was. She was just as friendly to me then as when we first met in 1941. I had been a medic in the Navy and told her I'd like to help her out while I was home, and she put me to work the very next day, tending to patients and taking x-rays. It certainly was a contrast to selling patients newspapers, but it gave me a good feeling knowing I was able to repay Ruby Gregerson a little for all the help and kindness she'd shown me years ago, and it was nice being home among friends again.

SUPPERTIME

Every evening at precisely 6:00 p.m., Manley Millard, the school and church caretaker, entered the Cathedral of the Immaculate Conception vestibule, grasped the thick rope connected to the bell in the belfry, and tugged at it until the bell rang six times, telling all the Crookston businessmen and shopkeepers that it was time to lock up and head home for supper.

Late one afternoon when I came home from school, my mom handed me a clean, empty, one gallon Karo syrup can and asked me to go to the creamery and get some buttermilk. I had done this before, and it was fun. The creamery was only three blocks from our 416 Woodland Avenue home, and I felt pretty important as I bumped the empty pail against my leg, crossed the bridge, and headed towards the Old Dam, near which the creamery was located.

When I entered the creamery, the big, cylindrical, wooden tubs were turning noisily, churning the milk to make butter. Surrounding the tubs were many creamery cans full of buttermilk which remained after the butter had been separated from it. That's what I was after, the buttermilk which was "free," and since it was 1936 and the country was still feeling the effects of the Great Depression, anything "free" was always welcome.

When Mr. Gamee, our Sampson's Addition neighbor and the creamery butter maker, saw me, he knew right away what I was after and called out loudly so that I could hear him over the roar of the machinery, "Go ahead and take buttermilk from any of those cans, Charlie! They're all full!" This was easy for Mr.

Gamee to say because he was a man who was big and strong, but for an eight year old boy who didn't weigh as much as the can he was about to pour buttermilk from, this was no easy feat. First, I had to pound the cover off the heavy metal can with my bare hands and then try to tip it so the buttermilk poured into my pail and didn't slosh all over the floor. I was usually successful, but if I wasn't, I tried to beat it before Mr. Gamee came around to check up on me.

At suppertime the table was set with a brick of creamy Land O' Lakes butter, a large pitcher of light brown Karo syrup, and a platter of golden brown buttermilk pancakes, one of my favorites! "Come and eat," my mom called, and she, my dad, sister Betty, brother Bill, and I began gathering and seating ourselves around the small, oil-cloth covered kitchen table to enjoy another one of my mom's deliciously prepared meals. After my dad made the sign of the cross and began saying grace, we all followed his lead. The pancakes were delicious, and I loved having mine slathered with butter and swimming in syrup!

Another one of my favorite meals was rice pudding with raisins. My mom would usually have a large kettle of it simmering on the stove when Dad came home from work, and right after he said grace, we'd all dig in. I liked mine with lots of sugar, cinnamon, and milk and usually ate two or three bowls full because that was it for out supper. How much we ate really didn't matter because Mom always prepared plenty for everybody.

One week, however, our mom had to be hospitalized, and her sister, Anne Erickson, came from Velva, North Dakota to take care of us kids. There were now five children in our family, and we were all good eaters! The first day Mom was gone, Aunt Anne stopped me before I left for school and asked, "Charlie, what would you like for supper tonight?"

"How about rice pudding with raisins," I said. "I really like that!"

"Okay. That's what I'll make for you," she said.

When we got home from school, Aunt Annie was already busy in the kitchen, and when Dad came home shortly after six o' clock, we sat down and were ready to eat. After praying, Aunt Annie served us our rice pudding in the same bowls Mom always used, but when we finished and asked for seconds, there were none! The pot was empty! Aunt Annie blushed many shades of red, apologized, and was terribly embarrassed for not having fixed us enough to eat. We kids just laughed about it, and this really got our aunt's goat! Guess what we had for supper the next night. You guessed it! Rice pudding with raisins! Enough to feed an army! Boy, did Annie ever show us. When we sat down to eat, she was smiling and said, "I felt real bad about last night, so I thought I'd fix rice pudding and raisins again. I hope I fixed enough for you boys this time." Did she ever!

Unlike buttermilk pancakes and rice pudding which were easy to swallow, meat was a different story. "Always chew your food thirty times before you swallow it," my dad would say. "That way you won't have to worry about choking on it." I think that was something they'd taught Dad in the army, and he was just passing on this valuable tidbit of information to us kids to save us from ourselves because he thought we wolfed down our food and didn't chew it enough. Unfortunately, this army formula didn't work too well for Dad one evening when we were having gristly liver and bacon with the rind left on it for supper.

Suddenly, shortly after we began eating, my dad hurriedly pushed himself away from the table, grew flushed in his face, and began gasping for air, but he couldn't breathe or speak! He was choking! "What, Frank? What's the matter?" my mom shouted excitedly as Dad sat there with his head cocked back, mouth open.

Then our Mom went into action! She reached right down my dad's throat with two of her fingers and pulled out a long strand of bacon rind. Instantly, Dad began taking deep breaths. "Thanks, Grace!" he gasped. "Thanks for saving my life!"

We kids just sat there, our mouths open, stunned at what had just taken place, proud of our mom for what she'd done, and thankful that our dad was saved!

Nowadays we have the Heimlich maneuver which could have been used in my dad's situation. I had an opportunity to use it one day when I was teaching junior high school at Santa Rosa, California.

It was lunchtime and all of the teachers and secretarial staff were in the faculty lounge, eating, talking, and laughing with one another when suddenly Fern Newlin, one of the school secretaries, threw her crossed hands to her throat and looked panic-stricken! She was choking! Neither she nor anyone else moved, so I helped her stand, stood behind her, and placed my hands around her waist.

That's when the situation became sort of dicey because Fern was a short, heavy-set woman, and I knew I was going to have to apply enough pressure to be effective, but I didn't want to apply so much that I'd hurt her. I'd never done this before, and it gave me a really scary feeling knowing that I might be responsible for her living or dying! In spite of this fact, I made a fist, grabbed it with my other hand, and pressed it into her abdomen with a quick, upward thrust as I had been instructed. Nothing happened! So, I tried again, applying more pressure this time, and it worked! Fern coughed up the food that was blocking her windpipe and left the room, sobbing!

Later in the day she stopped me and thanked me for helping her, and it made me think of how happy my mom must have felt when she saved my dad from choking.

DRIVEN

Although my parents never owned a car, that doesn't mean I never tried to drive one while I was living in Crookston, because I did, three times as a matter of fact. My first attempt was in the eighth grade during the winter of 1942 when I was working at Medved's Meat Market on Saturdays and helping Mr. Medved's son Jimmy deliver meat out in the Carmen Addition. Jimmy was driving the market's pick-up truck on a snow and ice-packed country road when he suddenly skidded to a stop and yelled, "Hop over here, Charlie. I'm going to teach you how to drive!" Suffice it to say that that lesson didn't last very long after my foot froze on the accelerator and we just about landed in a snow-filled ditch!

My second driving experience took place the following year when my uncle Jim bought an old 1929 Chevy which he let my cousin, Bill Carter, drive around town. The car was a big, old, black, boxy-looking four door which had running boards, plush mohair seats, and a stick shift which rose vertically from the floor between the driver and the passenger. "C'mon, Charlie," Bill called out to me shortly after having been allowed to take the monster car on its maiden voyage. "Let's go for a little spin!" I didn't object because I wanted to learn how to drive just like my cousin and I thought this just might be my chance.

"Okay," I said eagerly as I opened the door and hopped into the passenger side seat.

"Where should we go?"

"Just wait. You'll see," Bill answered as he turned the key in the ignition and the old monster roared with life. Then he let out the emergency brake, shifted into first, and smoothly left the curb from in front of his North Main Street home. I watched all of his movements like a hawk, how he clutched, how he shifted, and how he accelerated. "What do you think, Charlie?" Bill asked proudly as we turned onto the highway and headed north towards the New Addition. I didn't answer him. I was too intent on studying what he was doing with his hands and feet. When we neared "The Barrel," Crookston's favorite root beer and hamburger stop, Bill made a sharp left turn and said, "Let's take a drive out to the cemetery."

On the way back he turned up a steep hill, and that's when the ride got real exciting! The Chevy's old engine began sputtering when we got about a quarter of the way up, and I watched Bill suddenly slam the clutch to the floor with his left foot and simultaneously shift the car into second gear. The beast kept sputtering, coughing, shuddering, and wheezing as he eased his foot from the clutch, depressed the accelerator and began moving along slowly in sharp, short jerks. Beads of sweat began forming on his excited face, and then we came to a sudden halt right in the middle of the hill in front of Dr. Mercil's house. Bill looked over at me quizzically and said, "Well, Charlie, guess that didn't go so well. What do we do now?"

I said, "I think you're supposed to have the car in first gear when you're going up a hill." Bill said, "No, it's okay to have it in second." "I don't think so," I countered. "Here, Charlie," Bill said sharply as he extended his hand with the key in it towards me. "You give it a try!" I was sort of flabbergasted because my only other attempt at driving had been with Jimmy Medved. Nevertheless, I hesitantly took the key and said, "Okay."

To make a long story short, the same thing happened to me that happened to Bill, so I simply eased my foot off the brake and let the old dragon drift down backwards to level ground where Bill once again took command and drove us home.

My third and last attempt at driving before leaving Crookston happened early in the evening of our spring prom at Cathedral High School in 1945. My friend Ray O'Claire and I went with Lucy Derosier and Irene Altepeter. Irene was my date and she was the only one who had access to a car, so she drove. That is, until she reached my house on Woodland Avenue in Sampson's Addition. "Here, Charlie," she said as she gave me the keys. "You can drive." Ray was already cuddled in the back seat with Lucy, so Irene just hopped into the passenger seat in the front and said, "Let's go, Charlie!"

She must have noticed my hesitation because she pointed to the ignition and said, "Right there." I was such a fool! I should have just owned up to my inadequacy right from the start, told Irene I didn't know how to drive, and let her. She knew all about machinery and was a pro behind the wheel. My first two attempts at driving were dismal failures, and this was about to become a third.

Somehow, I drove us safely the three blocks from my house to the downtown area, but after I just about hit two cars between Main Street and Broadway, a distance of one whole block, I stopped the car, handed Irene the keys and said, "Here, Irene. I think you better drive."

About one year later when I was a Navy medic stationed at Annapolis, Maryland, I had my first successful driving experience. Here's how it happened. I was in the surgical room administering a shot of penicillin in beeswax to a sailor's butt, and unbeknownst to me my commanding officer, Dr. Mel Snowden, just happened to be standing in the doorway, watching me. "Dowdle," he said, "you really do that skillfully! I want you to go over to the Naval Academy and take the test for Pharmacist Mate Third Class, and I'd also like you to qualify for driving our ambulance."

"Yes sir!" I answered as Commander Snowden wheeled around and left for his office. I soon learned that in order to take the driving test I'd need a state driving license which I didn't have, so I wrote to Ray Espe who was the Polk County Clerk of Court in Crookston, and he sent me one, just like that, no tests, no nothing.

That was all fine, but now I had to teach myself to drive and get some practice before I presented myself at the Naval Academy for the test. I didn't have a car, but the dispensary had an old, black, 1930's vintage, stick-shift Ford sedan, and we were allowed to drive it, so I drove it all around the base every afternoon after work. After about a month of practice, I was ready for the driving test and went over to the Naval Academy to take it with a sailor friend who was also striking for Pharmacist Mate Third Class.

Oh my! Stretched out before us the length and width of a football field was an obstacle course! "All right, boys," the driving tester said, "the first thing I want you to do is to get in that ambulance over there and drive it between those stanchions while you're going at least forty miles an hour. Then back up between them going as fast as you can. Who wants to be first?" My buddy Jim Kelly raised his hand, and he began walking towards the ambulance. It was like a long, white, stretch limo. "How in the hell," I thought nervously, "was a person supposed to weave in and out between those posts while going over forty miles per hour without knocking any of them over!" Well, Jim Kelly did it, and I was next!

"Go for it, Dowdle," Kelly said as he walked away from the ambulance and I approached it. In that instant I decided to do just what Kelly suggested. After all, what did I have to lose, just a promotion to Pharmacist Mate Third Class and an increase in my pay grade, that's all! So I cranked up that that long, sleek, white ambulance and began zigzagging rapidly between the stanchions. "This is fun!" I thought, as I raced towards the end of the course and slammed on my brakes. Going backwards was a little different! I started out slowly, but then noticed that the tester was clocking my progress, so I gunned it and made it to the end of the course, but knocked over a couple of posts on the way.

"You did good, boys," the inspector said, "now I want both of you to go over to that table and take the written test, and if you pass it, you're qualified to drive an ambulance." We both passed the tests, driving and medical, and were promoted. The first thing I did the following Sunday when no one was around was try to drive our big, boxy, truck-like, gray ambulance with the large red crosses on the sides. This was a different animal altogether compared to the dispensary's old black Ford and the limo-like white ambulance in which we had just been tested, but after toying with the shift, I finally mastered the brute and was soon ready for any emergency. It's good that I was because it wasn't too long after qualifying that both Kelly and I were called upon to race the ambulance to the bay where a pilot's seaplane had caught fire and he was burned badly all over his body.

Four and a half years later during the summer of 1952, I bought my first car, a large, black, four-door, stick shift, thirties vintage Nash sedan that looked like a hearse. It had been sitting in the snow on a vacant lot in St. Cloud, Minnesota all winter, and it had an old two wheel trailer attached to its rear, just what I needed!

Let the bargaining begin! The owner said he wanted $50.00 for both the trailer and the car, which I couldn't afford, so I asked him if he'd take $25.00 and his answer was, "No." So I said, "I've got a real expensive, brown, alligator-covered portable radio. Would you take it and $25.00 for the car and trailer?"

"What are ya gonna use 'em for?" the man asked.

I told him I had just graduated from St. John's University, was married, had a baby daughter, was on my way to my first teaching assignment at Karlsruhe, North Dakota, and needed something to haul all our stuff.

"Let me see the radio," the man said, "and I'll let you know." That same day I ran home, got the radio, showed it to him, and we had a deal!

Driving home between St. Cloud and Crookston was a real adventure. We had to stop about five times at small towns and farmhouses along the way to fill up the radiator with water because the engine kept overheating and spewing steam from under the hood. "Guess that's what you get for $25.00 and a portable radio," I thought. We made it okay to Karlsruhe, but a week later when we drove to Minot on a Saturday morning, the engine started making a loud ka clunk, ka clunk, noise as we drove down the main street of the city and into a service station. "Sounds like you broke a rod," the service station attendant said.

He was right, so I simply drove that clunker right to the Nash dealership in town and immediately traded it for a newer used car, another Nash. This one had a radio, and seeing it was Saturday, we were able to listen to the Minnesota Golden Gophers play a football game on our way home. Each Saturday thereafter during the fall, driving to Minot and then listening to a Gophers game while driving home became one of our main forms or entertainment.

We lasted only one year at Karlsruhe because it was such a godforsaken place, and sad to say, our new (used) car lasted for only a little over a year, also. That was it! We'd had it with cars, and for the next two years while I was teaching at Perham, Minnesota, we walked wherever we went, to school, to church, to buy groceries, etc. During those two years at Perham, we were blessed with another baby daughter, so when it came time to pull up roots and leave Minnesota for a new teaching job in California, we once again needed a car.

This time, Tom Schmitz, a fellow St. John's graduate who owned the Perham Ford agency with his dad, came to our rescue. He came knocking on our door one summer day shortly before we were getting to leave for Arcata, California and said, "You folks need a car! Let me sell you one!" We told him we didn't think we could afford one, and as he looked directly into our eyes and spoke in his most persuasive voice, he asked, "How does $25.00

down and payments of $25.00 a month sound?" That sounded great to both of us, and in less than a month we were traveling across the country in a brand new, fire-hydrant red, four-door, 1955 Ford country sedan with our two young daughters in tow to the new teaching assignment in northern California.

Arcata was cold and unusually wet, so after three years, we pulled up stakes again and took a teaching job at sunny Santa Rosa, California. My wife had learned to drive while we were in Arcata, so she drove the Ford (this time with three daughters because we had added another) and I drove a u-haul with our furniture. When we stopped for gas, the pumps were sitting on a barely perceptible incline, and while the tank was filling, I walked towards the station to go to the bathroom. "Hey, mister," shouted the service station attendant, "your truck's moving!" It was, right towards the large plate glass window of an automobile showroom which contained two new cars! I raced towards the truck, flung open the driver's side door, jumped in and jammed my foot on the brake. The rear of the truck stopped one foot from the plate glass window. Can you imagine the damage that might have taken place? That evening after we all arrived safely at our new Santa Rosa home, my wife and I both knelt down and said a heartfelt prayer of thanks to God.

That old station wagon lasted for over ten years, until 1965, and when we finally got rid of it, we had added two more daughters to our family for a total of five, so it was time for a new car. This time we bought a tan, four-door automatic Buick Wildcat which had a wide bench seat in the front and a very spacious back seat. I loved that car! It was roomy, comfortable, and powerful! It was the perfect animal in which to teach my first three daughters how to drive because they were a little wild, too, but if they could tame that beast as it spit fire, they could learn to drive anything, and they did. Occasionally, I'd notice a new little dent or scratch here or there, but for the most part the girls did very well behind the wheel.

We owned other cars after the Buick: a dodge Dart, a Plymouth Volare, a Renault, and a Honda Civic. The Dodge was a great car! The Plymouth wasn't! All four windows shattered during the first month we owned it. I went into the dealership with a legalistically written piece of paper and said to the owner as I handed it to him, "I want to warn you that if my windshield ever shatters like the other four windows, and I have an accident because of it, I'm going to sue you!" I had a little problem with the Renault when I first got it, too. Although it was voted the "Motor Trend Car of the Year," the steering column actually dropped into my hands one day while I was driving in downtown Santa Rosa. Our last car was a silver, four-door, automatic, 1989 Honda Civic. She purred like a kitten. I loved that little gem! As long as I treated her right, she kept treating me right, and I guess that's the secret to owning a car.

DAREDEVILS

Every winter when it started to freeze, Manley Millard, school and church caretaker, would snake a heavy hose along the ground to the steepest part of a hill behind the Cathedral and create an icy slide which ran for about a hundred and fifty feet toward the bottom bank of the Northern Pacific Railroad tracks. We Cathedral Elementary School kids would take pieces of cardboard and slide down the hill on them on our butts, and it was great fun, really exhilarating!

In the sixth grade while I was still speeding down that icy slide on my rump, my classmate Johnny Noah was taking a run at it and careening down standing up in his high-topped, leather-soled boots! In the seventh grade while I was skiing down the gentle slopes of the golf course, Johnny was skiing down a toboggan slide in Crookston's Central Park.

The rickety wooden structure had been built near the Red Lake River years ago. It had feeble railings on both sides and a dilapidated base with boards missing, so as you climbed to the two hundred foot top, you could see what would happen if you fell through to the ground. The slide itself was two feet wide and had sides which were two feet high so the toboggans wouldn't topple over the edge as they sped down the icy chute.

About four or five kids would hop on a toboggan, tuck in their arms and legs, and shove off. When the toboggan hit the bottom of the slide and glided onto the frozen, slick river, the screaming kids would be carried for another two or three blocks on the hard ice. Oh, it was fun! And it was all free!

One Saturday afternoon while we were tobogganing, along comes my friend Johnny Noah with his skis and says, "I think I'll try skiing down the toboggan slide." My first thought was, "Oh, Johnny, don't do it! That thing is iced! If you lose your balance and fall over the side of the chute, you could be killed!" That didn't matter in those days because once you said you were going to do something, regardless of how crazy it seemed, you did it.

So, Johnny began climbing to the top of the slide with his skis over his shoulders while the rest of us stood mutely at the bottom, waiting nervously to see what would happen. Not a word was spoken as Johnny poised himself on the platform at the top of the chute, knees bent, ready to let go. He pushed off and came hurtling down toward us. I held my breath and prayed that he wouldn't fall. He didn't, and when he hit the bottom and shot out onto the ice, everyone screamed their congratulations to him.

In the eighth grade Johnny told me he went skiing in the ditches out in the country while his brother (I don't know if it was Tim, Dan, or Joe) towed him with a rope behind a car. Besides being an Olympic ice hockey player, I think given the chance, Johnny Noah might have been an Olympic skier, too. He may have been a "daredevil," but he was also a great athlete.

Another gutsy action I was an eyewitness to happened one summer near the Central Park entrance where the Northern Pacific Railroad bridge spanned the Red Lake River. The bridge was supported by large timbers which jutted out over the river at different elevations, and whenever older teenagers tired of playing a wild game of "tag" at the nearby swimming pool, they'd walk over to the bridge with their suits still on and continue their reckless play by diving from the timbers. It was 1940, and I was twelve years old at the time, just old enough to dare dive from the lowest ten foot elevation but not courageous enough to go higher like the older boys. That's when it happened, when the older boys were diving from the twenty and thirty foot elevations.

An older boy yelled, "Hell, for five dollars I'll dive from the bridge!" This, of course, got everyone's attention, and before you knew it, the five dollars was collected and the braggart began climbing up to the railroad track level and walking out toward the middle of the bridge. This by itself was scary to me because the railroad ties were spread about a foot apart and all one saw when he looked down between them was river water. Also, no one wanted to be caught out on the middle of that bridge when a train was coming because there was nowhere to go to escape from it but down to the river. I myself never ever walked across it. Was this guy crazy?

When he reached the middle of the bridge, all eyes were on him. I don't remember who he was, only that he must have been around seventeen years old. As he stared down at the water which must have been at least fifty feet from where he was standing, he made a perfect dive, surfaced immediately, and swam over to the shore to collect his five bucks. Kids were congratulating him and beginning to walk away towards the pool when Bill Medved yelled, "I'll jump from the arch over the bridge for ten dollars!"

Everyone gasped, knowing that to even get on top of the arch required climbing up another fifty feet on a slanting iron brace which was only a foot and a half wide, but the money for this daring feat was soon collected, and Bill Medved immediately began climbing to the top, firmly grasping the edges of the iron brace and moving hand over hand until he reached it. Without a moment's hesitation, he began walking towards the middle of the bridge, and when he reached it, turned, and stared down at the river.

You could have heard a pin drop among all the boys gathered along the river to watch him. Bill Medved was a muscular guy, a very athletic eighteen year old, but even he may have gotten over his head with this stunt. As he shifted a little from side to side and grasped the edge of the iron top with his toes, preparing to jump, murmurs began floating among the watching boys, wondering if he was really going to do it.

And then he did! He sprang from the top, his body plummeted towards the surface of the calm river, and his feet cut it like a knife! A cheer broke out from the boys on shore as they all waited for Bill to surface, but he didn't! For an interminably long time, we all waited and waited and waited, and stared at the smooth, flowing water, but no head broke through it. The boys began whispering and mumbling among themselves, wondering if Bill Medved had made it, if he was still alive!

Finally, his body came crashing through the surface as he gasped for air and looked around as if trying to gain a sense of where he was before swimming towards the shore. The boys cheered wildly as he approached them, and congratulations and questions like the following could be heard: "Good going, Bill." "That was one hell of a jump!" "What took you so long to come up?" "Was it worth the ten bucks?" Bill didn't say a word, just took the money when it was handed to him and walked away.

Bill had a younger brother, Jimmy, who was much smaller than he, but also very athletic and gutsy. I'll always remember the night football game Cathedral High School was playing out at Highland Park in 1940 when I was in the seventh grade and Jimmy was in the ninth. A big, lumbering fullback came plowing down the sidelines towards the goal when Jimmy streaked out of nowhere, threw himself into the air at the ball carrier's legs, wrapped his arms around them, and felled the man like a tree. Jimmy was tiny compared to his brother Bill, but like him, he had the heart of a lion and was very athletic. Another example of his courage was demonstrated to me when we were playing a football game against East Grand Forks. Jimmy was plunging into the line, playing his heart out, trying for a touchdown when he broke his collar bone. In spite of the intense pain, he continued carrying the ball a couple more plays, but then had to quit.

The last incident I'd like to describe is being told purely for comic relief because it concerns an amusing scene which took place in a potentially tragic setting. Howie Pederson, Clinton

"Kitty" Kleinschmidt, Alguts Nelson and I happened to be walking home together from high school late one fall afternoon when Alguts ran ahead of us, jumped up on the five inch wide railing of the old Sampson's Addition bridge we were about to cross, and ran across it, a distance of about two hundred feet. Kitty called out to him, "Alguts, get down from there before you fall and hurt yourself!" Of course, this is just what Alguts wanted, Kitty's attention, because Kitty was like a big brother to him, a strong, bright, handsome, older big brother.

"One of these days you're going to pull a stunt like that and land in the river!" Howie yelled. "Then maybe you'll come to your senses!" Alguts ignored them, and what Clint and Howie yelled at him simply added fuel to his fire. As we neared the middle of the bridge, Alguts had already reached the other side and began climbing like a monkey up the foot and a half wide iron bracing to the top of the bridge. "Watch this!" he yelled as he ran recklessly toward us. When he reached the middle, he stopped and looked down at us. As we looked up at him, amazed at what he was doing, Kitty yelled, "Alguts, you dummy, come on down from there before you fall and kill yourself!"

Alguts simply did an about face and walked along with us, he above, we below, to the other side of the bridge. When he reached the foot and a half wide iron bracing he had to descend to get to our level, he didn't climb down backwards. He ran down forwards, recklessly, carelessly, utterly unconcerned about the consequences of falling and hurting himself. I just pondered over Alguts' actions and knew I'd never be able to understand his devil may care take on life.

MARTHA LEHMAN

One winter during the Great Depression of the 1930's a middle-aged Crookston woman named Martha Lehman gathered a small group of us neighborhood boys at her Woodland Avenue home and taught us woodworking skills every Saturday morning. When you entered her house, clouds of smoke could be seen billowing from her dining room, not cigarette smoke because neither Martha nor her brother, a tinsmith, nor her father with whom she lived smoked. This smoke surged from a toaster which sat on the dining room table near a heaping plate full of charred toast. Next to the dining room was a large kitchen which contained all kinds of woodworking equipment. Neither Martha nor her brother were married, so each Saturday morning we boys became their kids, and she taught us woodworking skills which kept us all occupied and out of mischief.

The first thing we needed was wood, and if you were too poor to buy it, you had to scrounge for it. I usually found some behind the Red Owl Store on Main Street. Apple boxes were my favorites because they had nice wide sides and thick ends. The wood was pretty rough, so the first thing Martha taught us to do was sand it until it was perfectly smooth. This taught us a lot more than simply producing a piece of workable wood. It taught us endurance and patience until the job was well done. My wife Carmelle said her mother Josephine Johnson used to say, "When a task is once begun, never leave it 'til it's done. Be the labor great or small, do it well or not at all." That's exactly the way Martha had us approach our woodworking tasks.

The next step in the process was to decide what to make. I kept my first project simple, a birdhouse for wrens. It was easy to make because it had straight lines, and it was practical because I could use my apple box wood for it. Martha gave me a pattern to use, and I made the ends and bottom of the birdhouse out of the thick ends of the apple box and the sides and roof out of the wide quarter inch thick sides of the apple box.

Cutting out the wood pieces with a jigsaw wasn't easy for a beginner who had never used an electric machine saw. It had a narrow, vertically mounted blade for cutting curves and complex patterns and was difficult to keep on a straight line and at the same time watch so that fingers didn't get buzzed off. We had to take turns at the saw, but eventually I got mine cut out and then went to work once again, sanding the edges of the wood pieces.

Before nailing them together and completing the project, I drilled two holes in the front of the house, one large enough for house wrens to enter and the other smaller where a piece of doweling was glued for a perch. Then the nailing began, and with some assistance from Martha, it was soon completed. All that remained was to paint the house and put it up.

I chose the top of a tall, rounded post in the back yard of our Woodland Avenue home for the house wrens. That way cats couldn't get at them, and I could see clearly if the birdhouse had welcomed any new occupants. In the meantime, all during the winter and into the spring, I kept working on another project, making shelves.

These shelves were nailed onto all of the walls and into the corners of the walls of our house and they held all kinds of objects. They were all made of plywood and they were all stained a dark walnut. Funny, my mother never complained about them filling up the house, just kept putting them up and thanking me for them as fast as I turned them out. Near the end of spring when all of the snow had melted and the walls of our house were looking like a shelf menagerie, I was in for a big surprise.

Two house wrens had moved into my birdhouse! There they were, flitting back and forth, landing on their perch and bringing nesting materials into their new home, and I hadn't even been aware of it. Those wrens were so tiny. Couldn't have been more than five or six inches long, but they sure were spirited little creatures, and their constant movement and chirping at one another demonstrated their satisfaction with their new home.

This whole process turned out to be a win-win situation for everyone. It made Martha Lehman happy to see us boys learn new woodworking skills and develop other qualities, and it made me happy to see my mother and the wrens enjoying the shelves and the birdhouse. When it comes right down to it, I guess the most important lesson I learned that year was that a lot of our happiness depends on how much we care for others.

Near the beginning of summer, all of our woodworking projects were finished, and Martha took us on a fieldtrip to Maple Lake for a picnic and a day of play, her way of thanking us for allowing her to become a part of our lives. Near the end of the day, we all cut cattails, soaked their brown ends in kerosene, lit them, and ran around at dusk in a torch parade.

Thanks, Martha, for enriching our lives with new experiences and taking the time to care.

SURVIVORS

Survivors, people who struggle to keep on living productive lives in spite of difficult circumstances, are "special people" who seem to never lose faith in themselves.

The Cigar Man lived in a little one room guest house behind Theodore Garvick's big house on Pleasant Avenue. Every time I carried a pail of table scraps over to the Garvick house to feed their chickens, I'd stop at the little guest house and talk to the Cigar Man because his work and his "peg leg" fascinated me. I'd sit by his side in silence and watch him take big, brown, leaves of dried tobacco and roll, cut, and mold them until they became big, fat cigars. While I was watching his hands quickly and precisely shape the tobacco leaves into cigars, I'd sneak looks at his leg and wonder what it was like to have a wooden one. We talked occasionally, but I never asked him how he lost his leg because I thought it might embarrass him.

After he'd finish his work for the day, he'd place his fresh, custom-made cigars into used cigar boxes and take them downtown to sell them to saloons (Heck's, Acker's, Meng and Garvick's, Salem's), hotels (The Wayne on Second Street and The Crookston on Broadway), clubs (American Legion, Elks, Eagles, Veterans of Foreign Wars), and restaurants like The Grill on Robert Street and The Sweet Shop on Broadway which sold them to customers for a dime apiece. Like other Crookston survivors, the Cigar Man worked and remained independent during the "Great Depression" of the 1930's.

Frankie Berg may have had polio because his legs were shrunken and twisted, and he was confined to a wheelchair, but he worked, too. Sometimes when we'd meet on his way to work at Erickson's Meat Market, we'd talk as he gripped the wheels of his chair and skillfully propelled himself forward with his strong arms, and he'd tell me about his job. Frankie would crouch down on an elevated platform in the basement of the market, and when the animals were led down there, he'd shoot them in the head so they wouldn't suffer before they were slaughtered. Like the Cigar Man, this work provided Frankie with a means of support so he could remain independent.

Another man in this same category was Mr. Stainbrook, my friends Jack and Jimmy's dad. He worked out of a tiny shack right next to the Great Northern Railroad tracks where they crossed Robert Street, separating the downtown from the Flats and Sampson's Additions. Mr. Stainbrook walked with a limp, and my guess is that he injured himself while working for the railroad, probably while switching freight cars around, and the railroad gave him this new job. Whenever a train would come chugging down the tracks, Mr. Stainbrook would limp out to the middle of the roadway and hold up a stop sign, warning pedestrians and cars that a train was coming. The railroad could have put up mechanical, wooden, crossing arms, but instead hired Mr. Stainbrook to do the job so he could continue working and be independent.

Unlike the three older men mentioned above, Marguerite Bartholomew was a young, rosy-cheeked, teenage girl who attended Cathedral High School, but like them, she also had a problem with her legs. They were fitted in metal braces and wrapped with heavy leather straps, and she had to use crutches into which she slipped her arms. Polio had taken its toll on Marguerite's young, healthy legs, crippling them, but to see her moving around the school, struggling to throw her legs out in front of her in rhythm with the crutches so she could get from place to place, one forgot all about her disability. Perhaps that was because she was always very cheerful and energetic and never called attention to herself, and perhaps it was because her Cathedral High School classmates accepted her just the way she was and treated her just like everyone else.

I'm sure Marguerite's mom and dad had a lot to do with her positive attitude, too. Her father, Nick Bartholomew, who managed J.C. Penney's on Main Street, was a small, bustling, bundle of energy, always pleasant, polite, and eager to please his customers. Nick's enthusiasm for life and people must have rubbed off on his staff, too, because something happened at his store one evening that anyone who was living in Crookston at the time will always remember.

A customer entered Penny's at closing time, six o' clock, and asked the manager of the men's department if he'd mind staying a little late to help him pick out some new clothes. The manager was very accommodating and told the man he'd be happy to help him. The transaction took much longer than the manager expected because the man wanted everything new: sox, shoes, shirt, tie, and suit, but the manager's time was well spent. Not only was it a good sale, but two days later the manager found a brand new Buick parked in his driveway, compliments of the grateful customer. No one ever found out who he was because the Buick dealer was given strict instructions to not reveal his name, and he didn't, but it sure made a good story for the Crookston Daily Times and gave a lot of people something about which to talk. Some of them thought it may have been Mr. J.C. Penney.

What happened to that Penny's manager sort of reminded me of what happened in the book "Pay It Forward" in which people were encouraged to do acts of kindness for others without expecting anything in return. I guess we'll never know how the kindness those two men showed for one another played out in their lives nor how the lives of the Crookston townspeople were affected, but we do know that the incident got a lot of people talking and thinking after they read about it in the Crookston Daily Times. By the way, the author of "Pay It

Forward," Catherine Ryan Hyde, lives in my small community of Cambria, California.

Whereas Marguerite Bartholomew had to struggle valiantly every time she wanted to move forward, Darwin Ferrier, who captained the 1942 football and ice hockey teams during his senior year at Crookston's Northwest School of Agriculture, did it with ease. The marvel is that he was able to play both sports so well with only one arm.

The first time he came skirting around the end or crashing through the line, the pigskin tucked securely under his one arm, opponents had a tendency to want to take it easy on him when they tackled him so they wouldn't hurt him, but after the first collision which felt like they'd just rammed into a brick wall, all sympathy was rapidly set aside. The same was true of Ferrier when he played ice hockey. He could carry the puck down the ice, pass, stick handle, and score with one arm better than most of his opponents could with two, and he wasn't afraid to check, hard! It shook players up a lot when he hit them because he was short, stocky, fast, and tough, a natural athlete, and he played with the heart of a lion!

David Overton approached life in general that same way, with zest! The first day of school when he walked into my classroom, unaided, and blurted, "Hi, Mr. Dowdle! My name's David Overton, and I'm a new student in your ninth grade English class!" I knew I had a special student and a special challenge on my hands. You see, David was blind and was being mainstreamed into regular classes. To add insult to injury, he had no eyeballs, but this seemed like only a minor inconvenience to David.

As he approached my desk, he began clicking his tongue and spreading his arms and hands out in front of himself so he wouldn't bump into any objects. He told me that the tongue clicking produced an echo effect from any objects that were directly in front of him that needed to be avoided. I could not believe the skill this boy had developed. After introducing myself and getting over being just a little stunned, I placed my arm on David's shoulder and led him over to a row of desks that were directly in front of mine. I said, "I think I'll have you sit right here, David."

Immediately, he sat down and opened a case which he had carried into the classroom, and from it he extracted a braille machine which he set on his desk. This kid meant business! When class began, he listened very attentively and began typing all of his class notes in braille. The same was true when he'd be writing a composition for a grade. He'd simply give the braille copy to his braille teacher who'd translate it for me and put an inked copy in my mailbox. Then I'd grade it, and David and I would sit together and talk about how he'd done. I used to stand by my door in the morning just to watch him come weaving in and out among a mass of students on the way to my classroom. Kids would constantly greet him and pat him on the back as he nudged among them, clicking his tongue all the while. You know kids! Some of them tried imitating David, clicking their own tongues while moving around with their eyes closed, but they weren't very successful. Only David knew how to use the feedback from an echo to move in and out among them successfully without seeing. He was so good at it, in fact, that the kids encouraged him to try riding a bicycle on the outdoor basketball courts without bumping into anything, and he did! They all cheered wildly after that magical demonstration.

The last special person I'd like to tell you about is my father-in-law, William J. Kirkwood. Unfortunately, I got to meet the man only once when I asked permission to marry his daughter Marilyn. He gave it along with a little friendly advice. "It doesn't matter what you do in life," I remember him saying, "as long as you're happy doing it." Mr. Kirkwood died suddenly of a coronary attack in April, 1949 at the age of fifty-eight.

I think Bill Kirkwood was special because he accomplished so much in his short lifetime while he had tuberculosis.

He was a rural teacher in North Dakota, attended business college in Fargo, worked as a law clerk, and studied law independently. In 1921 he was admitted to the Minnesota bar and practiced law in Crookston in conjunction with owning the Crookston Credit Exchange until his death. Also, he was mayor of Crookston for twelve years during which time he was President of the Minnesota League of Municipalities. Most of what I learned about Mr. Kirkwood when I was young, I read in the Crookston Daily Times.

What I learned about him from Marilyn after we were married is what I think made him a survivor. All the time he was mayor and working for the growth and development of the community, he was suffering from tuberculosis, and at one time he was quarantined in the sanatorium for an entire year. During that time, Beth Kirkwood made frequent treks out to the "san," as we used to call it, to confer with her husband about business matters so that the family was able to survive financially. In a way, Beth was a survivor, too, because she helped keep the business afloat and often hiked from her Woods Addition home to the Carmen Addition sanatorium in all kinds of inclement weather whenever she had to see her husband about business activities because she didn't drive.

Is the airport which Mr. Kirkwood was instrumental in bringing to Crookston still named the Kirkwood Municipal Airport? I certainly hope so because that would be at least one landmark dedicated to a man who dedicated his life to Crookston.

My wife Marilyn loved her daddy, as she referred to him fondly, and would often play the piano and sing Irish lullabies with him the way he did with his mother, Mary Ellen O' Sullivan, when he was young. What this all boils down to is that Bill Kirkwood worked tirelessly for his family and his community while he was suffering from a debilitating lung disease, and that's why I think he was a survivor.

Legs, arms, eyes, lungs, they're all vital human equipment

which help us succeed in life when we've got them and they're working properly, and when we don't have them or they're out of kilter for one reason or another, some very special people are able to dig deep down into their souls and generate a spirit that helps them survive, regardless.

TEACHING

After completing twelve semester units in education courses during the fall semester of my senior year at St. John's University in 1951, I was ready to tackle two weeks of student teaching at St. Cloud Cathedral High School in St. Cloud, Minnesota.

As I approached the classroom of senior social studies students, the regular teacher greeted me with a big smile, handed me his roll book, and said, "See you in two weeks! Have a good time!" When I entered the classroom and looked into the faces of those seniors, I became very nervous, but after saying good morning and introducing myself, I settled down and started taking roll. The kids were cooperative and understanding, and after two weeks of teaching and testing which simply flew by, I knew that I'd chosen the right career.

Unfortunately, St. John's University didn't have a well-established career placement office, so job hunting became my next problem. I didn't know how to write a letter of application nor what to include in one for a teaching position until my friend, Dick Meng, a Crookston Central High School pal who was attending St. Cloud State Teacher's College at the time, came to my rescue. He let me use a business English book which answered all my questions, so after I composed a letter and my wife Marilyn typed it up, I was ready.

I sent letters to several potential school districts but heard nothing back from them. That summer of 1952 I had a job laying sewer pipe at Sauk Rapids, Minnesota, and the boss asked me if

I wanted to go to Texas with him and work in the oil fields when the job there ended. I was tempted because the pay was good, and I hadn't received one nibble from the applications I'd sent out. Then, near the beginning of August, we received two letters. The first was from a junior high school in Columbia Heights which granted me an interview. I arrived for it on a Saturday morning at nine o' clock, but the office was empty, so I just waited until 10:30 a.m. when a young woman entered from the outside, paused before me and asked, "We're you waiting for someone?"

"Yes," I answered. "I had a nine o' clock appointment with the principal."

"Oh, I'm sorry," she said as she walked hurriedly past me towards her office. "It completely slipped my mind. I'll be with you in just a few minutes." Just a few minutes was how much time she gave me when she finally did see me, and when we parted, she said, "We'll be in touch with you, Mr. Dowdle." The next week I received a letter from her telling me the position had been filled, and my spirits fell.

The second letter I received was from a small town north of Crookston, so I began feeling optimistic again, but when I read it, my heart sank! "Dear Mr. Dowdle," it said, "thank you for applying for a teaching position in our school district. The Board gave careful consideration to your application and found you to be well-qualified and with exceptional references from St. John's University. However, they decided that you would not "fit in" with our community and will not be hiring you. Good luck in your continued search for a teaching position."

"Fit in," indeed! This was the first time I had ever encountered religious prejudice in a job, and it angered me! Then it happened! I received a third letter, this time from St. John's University telling me about a high school teaching job in Karlsruhe, North Dakota. I applied, signed a contract (sight unseen) for $3200 a year, and two weeks later we were on our way to Karlsruhe. Maybe we'd "fit in" there.

As we turned off State Highway #2 and began driving ten more miles in the summer heat on a dusty gravel road towards Karlsruhe, I began wondering what I'd gotten my little family into. Here we were, out on the prairie, in a no-man's land. When we reached the town, our first stop was the school which looked like a big house. Next, we drove on a dirt road through the rest of the town and saw: a restaurant, two bars, a grocery store, a hardware store, a gas station, a garage, and a Catholic church. We had rented an upstairs apartment (also sight unseen) from an elderly couple who lived across the street from the school. It had one bedroom, a narrow hallway, a closet-sized kitchen, and a bathroom which we had to share with them. Their name was Gefroh, and we soon learned from them that every man, woman, and child in the town and surrounding farms was German and spoke German.

When I met the other high school teacher who was also the superintendent, he said that all of the students spoke German and English, but once they entered the school doors, the only language that was allowed was English. "I'll be teaching all of the English classes," he said, "and you'll be teaching everything else: general science, general mathematics, world history, business law, and psychology." I also coached basketball which was going to be interesting because we never played it at Cathedral High School in Crookston. We had ice hockey instead.

Another interesting facet of the job was the seating of the students. Because we had only two high school rooms, while I was teaching seniors one subject, freshman were studying in the same room. I thought this was going to present a problem, but it didn't. The first week of school while I was teaching the seniors business law in the afternoon, the superintendent entered quietly and walked unnoticed to the back of the room. While I was speaking, one of the freshman boys who was supposed to be studying was talking to his neighbor, and the superintendent (who was six feet six inches tall) walked up behind him, slapped him behind the head with his right open hand and yanked him out of his desk and stood him upright with his left. "Don't you ever let me catch you speaking again when you're supposed to be studying!" he said softly but seriously. Not only was the student stunned. So was I! I didn't have a discipline problem in that school for the rest of the year.

Those kids really studied. They had to because just like in Minnesota, they had to pass State Board Examinations in each subject. At the end of the school year, only two students failed them, one senior in business law and the freshman who was disciplined the first week of school in general math. In retrospect, I don't think that was bad at all. What was bad was our basketball season!

I coached the team just as if they were playing ice hockey, and it worked. We won our first six games! However, during Christmas vacation while we were home visiting with our parents in Crookston, one of the Karlsruhe locals taught the team a different system, and we lost the last six games. The 1952-'53 school year in Karlsruhe was a real learning experience, one I hoped I'd never have to repeat.

Near the end of the school year I began applying to school districts in Minnesota, and when a call came from Perham one day, I got very excited! "Home, home to Minnesota," I thought. "Just what I want!" We drove to Perham and arrived late on a Friday afternoon in May for an interview. The superintendent was out of town at a track meet, so the principal, P.A. Pfenninger, invited us to supper that evening and said we could talk about the job then. We ate a delicious meal, engaged in casual conversation, and then played a challenging game of Scrabble. When we were getting ready to leave, Phil said, "Well, Charlie, it's going to be nice working with you! You've got the job! We'll see you in September!" Little did I realize I was being interviewed all the time we were eating and playing Scrabble.

As we were leaving Karlsruhe, waving to friends and honking our horn, my wife and I couldn't stop smiling at one another and singing all the way out to the main highway we were both so ecstatic about being on our way back to Minnesota. As soon as we arrived in Perham, we rented a beautiful basement apartment from Otto and Evelyn Krueger and bought new furniture from Al and Martin Schoeneberger. We didn't have much money saved, but when these brothers found out I was a new teacher, they both said, "Charge as much as you want," and we did. Our next shopping was for a doctor, and we chose Al and Martin's other brother, Dr. Paul Schoeneberger, on the recommendation of his nurse who was also our landlady, Evelyn Krueger. Pfenninger, Krueger, Schoeneberger? These names sounded like we'd never left Karlsruhe, but we definitely had.

The school was a large brick structure which housed both elementary and high school students and had twenty-four teachers. I taught junior business to ninth graders and a "core curriculum" which combined world geography and English to eighth graders. This was definitely going to be a "piece of cake" compared to Karlsruhe, only two preparations instead of five, no basketball, and only twenty kids in each of my eighth grade classes. I was ready and roaring to begin!

The first day of school was very interesting because there were identical twins in one class, and I couldn't tell Laurie and Linda Hertel from one another because they dressed alike. It soon became obvious, however, that Linda's smile, speech, and behavior were different from Laurie's, and it became easy to tell them apart.

During the first year I organized a Current Events Club which met once a week in the evening after supper. Parents from town and the surrounding farms would drive their children to school and pick them up around nine o'clock after we'd finished our meeting and spent a couple of hours discussing world issues. The kids demonstrated so much enthusiasm and became so well-informed about what was happening in the world that I asked Superintendent Harold Kraft if they could share their knowledge with the whole school during a meeting in the auditorium.

On the appointed day, eight members of the Current Events Club sat on the stage as a panel of experts and took turns speaking on an important world issue to the assembly. When they were all finished, students from the audience got to question them. It was inspiring listening to eighth graders respond with so much composure and detailed information to questions from the audience, especially to questions asked by juniors and seniors.

The 1953-'54 school year whizzed by and I soon found myself searching for a summer job to supplement my teaching income when Superintendent Kraft asked Har Sandholm and me if we'd be interested in painting the schoolrooms, all twenty of them. We both said we would, so Mr. Kraft said, "Go down to Welter's Hardware, pick out whatever paint you want, charge it to the school, and go to work." We took the man at his word, and while we listened to the baseball games all summer, we painted each of those classrooms a different color such as: peach, chartreuse, lilac, pink, beige, and pastel yellows, greens, browns, and purples. When the kids entered their classrooms in the fall, they were startled at the change, but loved it!

In addition to having the same schedule and the Current Events Club as the previous year, I began coaching eighth grade basketball and announcing at the night football games. It was enjoyable, but I was looking for more of a challenge and an opportunity to earn an advanced degree and more money, so I applied in California.

The first week in June I received a call from Arcata, California. "Good afternoon, Mr. Dowdle," the superintendent said. "My name is Cliff Sorem, and I'm calling to offer you the English-social studies job for which you applied. We're looking for someone just like you who has had experience with a "core curriculum." He offered me a thousand dollars more than I would have gotten at Perham and told me Humboldt State College was located at Arcata, so I said, "I'll take it!"

"Marilyn," I said rather nervously to my wife as soon as I got off the phone, "we're going to California. I just took a job at a place called Arcata." After the initial shock had worn off, we sat down and began making plans for the trip. We now had two little daughters, but we didn't have a car because our old one died. God must have been listening in on our thoughts because the next day Tom Schmitz, a fellow St. John's University grad and co-owner of the Ford agency with his dad, came knocking on our door and said, "You guys need a car. Let me sell you one." And he did! For twenty-five dollars down and twenty-five dollars a month we took delivery on a brand new, four-door, fire-hydrant red Country Sedan one week before leaving for California.

Our trip out West was very pleasant until we reached Crescent City, California. Everyone there was wearing sweaters and mackinaws, and our girls were in little summer dresses. It was cold in northern California and very unlike what I had read in the books! As we drove south along the coast towards Arcata, stands of huge redwood trees lined both sides of the highway, small lumber mills dotted the landscape, and smoke rose from the tops of rusty upside down iron cones in which scrap wood was being burned, and I wondered if we had made a giant mistake coming to California.

The warm welcome we received from the administration and sixty senior high school teachers soon put that fear to rest. A different fear, however, was awakened when I looked at my teaching schedule. The first hour I was to be an audio-visual man, servicing and checking out equipment to all of the teachers, and during the second and third hours I was assigned a class of mentally retarded ninth graders. I didn't have a clue what I was going to do with them until a fellow teacher said, "Why don't you have them build a house and teach them how to live in it."

We did just that! First came the plans for a model house which was going to be built to scale, and next came the lumber from a mill located behind the school. The boys really got into it, measuring, cutting, nailing, and the beauty of the project was that they were able to see the progress they were making each day. After the house was completed, we figured out what it would cost to live in it. We took a field trip to a grocery store and made out a monthly food budget. We read the newspaper ads and shopped for appliances, furniture, clothing and other essentials and worked them into an annual budget. We bought a car and figured out what the payments for principal, interest, and insurance would be each month. These kids may not have been as bright as some of the others, but the daily tasks involved in building a house and living in it engaged them and gave them a sense of success and pride in knowing what it would take to begin living on their own when they got out of high school. My next two classes were ninth grade English, and it took quite a mental shift to adjust to them.

After teaching three years at Arcata Union High School and earning a master's degree in secondary education at Humboldt State College, we wanted to move farther south where it was warmer and didn't rain so much, so we applied at Santa Rosa which was forty miles north of San Francisco. The college told me that Santa Rosa hadn't hired anyone from Humboldt State College in years, but I applied anyway and got an interview.

When I arrived for it in the summer of 1958, I was told that the superintendent wanted to see me at his house because it was a Saturday, and he was busy cutting his lawn. It was hot, and he was sweating buckets when I pulled up and met him. He invited me into the house for a glass of lemonade, and we chatted.

The man's name was Dr. Lloyd K. Wood, and his first question was, "Why do you want to come to Santa Rosa?" I told him I liked being near San Francisco, the climate and beauty of Santa Rosa, and the opportunity my family would have to take advantage of the cultural activities in the area. I don't think I said one thing about teaching in the Santa Rosa schools during our whole conversation, but after an hour, he told me to go over and see the principal of Santa Rosa Junior High School.

When I did, Ray I. Johnson, the principal, greeted me with a big smile, shook my hand and said, "There's no need for me to interview you, Mr. Dowdle. Dr. Wood called and gave you his blessing, and that's good enough for me."

My schedule consisted of seventh grade English classes at all levels, including a newly-created one for kids whose IQ's were 130 and above. They wanted these kids to be challenged with something new and different, so I proceeded to assign them what I knew best, how to write a comprehensive research paper. We went through the process step by step: choosing a topic, using the library, note-taking and using sources, outlining, footnoting, and giving credit to the sources used in a final bibliography. One boy did his on snakes and even brought some of them to school to demonstrate how harmless they were and what good pets they made. One girl, a violinist, did hers on harmony, and I needed help interpreting the finished product when it came time to grade it. Not only were these kids challenged by this assignment, so was I!

After teaching seven years at Santa Rosa Junior High, I applied for and became the English Department Chairman of a new junior high called Rincon Valley. It was on the outskirts of Santa Rosa and was surrounded by huge oak trees and new homes. The students were bright, polite, and dressed like "preppies," and the ten English teachers in the department were all experienced professionals who were eager to begin their work.

I loved teaching and retired in 1988. Since then I often meet former students wherever I go. The first time I went to my ophthalmologist in Santa Rosa, he said, "Ah, Mr. Dowdle. Now I can get even with you for all that work you gave me in the ninth grade!"

"Remember, Danny." I said, "all that work is what helped you get through Stanford and medical school."

In April, 2101 when Carmelle and I flew to Zihuatanejo, Mexico for our honeymoon, a young Mexican man called to me inside the terminal, "Hey, Mr. Dowdle! It's me, Gustavo Guerrero! Remember? Ninth grade English!" I hadn't seen this boy in over twenty years, and here he was, calling out my name in a foreign airport. "You'd be proud of me," he said. "I speak better English than any tourist guide at the airport." The next day we met Gustavo's wife and children and had a chance to talk over old times.

Recently, we were paid a visit by a former seventh grader who is now a federal judge in San Francisco. I hadn't seen Susan since 1961, but she still remembered me and greeted me warmly, and I think that's where the payoff comes in teaching, in being remembered by your students and in learning that they have made successes of their lives.

THE ARMORY

Besides being a training facility for soldiers, the Crookston National Guard Armory on North Broadway was often used for some other very interesting activities. Area farmers used the building every winter to display their best grains and livestock during the Farm Crop Show, and when the Civilian Conservation Corps was formed in 1933, the Armory was the place Crookston's unemployed young men gathered before they piled into trucks and drove off to help conserve our natural resources. I was only five years old at the time and got very excited to see all them talking among themselves and waving to us as they left.

One winter a few years later, other older boys were involved in a very different kind of action at the Armory. Earl Wampler and "Dirty" Dick Raines from Texas were wrestling there one evening, and the boys were going to sneak in because they didn't have any money. They tried to get past the ticket taker at the front door, but that didn't work, so they walked downstairs to the basement and searched for a way, but all they found down there was a group of older men who were playing cards, smoking cigars, and wondering what us kids were up to.

It was getting late, and the wrestling match was about to begin when one of the boys said, "Let's go outside and see if there's a way to get in in the back." So, we all ran upstairs, went outside, plowed through the snow to the back of the building and began searching for open doors, but there were none.

Then one of the boys made an invaluable discovery. Near the ground he found a trap door that opened into a black abyss, and even lighting a match didn't let us see how far it was to the bottom. No one wanted to be first to jump and find out, but then one of the braver souls of the group crawled to the opening and said, "I'll drop, and if it works, I'll open one of the back doors so the rest of you can come in." So, this kid dropped, and everyone was listening intently as he crashed to the bottom. Then they heard the kid groan, move slowly, and whisper, "That was one hell of a drop! This is a damn coal bin!"

Within minutes the boy had one of the back doors open, and all of us entered stealthily and climbed a short flight of stairs to the stage which was located at the far end of the basketball court. Excited adults crowded the floor around the ring, and the balcony was jammed on three sides with screaming kids. The wrestlers were already bouncing around in the ring, and the crowd was getting extremely noisy and eager to see their favorite, Earl Wampler, defeat the Texan. It was easy for us to leave the stage one at a time, blend into the crowd, and get good seats.

When the action began, everyone started shouting encouraging words to Earl like: "C'mon, Earl! Throw him, Earl! Pin him, Earl!" But Earl must not have been listening because after about an hour of tangling with "Dirty" Dick Raines, he began tiring, and that's when the Texan demonstrated his trademark hold, the "Backbreaker!" Raines picked Wampler up, held him over his head, and began twirling him around like a helicopter getting ready to fly. Then, suddenly, he kneeled on one knee, slammed Wampler's back across his bent leg, flipped him onto the canvas, and pinned him. Earl just lay there, motionless, like he was never going to move again. They had to carry him to the dressing room on a stretcher, and I never did find out what happened to him.

Another sport which took place at the Armory during the 1930's was adult basketball. Crookston played teams from the surrounding towns, and my friend and former Cathedral classmate, Johnny Noah, remembered them playing the Harlem Globe Trotters, and I even remember seeing them play football players from the University of Minnesota one winter on a Sunday afternoon. John Scully and Eddie McWaters were two of Crookston's exceptional players. John was short and Eddie was tall, but both were fast, excellent ball handlers, and great shooters. I always liked watching these men play basketball because I knew them as friends, John as my kind and gentle newspaper manager and Eddie as a respected Crookston police officer. I never had any money to get into the games, so I'd always hang around the door where my uncle Jim was taking tickets until he finally relented and let me in free.

One didn't have to pay for all of the activities which took place in the Armory. One winter the Nash-Finch Company, a wholesale grocery business located on North Broadway, sponsored a "coffee" drinking contest at which, of course, the delicious Nash-Finch brand coffee would be drunk. Prior to this spectacle, the company served free coffee and doughnuts to the audience, and then the coffee drinking competition began. A dozen men, all sizes and shapes, sat up on the stage, facing the audience, and when the timer rang a bell, the men began guzzling cup after cup to see who could consume the most coffee in an hour.

About half way through the competition, after each contestant had drunk about thirty cups of coffee, loud burps and belches resounded throughout the Armory, the guzzling was replaced by sipping, and most of the men simply quit. About five minutes before the end of the hour, only two contestants remained, a short, stocky guy with a huge gut and a tall, lanky, beanpole of a man. The audience began cheering them on as the seconds ticked away, but the big guy began looking a little sick! With only a minute to go, the two men began chug-a-lugging their coffee in a valiant effort to outdo one another, and the bell rang! The big man abruptly left the stage and made a beeline for the front door. The skinny man just sat there, beamed and collected his prize as if nothing had happened.

Another free activity, which was very unlike the coffee drinking contest, was a visit made to the Armory by Father Hubbard, a Catholic priest and Alaskan explorer, who was invited by Father Bill Keefe to come to Crookston one winter to share his experiences with all of Crookston's students. They were excited because when he pulled into town, it was on a sled behind a team of huskies he had mushed all the way from Alaska. First, he showed us a film about his Alaskan adventures, and the rest of the program was devoted questions from the students. The next day, a Saturday, Father Hubbard drove his dogs and sled downtown to a vacant lot on North Broadway where everyone could see his dogs and examine his equipment.

I could hardly wait because I wanted to get closer to those dogs. So did a lot of other kids, but when the time came, none of us got too close because those huskies just stared at us like they were looking at their next meal! What we did get to do up close was crack Father Hubbard's big, long whip and imagine we were up in Alaska, driving a team of dogs along a cold, icy trail, just like he had done.

All of the activities I've mentioned were memorable, but none was as memorable as the dance I attended at the Armory on December 31, 1947, New Year's Eve. I had just been discharged from the Navy and asked a former classmate, Carmelle Johnson, to go to the dance with me. We had a lot of fun dancing the night away, swinging and swaying, doing the lindy hop and the fox trot, and just being with one another. Fifty-three years later, after our spouses passed away, Carmelle and I met again at Cambria, California, and the course of our lives was changed forever. We got married on April 21, 2001.

IT'S THE BERRIES

Chokecherries, gooseberries, and blueberries (Yes, blueberries!) all grew wild around Crookston during the 1930's and were free for the picking if you just knew where to find them. One summer day around 1938 when I was ten years old, I just happened upon a cluster of blueberry bushes out by the san (tuberculosis sanatorium) in the Carmen Addition while I was taking one of my woodsy hikes on the trail that bordered the Red Lake River in Sampson's Addition. Coming out of the woods I entered an open field in the center of which was a large cluster of bushes which bore bluish berries that looked very much like the same ones we'd buy in little, wooden one pint boxes at the Red Owl Grocery Store on Main Street.

Upon closer inspection and after putting a handful of them in my mouth for the taste test, I decided that they were the same. Never before had I discovered any blueberry bushes in any of my hikes around town, so this was a first. I had discovered a goldmine of edible fruit!

Mentally, I marked the place where I'd found the blueberry bushes and then hightailed it home where I picked up a water bucket before running back to the field. I don't know why I got so excited and why I was in such a hurry. The blueberry bushes certainly weren't going to rise up and disappear on me. I think I just got anxious about picking a whole bunch of them and surprising my mom when I got home.

Then it happened, a big, big problem. As I neared the blueberry bushes, I wasn't paying any attention to some small mounds of white sand in the field, and I stepped right in the middle of one of them. Within seconds hordes of red ants were crawling up my leg and biting the hell out of it! I panicked, ripped off my pants, took off my shorts, shoes and socks, and began dancing around in the field and brushing off the ants as fast as I could before they ate me alive! Am I ever glad I was alone in that field.

Before long all of the ants were gone, and I began picking blueberries, picking and eating, picking and eating, picking and eating until my pail was filled to the brim. It was a long walk home to 403 Pleasant Avenue, about a mile, and lugging that heavy pail of blueberries didn't make it any easier, but it was going to be worth it. I could just see the surprised look on my mom's face when I showed her what I'd found.

"Oh my, Charles! Where'd you get those?" she asked when I entered the house and showed her the bucketful of berries.

"Out by the san," I said, as I watched her inspect them and smile. "I found a whole bunch of them in a cluster of bushes in a field near the woods." Then I scooped out a couple of handfuls, washed them, and put them in a big breakfast bowl. "I think I'm going to have some. Do you want some, Mom?" I asked.

"No. You go ahead," she said. "I'll wait until supper." So, I took a bottle of milk out of the refrigerator and poured it over the berries, sprinkled a couple of teaspoonfuls of sugar on top of them, and began eating. I was in blueberry heaven! That evening and for the rest of the week the whole family enjoyed blueberries for dessert, and it made me happy to know that I was the one who had provided them.

Gooseberries were no big deal because bushes simply dripping with them were scattered all around town, behind the library by the old swimming pool, across the street from our house on a big old wooded lot, and in many other places. The thing about gooseberries was that they were sort of prickly and very sour! You knew that when you put a handful of those babies in your mouth and crushed down on them that the sour juice was going to make you pay the price. The nice thing about them was that they were plentiful and free.

Chokecherries were also very common around Crookston, and being extremely astringent, they contracted the soft tissue in your mouth when they were eaten, but it was worth it. Two tall chokecherry trees grew on the west side of our house next to a vacant lot, and when I didn't have anything else to do during some of Crookston's hot, humid summer days, I'd shinny up near the top of one of the trees and eat chokecherries. They were certainly well-named because they were very tart and always made me pucker up, but that didn't matter when I was up in that tree because I was like an eagle in its aerie, surveying the surrounding neighborhood action from my lofty nest and all the while enjoying the juicy berries.

One day later that same summer I discovered some chokecherries while I was roaming the Catholic part of the cemetery near where my grandma and grandpa, Laura and George Dowdle, were buried. I noticed a cluster of chokecherry trees in the nearby woods, and the branches were so heavily-laden with the black fruit that they were bending towards the ground. I had never in my life seen chokecherries as large and plump as those, and they seemed sweeter than any I had ever tasted, still astringent, but sweeter. This was just like the blueberry find I had made earlier in the summer out by the san.

The difference was I was farther from home, but that didn't matter. I got just as excited as when I had discovered the blueberries, and I ran home to get the bucket. After I got back and filled it to the brim, I lugged it all the way from the cemetery to my dad's and uncle Jim's Second Street barbershop so I could show them what I'd found. They were both very impressed. "For heaven's sakes, Charlie," my dad blurted, "where'd you get those big chokecherries?"

When I told him out by grandma and grandpa's graves in the cemetery, my uncle Jim got very interested and said, "Tell you what, Charlie. You stick around the shop until we close, and your dad and you and I will all drive out there together, and you can show us where you got them and we'll pick some more. And that's just what we did, but we stopped at my uncle Jim's North Main Street house first to get some more buckets.

When we got to the cemetery, we walked the short distance into the woods and I pointed up at the chokeberry tree branches which were fairly dripping with large bunches of the black fruit. "Oh my!" my uncle Jim exclaimed excitedly. "This is too good to be true! Tell you what, Charlie," he said. "Why don't you climb up that tree and hang out on that big branch, and we'll grab it and break it off and pick the berries on the ground." We did just that, and before long we had all the buckets full.

That evening my dad and uncle Jim made chokecherry jam out of all the berries we had picked, and it lasted all winter. I just loved spreading a thick layer of Land 'O Lakes butter on a piece of freshly baked white bread and covering it with chokecherry jam before downing it with a glass of cold milk.

I don't know which I could say were my favorites, chokecherries, gooseberries, or blueberries because they were all a gastronomic delight which I will forever associate with some of my favorite Crookston childhood experiences. Anyone for crabapples?

THE ROWBOAT

Early one hot, humid summer evening after supper when I was walking up Woodland Avenue toward Ade Ness'es little store to buy some candy, my neighbor, Virgil Issacson, called out, "Hey, Charlie, wait up for me a few minutes and you and I'll go for a swim above the old dam."

"Okay," I called back as I sat down on the warm curb and began waiting, "but hurry up because it's still plenty hot out here." As I sat watching the cars drive up and down Woodland Avenue in the debilitating heat, I began thinking about how refreshing it was going to be to go for a nice, cool swim in the river, and how freeing because we never wore suits and no one was ever there to tell us what we could or couldn't do.

"Okay, Charlie," Virgie yelled as he came walking quickly out of his house, "let's go." I didn't hesitate, just jumped up from the curb, ran across the street, and fell in walking alongside him like an obedient soldier. You see, Virgie had just graduated from the tenth grade at Central and was two years older than I, so naturally he was the leader.

It only took us about ten minutes of fast walking to reach the dam, but we still had to climb a hill to get above it where we swam. "C'mon, Charlie," Virgie yelled, "let's run the rest of the way!" We did, he in the lead and I lagging behind. When I finally caught up to him, he was already stripped and ready to go. "Hurry up," he said, "and we'll run and dive off the bank together." Sweating and tugging at my clothes, it didn't take long before we were both plunging off the bank into the warm Red Lake River water.

While we were both swimming around, Virgie yelled, "Hey, Charlie, look at that rowboat on the other side of the river. I wonder what it's doing there?" I didn't have a clue. There were no houses on that side of the river, so it was an unusual place for a person to leave a boat. We just kept swimming around for awhile, but I could see that Virgie's mind was on that rowboat, and when we climbed up on the bank to quit and dry off, I found out I was right.

"Let's swim across the river and go for a boat ride," he said. "We can hold our clothes over our heads and swim across with one arm." To me this didn't sound like a very good idea, and a lot of questions began entering my mind. What if I got half way across and got so tired I had to drop my bundle of clothes in the river? What would I do then? Wait until night and run home in the nude? Or worse, what if I got to the middle of the river and the current was so strong it swept me right over the dam? What then? "C'mon, Charlie, let's go!" Virgie yelled as he began tying his clothes in a tight bundle. I decided to try it, but I wasn't going to like it.

As I eased my body into the water, holding my clothes as high above my head as possible with my right arm, doing a scissors kick with my legs and a rapid side stroke with my left arm, I'm sure fear was written all over my face because this was definitely against my better judgment. I was scared because when we reached the middle of the river, the current did grow stronger, and I began thinking again about what would happen if I got so tired I couldn't swim anymore and went floating over the dam. That's when Virgie began yelling encouragement, and it became clear to me that we were going to make it. As we approached the opposite shore, I was so tired my right arm began dragging in the water, and my clothes got wet anyway, but at least we made it.

The boat was just sitting there with two oars and an empty two pound coffee can in the bottom. It didn't take us long to get dressed, put the oars in the oarlocks and shove off. We sat together on a bench in the middle of the boat and each pulled an oar. As we zigzagged slowly up the river, Virgie said, "You're going to have to pull harder on your oar, Charlie, or we're never going to get there." I didn't ask where "there" was, just kept struggling with my oar so I could keep up with Virgie and help to move the boat forward in a straight line.

Once we got the swing of things, we began making pretty good time. It wasn't long before we were going under the bridge, past the Peter George Grocery Store, and around the bend by the Mill Woods, all familiar landmarks. By the time we got beyond them, it had become dusky, and I became worried because all I could see were clusters of trees casting shadows on unfamiliar riverbanks. It became a little eerie, so I asked, "Where are we going to end up, Virgie?"

"Just wait," he said. "You'll see." So, I just kept rowing and getting more miserable by the minute because now mosquitoes began buzzing around us, trying to land on our sweaty arms and faces. "You're going to have to row by yourself for awhile, Charlie," Virgie said as he hopped to the back of the boat with the coffee can in hand and began bailing out water. Now I really began getting worried! Here we were, in a stolen boat that was leaking like a sieve, on a part of the river that was totally unfamiliar, and at night!

That's when I began hearing some faint strains of music coming from the nearby woods and realized, as I kept rowing and the music grew louder, that we were near the ice arena where oak flooring was installed each summer for roller skating. What a relief! Before too long, we rounded the bend, and I could see the bridge. "What'd I tell you, Charlie," Virgie said. He had stopped bailing water and was now sitting beside me, helping me row the boat to the shore under the bridge. When we reached it, Virgie jumped out first, I followed, and then we both tugged at the boat until it was high and dry.

As we climbed the hill to the street level and began walking towards the arena, Virgie said, "Let's go skating." I didn't see why not, so we bought our tickets, clamped the heavy, metal skates to the soles of our shoes, tightened the straps around our ankles, and we were off skating among the rest of the crowd. As I wheeled around the arena, the cool breeze brushing against my face and body, drying the sweat that had collected there, it felt good to be free of the boat, the river, and the mosquitoes, but the thought still lingered in my mind about the boat we'd taken that wasn't ours and about the swim we'd taken that could have ended tragically. Never again!

THE PLAYHOUSE

During the 1930's the Playhouse was a bar and pool hall for gentlemen, but during the early 1940's when World War II was being fought, the men left, beer stopped being sold, and it became a hangout for teenage boys. They smoked, played pool, and fed their loose change to the jukebox so they could listen to the music and songs being played and sung by Duke Ellington, Glen Miller, Nat "King" Cole, Frank Sinatra, Bing Crosby and the Andrews Sisters. And they smoked, and smoked, and smoked!

And what did they talk about as they played pool, listened to music, and smoked? Sex! They talked about sports, drinking, and fighting, too, but sex was the number one topic of conversation. For me, a seventh grader in 1940 when I first began going to the Playhouse, the older boys' talk provided the only course in sex education I ever received or needed because they described their behavior explicitly. For the most part, they bragged about the girls they'd met and "laid" at Maple Lake, Grand Forks, and Red Lake Falls, or they'd talk about how nice one of the local Crookston girls was or had been to them. I think a lot of the older boys' talk was just that, talk, and I say that for a reason.

One day the manager of the Playhouse, a young guy whose testosterone could almost be seen oozing from his pores, persuaded a star senior Central basketball player to walk across the street with him and meet two ladies who were ensconced in an upstairs apartment and waiting to meet them. The senior, who was liked by all the girls, was hesitant at first, but when he finally caved in and walked out the door with the manager, all of the boys stopped playing billiards, snooker, and rotation and gawked after him. When he came back about an hour later, it was obvious that this "man about town," who had always been talking big about the girls, had lost his virginity to an older, experienced woman because he had a silly smile on his face and was silent.

On another occasion some of the Playhouse boys got involved in a group sexual experience when on a winter evening a call came for a particular boy from a particular girl who was babysitting some kids with her girlfriend at a house in Sampson's Addition. The girl asked the boy if he'd like to bring a friend and come keep them company. What did the boy do? He announced this situation to a group of his friends, and when he went out the door, about a dozen of them left with him. I went, too, only because I was curious, it was late, and it was on my way home. The boys entered the house two at a time until they had all gone in and come out, and their loud, excited talk didn't leave much to the imagination concerning what had happened with the two girls in the house.

Maple Lake on Saturday nights during the summer was another place where the Playhouse boys met the girls. I got to go there one Saturday night with my older brother Bill, his friend Harold "Hoppy" Hopkins who drove an old, black four-door Ford sedan, and some other boys. We stopped at Mentor for beer, and Bill said, "Just go up to the bar, Charlie, put down a nickel and say, 'Gimme a draft beer.'" I did just as he said, and to my surprise I was asked no questions and a large mug of cold, amber-colored beer with white foam on top appeared like magic. This was living!

When we arrived at the Maple Lake Pavilion, all of the guys were happy and ready to begin dancing. The band was already playing, so the boys bought their tickets, entered, and began "casing" the place for the girls they wanted to ask to dance. By intermission time the dancehall was hot and humid, and the dancers were in a frenzy as the band finished with the "One O'clock Jump," a fast jitterbug number. Then everyone seemed to gradually disappear, and I couldn't figure out where they all went or why some of them were carrying blankets. On the drive home, I found out. To the car, to the beach, to the woods, to the who knows where just by the way they were talking: "Did you see that babe I had? She was really nice! Not as nice as the one I had! I could have stayed with her all night!" And that's the way the talk went all the way back to Crookston.

Every once in awhile on a Saturday afternoon, one of these real nice girls a boy had met at Maple Lake would come walking slowly by the Playhouse, looking for him because she was pregnant. If the boy for whom she was looking happened to be in the Playhouse, he would tear out the back door into the alley and would not be seen around there again for a long, long time. These guys wanted to have their fun, anonymously, but they didn't want to be responsible for the consequences of their actions. Unfortunately, it was the girl who was left to face the reality of the birth of a child, alone.

Of course, there were other ways of having fun and showing that you were a real macho man. One day Don Duckworth who was stocky and built like a bull was going to prove how strong he was by letting one of the smaller guys punch him in the gut while he held his arms high over his head. "C'mon, Hoppy," he called to Harry Hopkins who was walking by him. "Let me have your best punch! It won't even phase me!" Hopkins who was about five feet eight inches tall and 120 pounds wringing wet just ignored Duckworth at first, but then turned rapidly and buried his fist in Duckworth's midsection, right beneath his breastbone, and Don doubled over and couldn't get his breath for a long, long time.

Another time when my brother Bill and I entered the Playhouse, the bartender said something to him, my brother said something back, and the bartender came running from around the bar right at him, and Bill landed his fist right on the bartender's chin and knocked him down and just about out, and that was the end of that little conversation. Another time my brother who was about the same size as his friend Harry Hopkins got into it with a kid who was about 180 pounds and six feet tall and whose name was "Dinky" Anderson. No matter. When Dinky called my brother out, the two of them walked out the back door of the pool hall and into the alley, and everyone in the place followed them. That's always the way it was in Crookston. Whenever there was a fight, a whole gang of kids always surrounded you and watched, and made sure it was a fair fight. The one between my brother Bill and Dinky was fair alright, and it was also short and bloody. My brother beat the hell out of Dinky in spite of his size, and I'm glad it turned out that way because I loved my brother and would have felt really bad to see him get beat up.

Don't get me wrong. Fighting wasn't the only sport at which the Playhouse boys excelled. Football, basketball, and ice hockey occupied their time, too. By the time I was a senior at Cathedral in 1945, I still went into the Playhouse to play a little pool and talk with Jerry Knutson, Dick Meng, Bob Duckworth, Bill Monroe, Howie Peterson, Lee Gjesdahl, and my other friends from Central, but the whole scene had changed. All the guys I've been talking about had left for the service, and everything seemed calmer. There weren't fights, just about no one smoked, drinking was limited to an occasional beer on the weekends, and the boy-girl relationships seemed to stick closer to home and to take place at house and school parties. I won't say I didn't get quite an education from the older Playhouse boys of my generation, but I'm just happy I was younger and more of a passive observer than active participant in life during that time because it suited me better.

ICE SKATING

Each November during the 1930's after the leaves had fallen, the geese had flown south, and the football season had ended, the first snow started flying, the first freeze set in, and Crookston kids began looking forward to Thanksgiving feasts, Christmas presents, and ice skating. While some kids learned to skate on the Aunt Polly Slough in Jerome's Addition, my first experience was on a vacant lot next to Ade Ness's "little store" on Woodland Avenue in Sampson's Addition. Each winter the lot was flooded so all the neighborhood kids could come and slide on the ice and learn to skate. My first skates were two runners which were strapped to my boots, and skating amounted to walking and running on them, skidding, wobbling, falling, and then getting up and repeating the process until the skating skill was mastered.

When I got a little older, my folks bought me a pair of used tubular skates, and I walked to Central Park where all of the older kids skated and played hockey on two different rinks. It was fun skating in the park at night because lights lit up the rinks, a warming house managed by Milton O'Boyle was located nearby, and no one told you how fast you could go or whether or not you could play tag or crack the whip. The ice hockey rink was where the Cathedral High School boys (who were coached by Father Vic Cardin and later by Don Norman) practiced after school and played their games. It was also where elementary school kids who were interested in the game got together on Saturdays with their sticks and pucks to develop their hockey skills. We didn't have helmets, gloves, or shin pads in those days, and when we got whacked across the fingers or on the shins, it really stung. Some clowns would purposely whack you on the shins and then ask foolishly, "Did you feel that?"

Another skill all the kids developed early was the ice cleaning skill, especially after a heavy snow. Frank Zamboni didn't invent his ice resurfacer until 1947, so all of the snow had to be removed by hand. Horizontal boards that were about six inches high and six feet long were attached to handles and pushed around the rink until all the snow was in piles against the boards where it could be shoveled off. When the ice was flooded, it was usually so cold outside that it would freeze hard as a rock and be slick as glass and ready for skating in about ten or fifteen minutes.

In 1938 when the Works Progress Administration built the Winter Sports Arena, it was managed by Dwayne Palmer's dad. He flooded the ice with a big hose when it was needed, and sharpened our skates to a razor's edge for a quarter. The kids liked Mr. Palmer, and they loved the new arena because it had a lot of amenities like bathrooms, dressing rooms for hockey teams, and a large, heated, rectangular room the width of the arena where people could sit inside and watch the skating and hockey games if they wished.

Most people bundled up and went outside where they could get closer to the action during hockey games, and the kids brought their hockey sticks outside and slapped them against the boards as a way of cheering for their team. I was ten when the arena opened in 1938 and didn't get to play on Cathedral High School's team until I was a junior because there were too many other guys who could skate much better than I. Buddy Schraeder, Spanky Sullivan, Pete Prudhomne, Tommy Leblanc, Alf Sullivan, Jimmy Medved, my brother Bill Dowdle, Bill Sullivan, Les Martin, Stub Peterson, Johnny Noah, and Gene Theroux were just a few of them. They made up the 1943 Cathedral High School team managed by Pat McNamee and coached by Don Norman when I was a freshman.

When I was a junior in 1945, our team traveled to Winnipeg during Christmas vacation to play some Canadian high schools, but it was a disaster because they were too good. Also, they yelled at one another in French when they were going to make a play, and who could understand that! It didn't make much difference to me personally because I only got to play for a very short period of time and didn't know what I was doing out there when I did, anyway.

I just didn't understand the game that well and never skated that well. I knew that the puck had to go across the blue line before the player did, and I knew that the goalie could clobber you with his stick if you entered his crease, but I never really understood what icing the puck was all about. "Ice the puck!" somebody would yell, and I wouldn't know what he wanted me to do with it. My skating skill wasn't much better than my knowledge of the game. I was one of those guys who always had to keep his eyes on the puck in order to control it, and I never did develop a sense of struggling against or hitting a man like in football. We were always told to "play the puck, not the man," and I think that's what I always tried to do until one game the following year when we were playing at Thief River Falls.

Although I was a senior and still a little awkward on my skates, I found myself playing first string defense with Morrie Theroux because our star players had been kicked off the team for "turning pro," and I was all we had left. Turning pro? What happened was a group of my fellow seniors played with the Crookston Pirate team one Sunday, and when they accepted $10.00 and a steak dinner for playing, Father Keefe declared them professionals and gave them the boot. Well, there I was in Thief River Falls when this kid named Claffey came barreling down the ice all alone towards me. He threw a fake, but I caught him with my right hip and he did a somersault in the air and landed right on his butt. Claffey was stunned, but so were Morrie and I because we had the puck dropped at our feet and a clear sheet of ice between us and the goalie. I wish I could tell you that when we raced down the ice and converged on the goalie that we scored, but we didn't.

That game was my last high school hockey game because I quit school and joined the Navy on my eighteenth birthday on February 1, 1946, but it certainly wasn't the last time I skated, nor the last time I played hockey. When I was stationed at Annapolis, Maryland, I went skating in an arena at Baltimore on the weekends, and when I was at St. John's University, I went out for the team and made it during my junior year in 1951, but there was a problem.

Five guys from Cretin High School in Saint Paul stuck together, and it was difficult to break their ranks, but I did break something else one afternoon during scrimmage, and then I felt really ostracized. Joe Cascalenda, who was also a football star for St. John's, came streaking down the ice towards me with the puck, and when I poke checked him, he tripped, fell, and broke his leg. This did not set well at all with the other Cretin High School guys, but what could I do? It just happened. The next year was even more eventful.

I got married to Marilyn Kirkwood, a Cathedral High School classmate, on June 9, 1951, and we lived in Saint Cloud. To make extra money during the winter, I took a job with the Saint Cloud Recreation Department as an "ice cop" on the lake. I wore a badge and skated all around at night and just made sure the kids didn't harass or kill one another. I didn't go out for the Saint John's ice hockey team that year because there just wasn't the time, and my wife was pregnant. However, in January of 1952 when she was seven months along, she got to see me play for the first time.

Some alumni from Saint John's arranged to play the Saint John's University team on an outside rink in Saint Cloud one evening, and the alumni asked me to play with them. I had developed a lot more confidence in my skating ability by that time, so I agreed to play with them, and my wife agreed to come watch. She was standing outside by the side of the boards, big as you please, when another wingman and I got the puck and began streaking down the ice all alone. Just before we reached the blue line, I had the puck and was about to pass it when I was blind-sided by one of the Cretin High School guys.

It wasn't cool to wear helmets in those days, so when I got flattened, the back of my head bounced off the ice, and I woke up later in the Saint Cloud Hospital. Lights were shining in my eyes, and I could hear the doctors murmur, "It's a star cut. He's had a bad concussion. We'll have to shoot him with penicillin and watch him." Two weeks later after I got out of the hospital and was back at school, my joints started swelling up all over, and I discovered I was allergic to penicillin and could have lost my life!

I never did play the game again, but I skated at some of the places where I taught school. At Karlsruhe, North Dakota on a pond where I drove the local priest crazy in a game of tag, at Perham, Minnesota where I taught our little two-year-old daughter Kathleen how to skate, and at Santa Rosa, California where my daughter Ally used to go skating with me at the beautiful Redwood Empire Ice Arena built by Charles Schulz, the "Peanuts" cartoonist from Saint Paul.

About that time I thought I was never going to be able to skate again because an old back injury flared up, and I needed surgery. Fortunately, my family doctor recommended a skilled Santa Rosa neurosurgeon. His name was Dr. Winston Ekren, and to my surprise he was from Grand Forks and married to a Crookston girl who knew my wife. Enough said. When he learned that and that I also was from Crookston, I had it made! "What do you want to be able to do after this surgery?" Dr. Ekren asked. I told him I wanted to be able to ice skate, and he got a good chuckle out of that. The operation was successful, and it was pure joy I experienced one evening a few months later when I met Dr. Ekren out at the ice arena and the two of us were whipping around on the ice. I'll be forever grateful to that man!

I'm grateful to Charles Schulz, too, because he provided the beautiful arena and brought the Senior Olympics to town for the community to enjoy. Each summer during July ice hockey teams from around the world came to Santa Rosa to compete, and people could watch hockey being played from six in the morning until midnight if they wished, and it was all free! Charles Schulz was a very gentle, kind, generous, and talented Minnesotan who loved ice skating.

I guess once you've ice skated or played ice hockey, it never really gets out of your blood, but now that I'm seventy-seven, I think I'm going to play it safe and stick with walking and riding my bicycle along the Pacific Coast Highway to the Hearst Castle and back home to Cambria. Watching that ocean while your exercising may not be ice, but it sure is relaxing and nice.

CHILDBIRTH

When I was a child, I remember asking my mom where babies came from, and when she said the stork brought them, I believed her because she showed me a picture book, and sure enough, there was a big, old, white stork flying over a house, and it was carrying a smiling baby wrapped in what looked like a large white diaper that was knotted around the bird's long, red beak. That familiar legend about the stork bringing new babies into homes was a happy story, and it was good enough to satisfy my curiosity at that time.

However, when I was four years old and my sister Betty was born, I didn't see any old stork flying around our 403 Pleasant Avenue house. What I did see was a bunch of people: Dr. Nelson, my mom's sisters, Anne Erickson and Jeanette Trepanier, my dad, and my brother Bill, and I began growing suspicious of the old stork story. It wasn't too many years after that when I was told the truth, that babies resulted from lovemaking between a man and a woman, and that my older brother Bill, my younger sister Betty, and I were all made that way and were all born in the same house.

By the time my sister Catherine and my brother Jerry came along, we had moved to 416 Woodland Avenue, right across the street from the Bethesda Hospital, and that's where they were born. My mom didn't like it as well as giving birth at home. She always used to say, "There were too many bright lights, Charlie, and too much of a hubbub."

Let me tell you about real hubbub! That would be very early

in the morning, the day before our first daughter, Kathleen, was born in St. Cloud, Minnesota on March 25, 1952. At about three o' clock, my wife threw her open arms against me and the bed and shouted, "Chuck! Wake up! I think I'm having the baby!" She was lying in a puddle of fluid, and nothing either of us had read in Dr. Spock's "Common Sense Book of Baby and Child Care" had prepared us for this. We panicked! We didn't have a car, it had snowed the night before, and it was a three block walk to the hospital. Quickly, we put on all our winter clothes, left the house, and trudged to the hospital. When I look back on that morning, I can't believe what a fool I was, making my pregnant wife who was about to have a baby, plow through two feet of snow all the way to the hospital!

But, we made it, and I sat in a nice warm room by my wife's side until about nine o' clock when a nurse entered and said, "You may as well go to school, Mr. Dowdle, because nothing is going to happen for a while." When I came back from St. John's University later that afternoon, Marilyn was still in labor, and she wasn't too happy with me when I tried to hold her hand and comfort her. As a matter of fact, both she and the nurse wanted me out of there! There was a problem! The baby wasn't going to be coming out head first. It was going to be a breech delivery. After many hours of continued labor which lasted well into the next day, our first child was finally born, and my wife was totally exhausted!

The birth of our second child was traumatic, too, because "they" were premature twin boys that didn't make it! We were living right across the street from the hospital in Perham, Minnesota when they were born on August 9, 1953. Dr. Schoeneberger came out of the delivery room and shook my hand. "Congratulations, Mr. Dowdle," he said. "You're the father of twin boys!" Then his voice dropped, his expression changed, and he said, "But, sadly, I don't think they're going to make it." My heart sank! I didn't know what to say to him. I simply turned and began walking out of the hospital, numbed.

As I was crossing the street to go home, a teacher friend, John Klug, whose wife Ruthie had had two miscarriages, stopped his car near me and asked, "How's Marilyn doing?" I couldn't answer him. I was so shocked I couldn't speak, so as tears filled my eyes, I simply turned from him and walked slowly home.

Our boys, Michael Charles and Mark Edward, were six and a half months old when they were born, each weighed a little over a pound, and they lived only one day. The hospital didn't have incubators, so they lay their little heads inside oxygen masks to help them breathe, but it wasn't enough. I couldn't believe they weren't going to live because their little bodies had such good coloring and were so perfectly formed. I had a good talk with my God the day they were born and said, "Whatever You will." The boys were baptized and confirmed, and two days later after a brief funeral service, they were buried together in a little white casket in the Perham cemetery.

When my wife came home from the hospital, she said that she had had an "out of body experience" during the delivery, that she was above the operating table, watching the doctor and nurses working on her when she was delivering the babies. I didn't believe her and discounted what she was telling me at the time, but years later after I read Doctor Elisabeth Kubler-Ross's book, "On Death and Dying," it dawned on me that my wife was telling the truth and that I had just about lost her, too.

A year later our second daughter, Laure Jean, was also born prematurely at the same Perham hospital, but everything went well, thanks be to God!

In 1955 we moved to Arcata, California, and Marilyn became pregnant once again. She was real nonchalant when the time came to go to the hospital this time because she was an old hand at this birthing business and remained indifferent and coolly unconcerned when she began having labor pains. I was the one who got nervous and excited and wanted her to get a move on, but she just took her sweet time and said, "Don't worry, Chuck.

There's plenty of time." We had to drive to the hospital in Eureka which was eight miles away, and the longer Marilyn took, the more anxious I got to get moving. Finally, we left when her labor pains were about ten minutes apart, and I was greatly relieved.

After we'd been at the hospital for about an hour, the doctor walked in, examined my wife, and began walking away. "I'll come back later," he said. "I don't think your baby's going to be coming for a while."

My wife looked directly at him as he neared the door and in a very serious voice said, "I wouldn't leave right away if I were you, doctor! I think it's going to be sooner than you think!" Patricia Marie, our third daughter, was born fifteen minutes later on January 17, 1956. Like Archimedes when he discovered the test for the purity of gold, I felt like shouting, "Eureka!"

Northern California stayed too rainy and cool for us, so we moved to Santa Rosa where our last two daughters were born, Genevieve Suzanne on January 1, 1963 and Mary Maureen on January 24, 1966. When these two girls got married and began having their own babies, the excitement continued.

I had never seen the birth of a child because in those days fathers were always sent to a waiting room during the delivery, so when Genny invited my wife and I in to watch the birth of our grandson, Chad, we eagerly accepted. I was hunched behind the doctor, observing the whole process, and when the head crowned, I was in awe! All I could think was "miracle" when the baby's whole body came out of its mother. It was a spiritual experience, one which generated a love bond between my grandson and me forever.

The second Grandson with whom I feel especially close is Dean. He was a baby my youngest daughter Mary and her husband Tom wanted dearly because they had previously lost a child by a miscarriage, and that was followed by Mary having to have surgery to remove fibroids which had become embedded in her uterus, and it was questionable whether or not she'd ever be able to carry a child again, but she got pregnant and gave birth to two pound ten ounce Dean Kavanaugh at the California Pacific Medical Center in San Francisco on February 24, 2000.

The pregnancy wasn't without complications, however, because Mary had been attacked by a disease called pre-eclampsia. It's also called toxemia of pregnancy and attacks some women during the later months of pregnancy or just after giving birth, and it may result in the death of the mother, the fetus, or both, and it gave my wife and I a great scare when our daughter began having splitting headaches and her blood pressure began shooting through the roof! We prayed and were thankful that she lived in a city where specialists were available to treat her condition and save both her and her son.

Mary had to have a cesarean section, and little Dean had to stay in the hospital for a month, but he survived! I couldn't help thinking about our twin boys and what might have been the outcome for them had they had a facility like that available when they were born. I also began thinking about my mother, my wife, my other daughters, and women in general, and what truly amazing human beings they were, laying their lives on the line every time they gave birth to a child! It's good that we have a special day set aside to honor mothers. They deserve it!

FLIGHT

During the warm, summer evenings around dusk, a small airplane would sometimes fly over our Sampson's Addition house and head north towards the river and beyond. If I happened to be in the house when I heard the drone of its approaching engine, I'd run outside to our front yard and watch it until it became just a speck in the sky and then disappeared entirely. I was only five years old at the time, 1933, and I always wondered what happened to that airplane. It fascinated me!

When I got a little older, around eight, and learned that there was an airport north of town where the plane landed, my curiosity was somewhat satisfied, but now I began wondering what it would be like to parachute from an airplane. So, one Saturday winter morning after a heavy snowfall, I bundled up and took our large, black umbrella across the street to our neighbor's house and climbed their outdoor wooden steps to the second floor and the roof. "This was going to be fun!" I thought as I opened the umbrella and gazed down at the huge drift of snow below. And then I jumped! Instead of drifting down slowly through the air as I had seen pilots do in the movies at the Grand theater, I plummeted and sank into the bank. I didn't get hurt, but it sure was a big surprise from what I had expected to happen.

My interest in airplanes grew when I listened to older Crookston boys talking about going to Canada and joining the Royal Canadian Air Force to become pilots, and it continued growing when we entered World War II in 1941 and I was thirteen. Many different kinds of fighter aircraft were being invented at that time, and we kids could buy model airplane kits and build our own planes out of balsa wood and pretend to fly them just like in the war. It wasn't an easy process to build a model airplane, and it required a lot of patience, but I enjoyed doing it.

The first step was cutting out all the pieces which were printed on sheets of balsa wood. I'd lay the sheets on a flat piece of cardboard so I wouldn't cut through to our dining room table and use a thin, double-edge razor blade which would bend easily around the curves of the pieces I was cutting. By the time I was finished, the tips of my thumb and forefinger were a little shredded, but it got the job done. Sometimes a piece would crack in half while it was being cut, and I'd have to glue it together which brings me to the next step, gluing.

I started by pinning the plan for the plane on the same piece of cardboard I'd used for cutting and continued by putting all the pieces in their right places. I usually began gluing the wings and tail pieces together first and followed with the top, bottom and sides of the fuselage. By this time I'd inhaled so many fumes from the glue that I had to go outside and breathe some fresh air before finishing.

The third step was the assembly step, and this was great because now you could see all of your hard work paying off and your airplane taking shape. Small blocks of balsa wood were glued inside the fuselage near the tail and the nose so that small metal hooks at each end could be connected to a rubber band which was used to propel the plane.

The last step was relatively easy because it consisted of simply gluing tissue paper to the whole frame of the plane, and voila, it was done and ready to fly!

I'd wind the propeller up until the rubber band inside the fuselage just about reached its breaking point and then set the plane on the sidewalk and watch it roll down the old concrete runway and become airborne. After so many runs, the rubber band would become slack, and it would be time for the plane's demise which took place in a war setting on the Sampson's Addition bridge.

This war involved the plane, a match, and a pile of stones. For the last time the propeller would be wound taut, the plane would be torched, and it would be bombed with stones as it flew blazing through the air before crashing into the water.

Recently, when my wife's sister, Wanda (Johnson) Helgeson, and her husband Gene were visiting with Carmelle and me, Gene told me his buddy Denny Engen and he used to make model airplanes, too. They would make one at Gene's house and the next one at Denny's house. When they finished playing with them, they would also take them to a bridge, wind them up, set fire to them, and let them fly. While the airplanes floated down the river, the boys would pelt them with rocks.

Gene said Denny was always interested in flying, became a pilot a young age, and especially liked to fly helicopters. Both Denny and he joined the Army around the same time. In Gene's first tour of duty in Viet Nam with the First Cavalry Airborne Brigade in 1966, he was stationed at An Ky in the Central Highlands, and his unit came under heavy fire and needed to be extracted by helicopter. The chopper came, and as the men piled into it, the pilot saw Gene and yelled, "Helgeson, what the hell are you doing here?" It was Denny Engen, his old Crookston buddy whom he hadn't seen for twelve years. Gene shook his head and said, "What are the odds of that happening?"

Although there were no crashes of real planes in the Red Lake River during World War II, I imagine there were a few out near the airport at that time because Crookston was a training center for would be pilots from the South who added a lot of interest to the local scene, especially among some of the girls and older women who went gaga over these men in uniform who spoke with a different accent and loved to dance. Some of the older guys benefited from having the airmen train in town, too, because they were hired by the government to wind up the propellers before the training planes took off.

I sort of lost interest in airplanes during high school, but had it kindled again when I joined the Navy in 1946 and found myself working as a Pharmacist Mate with flight surgeons at Annapolis, Maryland. These guys were real daring do pilots and surgeons who flew into battle and performed surgery aboard ships and in the field with the marines. They were wild! I went on a flight with my Commander, Mel Snowden, in a seaplane one day, and I couldn't figure out what he was doing when he angled the nose of the plane toward the runway and had no intention of landing. We got closer and closer, and I kept thinking, "Pull up! Pull up! Do you want to get us killed!" And that's when he bounced the wheels off the runway, gunned the engine, and put the plane into a steep climb. It was about the same time that I had to feel my pants to see if they were wet. Evidently, this was a regular training exercise that the flight surgeons practiced regularly.

Another training exercise which I witnessed was aboard a baby aircraft carrier docked at Annapolis in 1947, and it, too, held a big surprise for me. One day I was sent aboard the ship to take care of any sailor who might get hurt while training to fire the catapult. I couldn't believe my eyes when among those sailors who were training was "Spanky" Sullivan, one of my classmates from Cathedral High School. It was a little like Gene's meeting with Denny Engen, but under very different circumstances.

I guess all this proves is that we live in a small world, a world that has been made even smaller by the invention of the airplane, but I think it also shows that we're blessed to live in a country with veterans who have been willing to risk their lives to help us live free!

VETERANS

When I was a kid during the 1930's, my dad, Frank Dowdle, would come home from work at his Second Street barbershop and often break out singing: "How ya gonna keep 'em down on the farm, after they've seen Parrreee! At the time, those words didn't mean a thing to me. Nor did the World War I uniform that was hanging in my bedroom closet.

And I never wanted to sit still long enough for my dad to tell me what happened during that war, but then one Fourth of July when he let me play soldier outside with his helmet and gas mask, I listened to him long enough to learn that he left the farm in Corydon, Indiana and was a barber in Crookston when he enlisted in the infantry in 1917. One of his brothers who stayed back in Indiana at that time, wrote him the following card:

Dear Brother,

I hear that you are going to war. Well, stick to Old Glory, our flag. I may have to go myself. If you have any chance of coming to see me, come. I want to see you. I would like to see you all. I am going to march in the parade this morning. I belong to the union and this is Labor Day. Well, this leaves me well.

Good-bye and love to all,
John Dowdle

Dad was twenty-seven years old when he enlisted and trained at Camp Dodge in Des Moines, Iowa and Camp Cody in Deming, New Mexico, twenty-eight when he saw action in France at Chateau-Thierry, St. Mihiel, and the Meuse-Argonne battlefronts, and twenty-nine when he arrived back in the United States in the summer of 1919. He said a lot of soldiers got really sick on the ship going to and from France, but I'm guessing that the great time they had celebrating in Paris after the war made up for it.

Once he got home, Dad moved his parents who had been living in Lockhart and Beltrami to Crookston where he opened a barber shop with his younger brother Jim at 120 Second Street. At the time business was thriving and Dad was living the life of a carefree bachelor, but he wasn't getting any younger, so he began looking for a wife, and how he met my mom, Grace Gretchen Van Raden, was quite novel.

She said, "I was sitting in a Crookston shoeshine parlor having my shoes shined when this older man walked in, began flirting with me, and just swept me right off my feet!" There was fourteen years difference in their ages. Mom was 19 and Dad was 33 when they got married two years later on June 26, 1922.

We were a pretty loose knit family. When I wasn't running around town or playing by the river or in the woods with my friends, I'd follow my brother Bill around, or I'd stop at the barbershop and visit with my dad. Many times I'd wait for the shop to close at six when the Cathedral bell would ring and walk home with him. I really loved my dad because he let us have plenty of freedom and was always supportive of whatever we wanted to try in life to better ourselves. He also had a great sense of humor and cared for people, especially veterans.

They'd often come into the barbershop, and because Dad was the veterans service officer for the VFW, he'd help them fill out the necessary papers to win the disability payments they were owed or to receive treatment at the Veterans' Hospital in Fargo. I think it's really a pity that veterans have to fight for what's due them after they've laid their lives on the line for their country, and that's the way my dad felt, too.

When the United Sates entered World War II on December 7, 1941, Dad closed the barbershop and began tending bar at the VFW Club, and I've never seen him happier than when he was serving and socializing with other veterans. Then, instead of stopping at the barbershop during the day and talking with Dad, I'd often go up to the VFW in the evening before he closed, sip a beer with him, and then walk home and talk. That's when he'd give me advice like: "Don't go into the Army like I did, Charlie, because all you do is crawl around in the mud all day and get shot at." And, "Don't become a barber, Charlie, because you have to strand on your feet all day." And, "Get an education, Charlie. That's something no one can take away from you."

Good advice, Dad! I joined the Navy, became a junior high school English teacher, and got four years of free college on the G.I. Bill. Thanks for being my friend.

SKI BUM

Before ever donning a pair of skis, shuffling along Crookston's icy, snow-covered sidewalks and streets during the winter months was all the preparation one ever needed to become a cross-country skier because the same maneuver was practiced daily. Another skill that was sometimes practiced by us idiot kids was hanging onto the rear bumpers of cars and sliding along behind them.

At the Woodland Avenue stop sign near the bridge, the driver of a car would know what we were up to and purposely gun his engine to get away from us. Of course, what would happen is that his rear wheels would simply spin, and we'd get sprayed with a little snow and breathe in huge draughts of carbon monoxide, but we boys were up to the challenge and would cling to his bumper like our lives depended on it. The trick was to hang on as long as we could and keep our balance even as the driver picked up speed and tried to shake us loose. Skiing on flat ground was rather tame stuff after practicing that maneuver.

My first skis were tall, wide, thick, old wooden things that barely moved, even when I went down a hill. And when I'd ski on flat land, my boots would keep slipping out of the leather straps because balls of ice would keep forming under my feet. Then I'd have to take the tails of my skis and ram them against these ice knobs so I could fit my boots into the straps and go again. It was no fun at all until I got new skis.

That happened when I was in about the seventh grade and John Scully gave us kids prizes for selling newspaper subscriptions to the Grand Forks Herald, Minneapolis Tribune, and St. Paul Pioneer Press. In addition to several pairs of sheepskin-lined leather mittens, I won three sets of skis. They weren't the modern kind like we have today with boots and bindings, but they were shiny, sleek, and tall and had my old ones all beat. Besides, I'd discovered a new way to hold my boots in the leather straps. First, I'd cut two one inch wide circles of rubber from an automobile inner tube and slip one over each boot. Then I'd snap the front part under each toe and voila, they served the same purpose as heel and toe bindings do on ski boots.

Now I was ready to do some real Nordic skiing! No more of this flat land stuff for me! I started on some of the small hills in Sampson's Addition, crossed the river to Darkow's to take on bigger hills, and ended up at the golf course to do some jumping. We're not talking long distances here, maybe ten or twelve feet in the air after we'd left the jump, but it was fun, and my rubber bindings worked perfectly. If I fell, they snapped right off my feet and everything was fine.

But, my friends and I needed more of a challenge, and we kept looking for one until we found it right in our own back yard above the Old Dam. The hills there went straight down and right out onto the river, so we piled up snow for a jump about halfway down the run and decided to try it. We made a big engineering mistake. We angled the jump skyward at about seventy degrees, so the first time we went over it, the tips of our skis reached for the sky and then went straight down into the hard, snow-covered ground, and we went tumbling down the hill, and our skis snapped off our feet and went shooting out onto the frozen river. After some minor adjustments to the jump, this became our favorite place to ski for the rest of the winter.

After I left Crookston, I never tried skiing again until I was twenty-two years old and going to St. John's University at Collegeville, Minnesota. The school had a ski run that was about a block long and a tow rope to pull you back up the hill. That was great! I'd never before experienced being pulled back up a hill.

Well, St. John's couldn't hold a candle to the next place I skied. That would be at Squaw Valley, California with my son-in-law, Dennis Tatman, when I was sixty years old. I was recently retired and thought it would be a lot of fun to try mountain skiing just to see how it would differ from the banks along the Red Lake River, the smooth, gentle hills at the Minakwa Country Club, and the steep incline behind the Old Dam. Boy! Was I in for a surprise!

It was beginning to snow a little when we got there in the morning, so they said the slopes were going to be fast because it had melted a little the day before and frozen during the night. This was fine with me because I was eager to get started and hop aboard a ski lift for the first time in my life. The problem was I wasn't fast enough when I went to get on the chair, and the guy shoved me out of the way and onto the ground so I wouldn't get hurt. Well, I did get hurt a little because I banged my shin on the metal part of the chair lift when he shoved me out of the way, but I wasn't going to let that stop me.

The second attempt was successful, but it was a little scary having to get off so fast at the top and get out of the way so the person getting off behind me wouldn't knock me over. I did it, breathed a sigh of relief, and began heading down the beginner's slope which was like nothing I'd ever experienced in Crookston. It was high, it was a long way down, and I slewed from side to side sort of like I would with hockey skates so I wouldn't pick up too much speed. At the bottom I again caught the lift to the top, and after a few times, I had this hill mastered and went on up to the intermediate slope.

By this time the snow had begun falling harder, and the goggles I was wearing began fogging up, but I was still having fun. The intermediate slope was much, much higher and longer that the beginner's slope, and in some places it even had tracks which you could enter with your skis and follow them right down to the bottom. I tried this once and they took me right between a couple of trees and over a small jump, a jump that was about ten feet high. I sort of panicked when I approached it because I knew I was going to have to either fall down in the tracks or go over it. I decided to go for it, and when I flew over that thing, I didn't know what to do with my skis. Well, they knew what to do with me, and after hitting the ground and tumbling into the snow, they left me!

After getting them back, I tried the intermediate slope a few more times and was about ready to quit when my son-in-law, who was a real "hot dog." skied up to me and said, "Hey, Chuck, why don't you try the advanced slope where I've been skiing before we go home."

I hesitated at first, but then like a dummy said, "Okay," and began following him for a ways along a ridge. By this time the snow was really blowing, and you could barely see in front of you, but when Dennis stopped, pointed down, and said, "There it is," I couldn't believe it! I even get chills now when I think about it. It went straight down and had big bumps all over it. "Go ahead, Chuck," Dennis said. "Try it! You can do it!"

I don't know what ever possessed me to ski down that slope, but I let go, and before I was a quarter of the way down I knew I was in big trouble! It was like skiing on ice! I started cutting from side to side like I was on hockey skates to slow down, but that didn't help. I just kept picking up speed and losing my balance while hitting one mogul after another. That's when I decided to lower my body to the ground while trying to stop and slide down the rest of the way on my side. It was terrible! I felt my head, neck and body crunch as I slid over many moguls on my way to the bottom of the hill.

I ached every time I took a step that night when we went to dinner, and when I went to my doctor the next morning to see if I had broken any bones, he looked at my body which was totally black and blue from my waist to my feet and said, "My goodness, Mr. Dowdle, what have you been doing?" When I told him I'd been skiing at Squaw Valley with my son-in-law, he got a funny grin on his face and said, "Well, at least you didn't break any bones, and that thick pad of fluid under your black and blue body will go away soon.

Soon was about a month, and it took me about that long to get rid of all the aches and pains, too. I guess I thought I was a pretty macho man until I met that mountain. Now I know better. Never again!

www.ingramcontent.com/pod-product-compliance
Lightning Source LLC
LaVergne TN
LVHW091715070526
838199LV00050B/2413